BOSTON 1700-1980

BOSTON 1700-1980
The Evolution
of Urban Politics

edited by

Ronald P. Formisano
and
Constance K. Burns

Contributions in American History, Number 106

Greenwood Press
Westport, Connecticut • London, England

Library of Congress Cataloging in Publication Data

Main entry under title:

Boston, 1700-1980 : the evolution of urban politics.

  (Contributions in American history, ISSN 0084-9219 ;
no. 106)
  Most of these essays originated in the Boston
Political History Project, which celebrated Boston's
350th anniversary in 1980.
  Bibliography: p.
  Includes index.
  Contents: Introduction—Town meeting politics in
colonial Boston / G. B. Warden—From deferential-
participant to party politics, Boston, 1800-1840 /
Ronald P. Formisano—[etc.]
  1. Boston (Mass.)—Politics and government—
Addresses, essays, lectures. I. Formisano, Ronald P.,
1939-   . II. Burns, Constance K. III. Series.
F73.35.B69   1984   320.9744'61   83-18415
ISBN 0-313-23336-5 (lib. bdg.)

Library of Congress Catalog Card Number: 83-18415
ISBN: 0-313-23336-5
ISSN: 0084-9219

First published in 1984

Greenwood Press
A division of Congressional Information Service, Inc.
88 Post Road West
Westport, Connecticut 06881

Printed in the United States of America

10 9 8 7 6 5 4 3 2 1

Copyright Acknowledgments

Contents

8.   William V. Shannon, *Boston's Irish Mayors:
     An Ethnic Perspective*   199

9.   Martha W. Weinberg, *Boston's Kevin White:
     A Mayor Who Survives*   215

10. J. Anthony Lukas, *All in the Family:
     The Dilemmas of Busing and the
     Conflict of Values*   241

     CONCLUSION
     Ronald P. Formisano   259

     BIBLIOGRAPHICAL ESSAY   279

     INDEX   285

     ABOUT THE CONTRIBUTORS   295

Tables

BOSTON 1700-1980

Introduction

By American standards, 350 years is a long time. In 1980 when Boston celebrated 350 years of recorded existence as a principal urban place, it seemed appropriate to include in the public activities some reflection on the history of these centuries. For clarity such reflection should be limited to a single theme, and it should be relevant to the past of the city as well as to the present. An examination of the politics of the city seemed to fit the criteria well. Boston's Puritan founders had developed a unique form of popular representative government in the Town Meeting; in the colonial and pre-revolutionary period "the first urban political machine" had originated in Boston; politics began to function in the nineteenth century as a vital assimilator of immigrants of different ethnic and religious character into the city fabric; and in the twentieth century Boston has gained a reputation for being one of the most politically active, or, from a negative point of view, one of the most "politics ridden" cities in the nation. Historians have not neglected Boston's political history, but they have tended to focus on individual periods or fragments of time, several decades at the most. A comprehensive one- or multi-volume history of the politics of Boston does not exist.

This book begins to fill that need with a series of essays dealing with each major phase of Boston's politics, from the eighteenth-century town meeting which became so visible in the American Revolution to the contemporary city managed by a four-term mayor (1969-83) and a large, if fragmented, bureaucracy. Although the essays differ in their approaches, methods, and foci, this anthology provides in broad outline a virtually continuous narrative of the structure and dynamics of Boston's politics at each distinctive phase of its development from the 1700s to the 1970s. The authors take the reader through the politics and social settings of the unstable colonial town, the early nineteenth-century international seaport, the antebellum "Athens of America" with its Brahmin elite, the growing urban center of industry and immigrants, the declining twentieth-century manufacturing and financial city, the rebounding service and high-technology metropole, and, finally, to the present inner city struggling with racial discord and trying to come to terms, as J. Anthony Lukas puts it, with a historic conflict between community and democracy.

Beginning in 1630 as a settlement of English Puritans, indeed, as a "Holy Commonwealth" embodying the ideals of the left-wing of the English Reformation, Boston evolved rapidly into "the premier entrepot of New England," a Yankee traders' town that "outfitted and operated much of the complex Atlantic commerce of the seventeenth and eighteenth centuries and supplied arriving colonists throughout the period."[1] Although the city was transformed by the secular influences accompanying commercial prosperity into a cosmopolitan cultural center, the traditions of Puritan civic moralism remained strong even after the American Revolution. Despite the breakdown of religious consensus and the rise of liberal religious creeds and pluralism, Boston was the place in which theaters were closed in the 1790s as "immoral," and a man was tried in the 1830s for the criminal offense of "blasphemy." Yet while "banned in Boston" became a catchword for the degeneration of religion into prudish moralism, the city also became known for its non-conformists, dissenters, and radicals in religion, culture, and politics.

Until the early nineteenth century issues of public morality arose among a Yankee population that was remarkably homogeneous compared to other seaboard cities such as New York or Philadelphia. The Yankees, as Samuel Eliot Morison once pointed out, were not "all English" nor of "pure Anglo-Saxon stock." Yet "[t]o outsiders, as late as 1824, the population of seaboard Massachusetts seemed, and was, racially homogeneous as that of Brittany.... It was Yankee, a new Nordic amalgam on an English Puritan base.... A race whose typical member is eternally torn between a passion for righteousness and a desire to get on in the world."[2] After 1830 Boston's ethnic character began to change with the steady influx of Irish Catholics from the Celtic periphery of Britain—a people who had experienced English oppression for generations. At first the Irish immigrants fit into the scheme of things, adapting with occasional unruliness to firm Yankee dominance of all social, political, economic, and cultural institutions.

During and after the War of 1812 the Yankee merchants had put enormous amounts of capital into textile and footware factories in the hinterland of eastern Massachusetts and neighboring states, mostly outside of Boston. By mid-century the Irish increasingly provided a major element of a cheap labor force operating the factories, and had also lent their skills and backs to the building of the canals, turnpikes, and railroads of the new mid-nineteenth century transportation network.

In Boston itself the Irish population grew steadily throughout the nineteenth century, eventually producing a middle class and pushing its way into the lower echelons of city government and public works projects. By the last two decades of the century the Irish were numerous enough to dominate the city politically, and elected an Irish mayor in 1884. The advent of Irish political hegemony would not come as suddenly or as bitterly as folklore remembers it. Still, it was a dramatic and even traumatic—especially for the Yankees—socio-political process. After the first decade of the twentieth century, Boston became a city whose politics were dominated unequivocally by an Irish Catholic majority, a group which had been, a short sixty years before, a despised minority.

Several essays in this volume focus on the pivotal cultural-political transition of the period 1880 to 1920. Aside from its being perhaps *the* major change in the long sweep of Boston's political history, its legacy continues to shape politics and governance in Boston today. As the Yankees retreated from politics (although not from the boardrooms of banks, insurance companies, or cultural institutions), they called upon their allies in the legislature to contain the newly arrived Irish political leaders in Boston by creating a fractured structure of power, nonpartisan elections, independent watchdog commissions, and fiscal restraints. The resulting array of checks and balances institutionalized Yankee distrust of the city's new political rulers.

During the first half of the twentieth century the Yankee-Irish conflict, with its roots reaching back to before the Civil War, continued to be the major visible political fault line in Boston. Indeed, in no other American city did the struggle between "Puritan and Celt" take on such epic proportions.

Yet the essays here show that even as the Irish takeover of 1900-1910 took place, *intra*-Irish political factionalism was perhaps as important to the outcomes of elections. The numbers of Yankees as a voting group steadily declined as native-stock Protestants moved out to the suburbs or further away from the city. Even before the 1940s their numbers made them a relatively minor force at the polls, but as a symbolic presence they remained quite important—even necessary—politically. As a reference group the Yankees could be manipulated for political mileage by Irish candidates long after the reality of their influence at the ballot box had dwindled to insignificance (partly, of course, because their financial, social and cultural power persisted in Boston's boardrooms). Yet all along divisions among the Irish based on class, neighborhood, or rivalries among ward bosses were at least as important as the battle between the Irish and what Curley contemptuously called the "codfish aristocracy."

Even before World War II the Yankee-Irish feud had become mostly shadow-boxing, and after the war it rapidly lost its political utility. With the political mobilization of Jews, Italians, unions, the elderly, and others, coalition-building politics has characterized city elections since 1945. Irish factionalism, already there for decades, adapted to a political arena now populated by other ethnic, religious, and economic interest-groups thrown together in what has been aptly called "street-fighting pluralism." In the 1970s and 1980s the blacks of Roxbury, Mattapan, and North Dorchester, whose population grew rapidly during the 1950s and 1960s, have added still another group to the electoral scene.

The focus on cultural conflict and on politics in these pages is not characteristic of the "new urban history" which has flourished in academic circles in the past two decades. Politics in particular has been "characteristically a subordinate theme" among the "young scholars" of the new urban history.[3] But politics dominates this volume. Readers will not find tables delineating rates of occupational or socio-economic mobility; the authors have not engaged in census linkage, or family reconstitution. The essays here do not undertake, in short, studies of "urbanization" or "city-building" as social processes.[4]

Yet the essays in *Boston 1700-1980: The Evolution of Urban Politics* can be said to reflect several positive trends found in the "new urban history" in recent years. Firstly, the authors have eschewed the traditional organizing categories of "problems" or "reform" and have not approached the city as a failed social organism. The essays dealing with the late nineteenth and early twentieth centuries, particularly, have avoided casting the city's politics in terms of the classic "duel between reform and bossism." That scenario has exercised a powerful influence over the writing of urban political history. "Whether the approach was quantitative or traditional, urban government of the period 1850 to 1940 was seen as a clash between upper and middle class reformers seeking centralized, efficient, moral rule and the political machines dedicated to rewarding party loyalists and securing the mass of immigrant votes through favors and service. This was the dichotomy that seemed to typify urban rule during the last half of the nineteenth century and the first decades of the twentieth century, and this has been the framework of the leading historical accounts of municipal government in America."[5] But the essays by Blodgett, Burns, Kleppner, and Weinberg, for example, do not approach the politics of the industrial city as if it were a debate, as another historian has put it, between Lincoln Steffens and George Washington Plunkett, between a muckraker and a ward boss.[6] In addition, the historians in this collection are for the most part quite self-consciously pluralists—in method, substance, ideology, and taste.[7]

There is no model for considering urban politics over centuries. The lack of a general political history of Boston is not a particular deficiency of Boston, but a characteristic of the history generally of American cities. There was a time when local historians wrote about city politics as a succession of mayors, taking the reader through one administration after another, much as national politics was organized according to a "Presidential Synthesis." When Boston celebrated its 250th anniversary in 1880 and Justin Winsor assembled his magisterial four volumes on the city's history, there was a section on the government of the city, organized according to a "mayoral synthesis," but there was very little in it about the actual politics of the city, and almost nothing concerning the social basis of group conflict.

Readers will encounter here many of Boston's best-known political leaders: Sam Adams, John Hancock, Josiah Quincy, Patrick Maguire, Martin Lomasney, Josiah Quincy, Jr., John F. Fitzgerald, James J. Storrow, James M. Curley, and Kevin H. White. But no "mayoral synthesis" imposes itself on the organization of any of these essays. Rather, readers encounter a series of different leadership styles derived from the changing social, economic, and cultural milieux of the city.

We have divided the essays into three sections: The Colonial and Revolutionary Town; the City; and the City at 350. But the political history of the town and city might be schematized in a slightly more refined fashion: 1630-1700, Pre-political Period; 1700-1776, Provincial Capital; 1776-1822, Patriot and Federal Town; 1822-1870, Yankee City; 1870-1910, Ethnocultural Transition; 1910-1960, Irish City; and

1960– , the "New Boston." Within these periods, cycles appear in which times of equilibrium and routine alternated with times of conflict and public innovation.

On the other hand, certain constants also have been present. Edward Banfield and James Q. Wilson, for example, have defined the politics of modern big cities as the mediation of tensions among groups and the delivery of services.[8] This definition seems applicable not only to twentieth-century Boston but also to the Yankee City and Provincial Capital. Similarly, in the late seventeenth century conflict between local and cosmopolitan (imperial) groups played an important role in Boston politics—yet surely political struggle between locals and cosmopolitans did not end when the British left Boston. In later generations this particular dichotomy would be overlaid by ethnic, religious and socio-economic divisions. In the seventeenth and eighteenth centuries conflicts over services concerned markets, while in the late twentieth century racial, ethnic and socio-economic groups are competing over such services as education, police and fire protection, and housing. But through it all, Boston has endured, and 1980 marked an important historic anniversary.

This collection originated in events during 1980 commemorating Boston's 350th Anniversary, specifically in the creation of Forum 350, the Boston Political History Project. A number of distinguished scholars and knowledgeable public figures came together in a series of conferences and lectures at the John F. Kennedy Library, sponsored by the Kennedy Library, Boston College, and the Office of Mayor Kevin White. The events were funded by the Lowell Institute, the Massachusetts Council for the Arts and Humanities, and the Massachusetts Foundation for the Humanities and Public Policy. The scholars' charge was to consider the relation of politics to the city in the periods of their particular expertise. The focus in several chapters on ethnocultural conflict, and especially on Irish-Yankee relations, resulted in large part from the concerns of scholars who have studied Boston. The papers in general presented an historical perspective for understanding the main outlines of Boston's political history.

For these and other reasons the editors, both participants and one the organizer of the conferences and lectures at which most of these essays were presented, decided to bring together several of the papers in one volume. Aware of the lack of any comprehensive history of Boston's politics, the editors have tried to bring this book as close as possible to filling that need. The essays by Paul Kleppner and Constance Burns were written for this collection, while Martha Weinberg's originally appeared elsewhere.

The contributors are mostly historians well known in their fields and include a political scientist, a prize-winning journalist, and a distinguished public servant. They bring different backgrounds, perspectives and methods to their particular studies, yet the editors believe that this anthology contains a degree of coherence unusual in works of this sort. The editors hope, moreover, that publishing these essays will not only preserve the fruits of a conference and series of lectures which were well received by the public but also will stimulate further scholarly research and writing into Boston's diverse and complex politics.

Ronald P. Formisano
Constance K. Burns

Notes

1. Michael P. Conzen and George K. Lewis, *Boston: A Geographical Portrait* (Cambridge, Mass.: Ballinger Publishing Co., 1976), p. 10.

2. Samuel Eliot Morison, *The Maritime History of Massachusetts, 1783-1860* (Boston: Houghton Mifflin Company, 1961; originally pub., 1921), pp. 21-22.

3. Edward Pessen, "Fruits of the New Urban History: The Sociology of Small Nineteenth-Century Cities," *Journal of Urban History*, 5 (November, 1978), 95.

4. Eric E. Lampard, "American Historians and the Study of Urbanization," *American Historical Review*, 67 (October, 1961), 49-61; Roy Lubove, "The Urbanization Process: An Approach to Historical Research," *Journal of the American Institute of Planners*, 33 (January, 1967), 36.

5. Jon C. Teaford, "Finis for Tweed and Steffens: Rewriting the History of Urban Rule," *Reviews in American History*, 10 December, 1982), 135. See also, Samuel P. Hays, "The Changing Political Structure of the City in Industrial America," *Journal of Urban History*, 7 (February, 1981), 205–18.

6. Michael Frisch, "OYEZ, OYEZ, OYEZ: The Recurring Case of *Plunkett v. Steffens*," *Journal of Urban History*, 1 7 (February, 1981), 205–18.

7. Michael H. Ebner, "Urban History: Retrospect and Prospect," *Journal of American History*, 68 (June, 1981), 84. See also, Kathleen Neils Conzen, "Community Studies, Urban History, and American Local History," in Michael

Kammen, ed., *The Past Before Us: Contemporary Historical Writing in the United States* (Ithaca, N.Y.: Cornall University Press, 1980), pp. 270–91.

   8. Edward Bantield and James Q. Wilson, *City Politics* (Cambridge: Harvard University Press, 1965), pp. 18–32.

Part I
The Colonial and
Revolutionary Town

1

Town Meeting Politics in Colonial and Revolutionary Boston

G. B. WARDEN

Contrary to popular notions, politics did indeed exist in Boston before the Irish Potato Famine of 1847. True, modern Boston's political concerns with busing, the BRA, Combat Zone and budgets may seem remote from John Winthrop's harmonious "city on a hill" in the seventeenth century or Samuel Adams's "Christian Sparta" in the eighteenth. Willy-nilly, modern Boston and ancient Boston share some common denominators which help to place the political system of town meetings and caucuses within a recognizable perspective.

Then as now, for example, the community was plagued by runaway inflation, rising prices, increasing taxes, chronic shortages of food and energy, threats of declining commerce and industry, and mounting indebtedness, public and private.[1] Socially, Old like New Boston suffered from disruptions in the character of neighborhoods, inadequate schooling, erosion of family values, and violence in the streets at an alarming level. One religious denomination predominated but not without challenges from others outside nor from dissension and controversy within, adversely affecting traditional values of public virtue and private morality. Popular notions or myths about modern Boston politics, deals, ward-heelers and the "boys in the back room" may not be far different in many ways from the small, select church-member political elites of the 1600s or Sam Adams's cronies meeting in smoke-filled taverns, pulling strings to control a local government of low-paid, not very efficient bureaucrats, trying to fend off interference from other government agencies and trying with variable success to avoid charges of graft, corruption, nepotism and scandals in public contracts.

It is not possible here to go into every detail of Boston politics from 1630 to 1775 in all their complexity. Still, it is necessary to sketch out some of the major significant characteristics of the political system and its operations during the colonial and revolutionary eras, in order to provide an introduction for contrasts and comparisons with later political developments.

For example, one could start with a not entirely facetious question like why and how the Bostonians developed the town meeting system in the first place. An older generation of historians wasted enormous amounts of ink and energy trying to answer that question and tracing the town meeting back to the ancient Greek *polis*, the Biblical Holy City, pre-imperial Rome, Teutonic folk assemblies, English parish vestries, municipal boroughs, university governance, craft guilds and manorial courts. Some elements of those precedents can be detected in the early town meeting system, but the fit is not quite exact. Some of the earlier European or English groups were popular assemblies, a few had annual elections, others had local legislative powers, but, as far as we can tell, none had all those ingredients together which characterized the town meeting system from the very start. Indeed, the available evidence suggests that the Bostonians and other New Englanders had no single precedent in mind when the town meetings began. By gradual, intermittent accretions, towns were given powers and formal organization by the General Court of the colony over local matters that the legislature itself did not want to bother with. Rather than some mystic continuity with a patchwork of Old World local governments, perhaps the mundane mechanics of land distribution and basic sanitary regulation help to explain how the town meetings began in each community and became the uniform standard political organization throughout the region.[2]

Because Boston was settled by Puritans as an experimental example of a "godly community," it is tempting to imagine a close connection between the origin of the town meeting and the creation of the independent Congregationalist form of church government. There were similarities as well as differences. Both depended on a form of popular consent, and in the early years only church members (about 33 percent of the adult males) could vote for town officials or the pastor and elders of the church. But the church was created after the town began, the church had no annual elections, and church members could not freely challenge the rule of the elders.[3]

A property qualification for voting supplemented church membership after 1647, and the religious requirement itself was ended in 1692. Though Puritan doctrines and procedures also changed dramatically between the seventeenth and eighteenth centuries, the town meeting and town government changed very little. At the initiative of the annually-elected Selectmen or upon popular petition, the town constables warned the freemen and other inhabitants when a town meeting would convene and what the general agenda would be. At the appointed time, the voters and other inhabitants would gather at the Town House at the head of King (now State) Street. An *ad hoc* Moderator would be chosen to run the meeting, after everyone settled down. A prayer by a local minister would follow, though that happened less often in the eighteenth century. The Moderator would then proceed to the business at hand. In the legally prescribed March and May meetings, the duly qualified freemen would cast handwritten secret ballots for town officers and for Representatives to the General Court, respectively. Finances and taxes were the main order of business at the May meeting. Other town meetings were held throughout the year about ongoing concerns or special issues. Technically, only freemen could vote on such matters. But most decisions were made by voice vote, and, since any other non-freemen could attend, make motions and debate issues, it might have been difficult to keep them from shouting along with the regular voters.[4]

The by-laws and orders of the town meeting were limited to the "prudential" affairs of the town, though that term was never clearly defined. By itself the town meeting could not impose a fine of more than twenty shillings for any violation of town by-laws. And collecting such fines depended on the questionable vigilance of the overworked constables as well as the co-operation of the judicial magistrates appointed by the General Court for Suffolk County before 1692 and, afterward, the county's Justices of the Peace appointed by the royal Governor. In substance the by-laws being enforced varied widely in their detail and scope. A large but not unlimited amount of discretionary power fell on the Selectmen in their frequent meetings, the constables and the two hundred other officials elected every year for regulating specific economic activities, public health and other details of everyday town life.

Such procedures of the town meeting government were relatively simple in formal terms yet intricately complex in informal, personal ways. All officials, for example, were part-time amateurs without any fixed, permanent bureaucracy. Only schoolteachers and watchmen received any regular wage from town taxes. Most officials served the town for free. Some might receive reimbursement for personal expenses on the town's behalf. Inspectors collected fees sometimes amounting to lucrative sums but not enough to live on alone. Though fortunes were made on war supply contracts given by the General Court or Crown, it would have been difficult for anyone to grow fat off the town payroll.[5] Even after the Caucus was organized in the eighteenth century, no one could expect to make a living solely as a politician, despite the occasional "deal."

The scarcity of political plums could not encourage the development of full-time bureaucrats or professional politicians in the modern sense. Personnel turnover was heavy in unpopular jobs like that of constable who was both peace-keeper and, until 1733, tax-collector. Considerable continuity prevailed in a few positions throughout the limited hierarchy, but no one had tenure or civil service protection. Getting elected, staying in office or getting some public work was much less organized than today and depended in large part on the informal, person-to-person, face-to-face networks expectable in a small town of five to fifteen thousand people.

We may never know how those networks operated exactly. In such a small town, those involved in public life rarely wrote down what they did, how they politicked and what their techniques were. The usual categories of family connections, marital alliances, wealth, occupational affiliations, neighborhood, church membership, education and other characteristics do not provide clear indications about how people entered public life in Boston or exercised influential power.[6] Many rich people never got involved in town politics, and some poorer people who did participate could exercise timely influence on a few key issues in local governance.

Similar mysteries surround the town meeting itself. The extant records provide few dramatic surprises or clues about the extent of public participation and conflict. Many votes and decisions appear to have been routine, though the phrase "after some discussion" hints at more controversial and divisive debates. Both before and after 1700, the available letters, diaries, sermons, pamphlets, voting patterns and newspaper items say little about what went on behind the scenes or at the Town House.

The informality of the town meeting system and the networks of personal influence indeed make it difficult to distinguish specialized political activity from the wider context of everyday local experience. Modern distinctions among politics, religion, society and economics overlapped each other in the town meeting system. Governance itself was kept to a minimum and depended more on changing circumstances than on deliberate policy or organized activity before the eighteenth century.

The approximate correspondence of the town meeting system with wider, overlapping social, economic and religious elements in the community was never entirely complete and began to disintegrate considerably after 1700. Politics became more organized and specialized, economic activities bred conflict, and religious and social values became more divisive. The complexities of town meeting politics induce me to avoid any hard and fast characterizations for a given period or for changes over time. There are, however, other structural or conceptual models which other historians have proposed—theocracy, traditionalistic corporate communal consensualism, secularism, modernization, Anglicization, bourgeois consensus and stratified class conflict.[7] Each has some merit, but they also involve severe evidentiary, methodological and interpretive problems as completely sufficient or satisfying generalizations.

The Bostonians themselves often had trouble classifying their complex experiences, and I am personally persuaded that an appreciation of that confusion, uncertainty, instability and unpredictability provides a better understanding of town meeting politics than neat, abstract models may provide.[8] Even I have to qualify such a surmise by pointing out that many Bostonians after 1700 were trying earnestly to create greater certainty and stability in local politics and government. Such attempts never quite succeeded, leaving behind some contradictory paradoxes. With variations, instability tended to become a stable, accepted norm in the community, in politics and government, providing a flexibility and pragmatic adaptability well-suited to changing local conditions. At the same time, attempts to impose certainty, order and stability in local trade, regulations and governance tended to create conflict, magnifying persistent instability and uncertainties to troublesome and potentially revolutionary extremes.

My emphasis on the paradoxes of instability may seem extremely bizarre, because many historians have assumed that the pre-modern period was far more stable, static, placid and traditionalistic than modern, urbanized, industrialized society. At a shallow, superficial level pre-revolutionary Boston does seem very static. For example, the recorded total population of the town went from 12,000 in 1720 to 16,000 in 1775. The organization of maritime commerce, crafts and finance in 1775 were approximately what they had been a century before.

Yet such stable appearances can be deceptive. In terms of total population, inward and outward migration was abundant each decade, while thousands may never have been counted. In economics, wars, smallpox, chronic depression, loss of industry, famines, droughts, fuel shortages, food riots, depreciating currency, outward cash drains and the absence of insurance, banking and corporate investment made everyday trade and planning extremely complex, risky, uncertain, unstable and unpredictable for rich, poor and middling Bostonians.[9]

The town meeting system and its informal political networks of the seventeenth century could not adequately cope with the unstable social, economic conditions of the eighteenth. Annual elections, part-time amateur officials, limited jurisdiction and transitory town by-laws could not deal with minor emergencies, much less long-term uncertainties. Attempts to create municipal incorporation or more royal appointees in the town might have provided more stability, but they failed. In chicken-and-egg fashion, the nature of the town meeting system itself contributed to persistent, long-range uncertainty in the basic management of public services and everyday life.

As noted before, other attempts to create stability occurred inside and outside the town meeting. As local conditions became less cohesive and more disintegrated, the clergy, for example, became more secular and organized, first to challenge older orthodoxy, then to defend itself against revivalism from below and later to oppose episcopacy from above.[10] In social relations, families tried to create more manageable order by having fewer children, supporting education, promoting apprenticeship and arranging marriages and inheritances with greater care than before. In economics, an inflated public currency seemed to be the magic panacea uniting debtors over the decades. Creditors, however, sought economic order by frequent, unsuccessful attempts to create public or private banks. They tried and failed to impose strict regulations on retail trade, causing riots in the 1730's. By 1750 they succeeded in converting the local inflated currency to a sound fiscal basis, but that too caused riots.[11]

Amidst all the confusion, the structure and organization of the town meeting remained virtually unchanged. After 1733, more wards were added to organize the militia, constables and public fire companies. At the same time, tax collectors separate from the constables and assessors separate from the selectmen were added. Just before the 1770s the Overseers of the Poor were legally incorporated to cure the chaos rampant in earlier management of the poor, the sick and the migrants. The town meeting system stayed the same.

The basic continuity of local administration amid continuing instability was affected by two fundamentally different developments—the creation of a royal establishment in the colony after 1692 and the development of the Caucus in the town after 1720. Of the two, the Caucus was the more enduring and significant, even though its origins and operations remain obscure. In part, the Caucus was one attempt to provide a coherent political management for the somewhat loose town meeting system. The new influence of royal officials in the county and provincial governments may also have illuminated the need for a countervailing organization in the town meeting. The Cookes, Noyeses, Colmans and Clarkes who developed the Caucus were young merchants and doctors who had tried and failed to get provincial and royal approval for a private bank in 1715. Thwarted by the Dudleys and the Belchers in the royal establishment, the young merchants turned first to the General Court in order to manipulate the provincial currency through inflation. In order to get elected to the General Court, the Caucus had to organize elections in the town meeting. Though their methods in the smoke-filled back rooms remain mysterious, they did seem to use liquor to oil the political machine, arranged for tax rebates, used the fire and militia companies in each ward as a communication and action network and cultivated occupational groups like the caulkers as well as social organizations like the Masons.[12]

The idea of a semi-secret group of a few political managers ran counter to the general democratic nature of the town meeting system of elections, voting, officeholding and popular participation. The leaders of the Caucus doubtless had private, personal motives for wheeling and dealing behind the scenes, but they still could legitimately claim that their organization promoted the public welfare and popular will against other selfish, privileged groups in the royal establishment. The Caucus kept the town meeting behind popular demands for inflation over three decades, opposed regulated markets as consumers wished, opposed the increase of royal patronage and influence and persistently defended the town meeting against attempts to make Boston an incorporated municipal borough or a separate county, both antithetical to popular interests. Though their personnel and methods were less than democratic, the results of their organization reflected popular attitudes and needs. On occasion, the leaders of the Caucus found themselves at odds with the electorate; they did lose elections and crucial votes at times, especially during the chaotic 1740s. The Caucus was not all-powerful or a completely closed shop.

The fortunes of the Caucus and popular government in the town meeting depended in part on the variable influence and competence of the new royal establishment after 1692. The Cookes and the early leaders of the Caucus claimed that they were defending the "old charter" government of the seventeenth century against the "innovations" associated with the new royal government after 1692. The royal governors appointed by the Crown could be effectively controlled or thwarted by the General Court, though Governor Shirley in the 1740s succeeded more than his other colleagues. The Governor's Council (then the upper house of the General Court) was elected annually by the Representatives, subject to the governor's veto. The Governor and Council made appointments for the military and judicial officers in the counties, but the General Court as a whole controlled the salaries of all royal officials except the customs officers. As far as local government in Boston was concerned, the new royal establishment of appointees for life had little direct authority except for the Justices of the Peace of Suffolk County and the Customs officers.

Though royal appointees had little success in the town meeting, Caucus or local government, the royal establishment represented a political system superior to and outside the control of popular opinion. Most Bostonians suspected it of evil intentions on that basis alone, and royal influence provided a perennial whipping-boy, scapegoat or bugaboo for the Caucus at elections or on crucial policy decisions like strict regulation of markets, municipal incorporation, currency reform and other unpopular measures.

The royal establishment, however, could exert an important *indirect* influence on local affairs. During wartime, the governor's influence over lucrative war contracts could woo important leaders like the Hancocks and Waldos away from popular will in town meeting or General Court. Judgeships in the county governments would never make anyone rich, but they were steady jobs with potentially high fees, status and prestige far beyond the gifts of elective politics. Culturally, the duelling, coffee-house idlers, mixed dances, concerts, fancy clothes, carriages, houses, country estates, and other provincial affectations of Englishness represented alluring challenges to the frugality, industry, piety, virtue and residual Puritanism associated with town meeting politics, middle-class values and popular attitudes.[13] The threats, though, were more potential than actual in their corruption of local public ideals of morality and whiggishness. Noticeable as Anglophilia often was, Anglophobia tended to be more persistent and dominant.

Far from fitting neat stereotypes, the royal appointees were often less aristocratic and elitist than one might expect, and the elective officials were often richer and less democratic than one might suppose.[14] Appearances and biased rhetoric may make them look separate and distinct, in view of their different sources of influence, but neither group behaved according to clearly opposite standards.

The groups' limitations and convergence need emphasis to avoid simplistic abstractions about "aristocracy versus democracy," polarized social stratification and class conflict in Boston's politics during the colonial period and especially in the pre-revolutionary years. One can detect (or inject) such elements in any analysis of colonial Boston, but they fall short of being entirely satisfactory in understanding the whole complexity of town meeting politics. If class conflict were a proper model to characterize the town at any time, the Bostonians should have behaved far more radically than they actually did.[15]

Imperial policies and constitutional issues after 1760 cannot be blithely dismissed in the political agitations which took such an extreme and unique form in Boston. Like newer class-conflict interpretations, the older constitutional ideas need to be considered within the larger context of instability in the town. After all the diverse uncertainties in Boston since the 1720s, the townspeople after 1760 had to endure the end of the French war, a post-war depression, a disastrous fire, a smallpox epidemic, another currency controversy, anti-episcopalian agitation, shattering bankruptcies, credit crunches and an escalating spiral of dislocations caused by English taxes, boycotts and repeal in 1765, 1768 and 1773. The aggravation of the town's usual problems made the "innovation" of English taxation even more unbearable, accounting in part for the extraordinary paranoia and violence of the Bostonians' protests and arguments. England's attempts to impose order in the town only magnified disorder.

England's changing imperial policies unsettled the precarious organization, personnel and activities of both the royal appointees and the Caucus in Boston. The older elite coalition that Governor Shirley had developed in the 1740s began to die off, leaving Governor Bernard after 1760 with the dubious support of such unpopular local figures as Thomas Hutchinson and Andrew Oliver at the top of the royal establishment along with a gaggle of inexperienced younger sons and nephews at the bottom. Bernard compounded the problem by trying to create an artificial base of support by lavish appointments of county justices of the peace. Such a tactic may have worked in England or the southern colonies, but it backfired in Boston and Massachusetts. The new appointees who were loyal were also ineffectual; those who were effective were whigs in opposition to him. Whiggishness also infected hitherto loyal allies in the Governor's Council. The "old order," such as it was, began to crumble at the top and the bottom in the crucial years after 1760.

The Caucus and town meeting remained intact, but they too had to face fundamental changes in personnel and tactics. Except for Samuel Adams, almost all the revolutionary leaders in Boston were not Bostonians. James Otis, John Hancock, John Adams, Josiah Quincy, William Molineux, Joseph Warren and Thomas Young all came from outlying areas and were relatively new to Boston politics. With the "black regiment" of the clergy, they formed a working alliance of merchants, doctors, lawyers, distillers, craftsmen and printers whose networks of influence covered the whole community, from the muscular, thirsty dockworkers to the frugal ladies brewing sassafras tea and spinning home-grown wool in protest against taxed importations. It is also remarkable that except for Otis, Hancock and the Adamses, none of the other revolutionary leaders held any elective office in the town meeting. Revolutionary agitation naturally involved the Caucus and town meeting, but, given their usual limitations, they were supplemented by other "outside" organizations—the Loyal Nine, the Sons of Liberty, the Merchants Club, the Committee of Correspondence and "the Body of the People," the amorphous but increasingly larger group of townspeople and neighbors who gathered on important issues beyond the scope of the town meeting.

These other organizations duplicated the personnel, structure and procedures of the town meeting and Caucus to a large extent. Still, for purposes of protest and agitation, a new division of labor was necessary to allow the town meeting and Caucus to carry on town business as usual, while the outside organizations provided the noise and muscle.

As during the Dominion of New England before the Glorious Revolution in 1688, the Crown eventually tried to suppress the town meeting as an obvious source of legal opposition. But it was too late. By 1774, the "spin-offs" from the Caucus and town meeting had created the Committee of Correspondence, the Provincial Congress, the Minutemen and the Solemn League for economic pressure—in short, a revolutionary *de facto* government surrounding the precarious peninsula of *de jure* royal government in Boston six months before the actual shooting began.[16]

Retrospectively, the Revolution in Boston before and after 1775 looks more orderly, inevitable and organized than it may actually have been. The leaders were rarely unanimous. Crowd actions were sometimes spontaneous, sometimes manipulated. Merchants wavered continually on means and ends, according to shifting, contradictory calculations of self-interest. Most Bostonians who joined protests over specific issues had little awareness of possible future consequences or conscious willingness for violence, revolution and independence to result. One may even doubt that a revolution occurred, in the usual, modern meanings of the term.

If the origins of the Revolution in Boston had few unequivocal sources in economic inequality, social stratification and class conflict, the same cannot be said for the results of the Revolution. Pre-war Whigs, Loyalists and indifferent moderates came from all socio-economic groupings rather than from distinct, isolated classes. But post-war inequalities of wealth and political power were far more extensive. Very little structural change had occurred to affect the poor workers and middling craftsmen, but the banks and protected corporate privileges developed during and after the war magnified the ability of the wealthy to increase and protect their wealth.[17] Such financial changes greatly diminished many of the economic uncertainties which had plagued the town, but as will become evident in the next chapter, at an enormous socio-economic cost to traditional values and community relations.

The socio-economic results of the Revolution influenced some changes in the town meeting and local government, without altering their basic structure. The two remarkable elements of pre-war agitation—new outsiders and outside organizations—played their part again in the postwar political systems. By an odd, mind-boggling demographic quirk, none of the prewar leaders except John Adams had any surviving sons to perpetuate the old whig leadership into the new post-war regime.

Instead, new and extremely wealthy outsiders, mainly from Essex County, migrated to Boston to fill the gaps left by the departing Loyalists and fading old Whigs.

At the same time, the Sons of Liberty, Committee of Correspondence, and other organizations outside the town meeting before 1776 had demonstrated that decisive policies could be effected without the popular, democratic but clumsy machinery of the town meeting. During the war when adult males, taxpayers and money were in short supply, the local government found it expedient to finance regular operations from loans and voluntary subscriptions. For similar reasons, many routine operations and special projects were delegated to special on-going committees and commissions. These continued after the war and became less dependent on the vagaries of annual elections and changeable town meeting by-laws. As a result, within a decade after independence, the important regulation of police, health, markets and public education were in the hands of commissioners separate from the old town meeting structure.

As local governance became more stable and coherent through outside commissions, the town meeting itself became less of a central arena for politicking and electioneering. Far bigger plums and prizes were now to be sought in elections and appointments to the new state and county governments. Lobbying in the General Court could produce the corporate privileges to build hospitals, bridges, markethouses, landfills and other public works projects beyond the town meeting's limited finances and jurisdiction.

There were even proposals in 1784 to abolish the town meeting altogether and incorporate Boston as a municipal borough with a mayor, aldermen and common council. As with earlier proposals, such changes would have made local politics and government more stable, consistent, organized, and elitist. The Bostonians would have none of that rationality at such a cost to their accustomed ways. Pamphlets dating back to 1715 were reprinted against incorporation, and mobs took to the streets to agitate more violently against the end of the town meeting.

If post-revolutionary rationalism and social stability could produce a new religion, Unitarianism, which denied the divinity of Christ in the capital of Puritanism, the days of the town meeting were clearly numbered. Modern economic mechanisms have little love for the democratic irrationality and popular sentimentalism associated with the town meeting system. As the population tripled in the forty years after 1780 and as the local economy grew more stable and predictable with overseas

commerce, insurance, corporations, banks and early industrial enter-
prize, the affairs of the town needed more order than part-time amateurs
could provide.

Still, although we can officially date the demise of the town meeting
system with municipal incorporation in 1822, it may not be so dead as
we think. The Caucus as the original, quintessential political machine
lived on and proliferated at the ward level and in the political clubs and
cliques which still survive. Later immigrant groups may have thought
they were rejecting and reinventing politics anew, but in fact they were
merely adopting and adapting the Caucus to promote their own local
organization and their own ethnic interests.

Finally, it is not entirely clear that town meeting politics is dead at
all. If the modern city is as ungovernable, disintegrated and fragmented
as people say, then modern Boston as a coherent social, political entity
may not exist at all. Instead, it may be more valid to consider modern
Boston as a loose confederation of twenty or thirty "colonial" villages
squished together by historical accidents and necessities rather than by
a common purpose and common values. Some of the "colonial" villages
within modern Boston may hark back to other Old World countries than
England.[18] But, even with modern improvements in transportation, bureaucracy, politicking and communication, the new colonial villages
enjoy as much unity, stability, certainty and harmony as colonial Bostonians had—that is to say, not much.

Notes

1. For general patterns of life in colonial Boston, see Darrett B. Rutman,
Winthrop's Boston: Portrait of a Puritan Town, 1630-1649, (Chapel Hill, N.C.:
University of North Carolina Press, 1965); G. B. Warden, *Boston, 1689-1776*
(Boston: Little, Brown, & Co., 1970); and the relevant portions of Carl Bri-
denbaugh, *Cities in the Wilderness* (New York: Ronald Press Company, 1960)
and *Cities in Revolt* (New York: Alfred A. Knopf, 1955); as well as Gary B.
Nash, *The Urban Crucible* (Cambridge: Harvard University Press, 1979).

2. Rutman, *Winthrop's Boston*, pp. 60-62.

3. See Perry Miller, *Orthodoxy in Massachusetts* (Cambridge: Harvard
University Press, 1933), pp. 148-186.

4. See Robert E. Wall, Jr. *Massachusetts Bay: The Crucial Decade* (New
Haven: Yale University Press, 1972), p. 39.

5. See the printed Town Records and manuscripts in the Boston Public
Library.

6. See G. B. Warden, "Officeholding and Officials in Boston, 1692-1775," *New England Historic and Genealogical Register* 131 (1977), 267-290.

7. For theocracy, see James T. Adams, *The Founding of New England* (Boston: Atlantic Monthly Press, 1921), pp. 146-174. For communalism, see Michael Zuckerman, *Peaceable Kingdoms* (New York: Alfred A. Knopf, 1970). For secularism and modernization see Rutman, *Winthrop's Boston* and Bernard Bailyn, *The New England Merchants in the Seventeenth Century* (Cambridge: Harvard University Press, 1955). For Anglicization, see John M. Murrin, "Anglicizing an American Colony," Ph.D. diss. Yale University, 1966. For bourgeois consensus, see Robert E. Brown, *Middle Class Democracy and the Revolution in Massachusetts* (Ithaca, N.Y.: Cornell University Press, 1955). I have reviewed the class-interpretation articles by Henretta, Kulikoff and Lockridge in "Inequality and Instability in Eighteenth-Century Boston," *Journal of Interdisciplinary History* 6 (Spring 1976), 585-620, but see also Nash, *Urban Crucible*, pp. 282-384.

8. See Warden, "Inequality and Instability," pp. 613-620.

9. See G. B. Warden, "The Distribution of Property in Boston, 1692-1775," *Perspectives in American History* 10 (1976), 98-99.

10. See Alan Heimert, *Religion and the American Mind* (Cambridge: Harvard University Press, 1966) and Carl Bridenbaugh, *Mitre and Sceptre* (New York: Oxford University Press, 1962).

11. See the marital alliances in Jules D. Prown, *John Singleton Copley* (Washington, D.C.: National Gallery of Art, 1965), I; for the economic reformers, see Warden, *Boston*, pp. 102-148.

12. See G. B. Warden, "The Caucus and Democracy in Colonial Boston," *New England Quarterly* 43 (March 1970), 19-45.

13. See Murrin, "Anglicizing," and Nash, *Urban Crucible*.

14. See Warden, "Officeholding."

15. See Warden, "Inequality and Instability," pp. 612-613.

16. For the Revolutionary years, see Warden, *Boston*, pp. 148-341; Hiller B. Zobel, *The Boston Massacre* (New York: W. W. Norton, 1978); Benjamin W. Labaree, *The Boston Tea Party* (New York: Oxford University Press, 1964); Richard D. Brown, *Revolutionary Politics in Massachusetts: The Boston Committee of Correspondence and the Towns, 1772-1774* (Cambridge: Harvard University Press, 1979).

17. There is no good history of Boston between the Revolution and 1822, but see Harold and James Kirker, *Bulfinch's Boston* (New York: Oxford University Press, 1965); Oscar and Mary Handlin, *Commonwealth* (Cambridge: Harvard University Press, 1969); Stephen E. Patterson, *Political Parties in Revolutionary Massachusetts* (Madison: University of Wisconsin Press, 1973) and Van Beck Hall, *Politics without Parties* (Pittsburgh: University of Pittsburgh Press, 1972).

18. As indeed some do: see Herbert J. Gans, *Urban Villagers: Group and Class in the Life of Italian Americans* (New York: The Free Press, 1962).

Part II
The City: Brahmins, Yankees, and Immigrants

2

Boston, 1800-1840: From Deferential-Participant to Party Politics

RONALD P. FORMISANO

Boston of the Federal Era (1800-1825) seems almost familiar. Some of its architecture—the Harrison Gray Otis House, Bulfinch's state capitol, Quincy Market—remain and recall not only its pre-industrial neo-classicism, but also the Federalist patricians, those intensely public men whose political style belonged so distinctively to that time. The apparent familiarity is deceptive. Just as the Federalists and their Jeffersonian rivals possessed their own architecture, they had their own political culture which had deep roots in the 18th century. Federal politics, though beginning to depart from colonial customs, remained, especially at the local level, as G.B. Warden suggested in the last chapter, far removed from the organized party politics constructed by a later generation. Not until the late 1830s, indeed, did a two-party system founded on a regular convention system become well established.

It will surprise no Bostonian to learn that Boston was once an oli-garchy: when has power in the Hub not been concentrated in the hands of a few? But Federal Boston was a peculiar kind of oligarchy, a mix of aristocracy and democracy, with the former in part a meritocracy. Though national and state politics became invested with high partisan feeling, town politics moved to a different beat. Even after the town became a city in 1822, local affairs were conducted along non-partisan lines and machine-like political parties were still unknown. In the 1820s, however, signs of change sprouted continuously. Social movements arose for the first time and new interest groups emerged raising populist cries of protest against established elites. Shifting in and out of political activity, these new movements and groups pushed along the transition to the organized mass politics which would become the principal frame-work for politics for the rest of the nineteenth century.

The Federal Era's style of politics may be characterized as "deferential-participant," a term which captures its somewhat conflicting mix of aristocratic, oligarchic, and democratic elements.[1] Most adult males participated primarily by voting in some elections while maintaining deferential attitudes toward a recognized elite of wealth, status, and talent. In this world gentlemen were known by their dress, speech, and bearing, and the middle and lower classes followed the lead of notables and elected them routinely to the higher public offices. It was a world in which deference to one's social betters did not necessarily imply servility or obsequiousness, and in which respect for social rank was quite compatible with integrity, self-respect, and one's own sense of importance.[2]

In the 1820s this political world, under strain since the American Revolution, began to change more rapidly than ever before. Yet the ethos of the town lingered on, even though the population was now 45,000 and rising rapidly. On the world scene Boston was virtually a small maritime empire, and with merchant and manufacturing wealth flowing to public and cultural institutions, its boosters touted it as the "Athens of America."[3] Yet many of its citizens retained a town mentality, and in politics they still followed the Federalist merchant princes.

Town politics during the Federal era followed its own pattern separate from Federal-Republican party warfare, and was highly consensual. The rich merchants and lawyers met with less challenge in town meetings than in national or state politics, and invited cooperation in local affairs by shedding their frequently imperious manner. In the 1820s city politics remained non-partisan, and by then the old parties were in disarray. At the same time, however, new currents of political action arose. All over the United States populist movements appeared, as middle-class and ordinary citizens launched protests, reforms, and a variety of schemes for society's improvement. In Boston, populism also thrust new groups into public prominence, though Boston's populism was more restrained than democratic protests elsewhere. But the new currents of political action and changing social conditions steadily eroded the consensus and deferential style of the old politics.

By the early 1830s, more radical movements of social protest emerged and disrupted politics while political party organizations slowly formed amid the turmoil. Boston, meanwhile, prospered mightily, with expanded maritime enterprise joined by the wealth of manufacturing magnates who expanded into banking, insurance, and railroads. Population grew too rapidly, however, and the new city's still old ways of coping with basic public needs grew even more inadequate. By the mid-1830s mob violence and the need to create professional departments of police and firemen signified the city's changed social character. It was no longer a setting which could support deferential-participant modes. Eventually political parties led partly by professional politicians would also impose order on much of political life. The parties had developed, however, outside of city politics in the arenas of state and national elections. By the late 1830s the new Whig and Democratic parties gradually aligned a reactivated mass electorate into two huge camps. And after 1835 party politics pervaded city nominations and elections as never before.

The Federal Town 1789-1822: Prospero's Boston

The town of Boston had forged a strong sense of community during the momentous events of the late eighteenth century. Boston merchants, supported by shopkeepers, artisans, and laborers, had led in bringing about the American Revolution and then in the movement creating a national Constitution in the 1780s. In the new federal government Boston merchants and lawyers and their allies from other parts of the state but especially from Essex County enjoyed much influence, and Congressional law provided various bounties and protection to the maritime industries which were the foundation of Boston's wealth. Washington's successor in the Presidency, John Adams, was essentially a Boston man, and the Bostonians believed that their large influence in national affairs was only natural. But opposition developed to the Washington and Adams administrations which, though it centered on foreign policy, and especially on relations with the former mother country, also involved the question of how strong and energetic the national government ought to be. Opponents of close relations with England and of a "consolidated" government formed an intra-sectional alliance which was led prominently by Virginians and New Yorkers and which succeeded in electing Thomas Jefferson to the Presidency. Boston's leading men had tied themselves closely to the policies of Washington, Adams, and the first Treasury Secretary, Alexander Hamilton, whose first tenet of energetic government was to bind the interests of the commercial and financial men to the federal government. Now the Boston elite found themselves not only out of power and influence, but increasingly at odds with the national administration. Further, a Jeffersonian Republican opposition grew within Massachusetts and Boston, led by merchants in the French trade and others on the margins of power, and began to contest state and federal elections.[4]

The European wars following the French Revolution and the rise of Napoleon had created a marvelous opportunity for the ships and shipowners of Boston. Neutral trade brought rich profits, and also great risks and blatant encroachments by France and England on the young nation's ships and seamen. Jefferson insisted that neutral rights be respected, but would use no weapon more lethal than embargo. He kept American ships at their wharves, in short, to punish the Great Powers. The Bostonians, with idle ships dismantled and rotting, thought *they* were being punished. With President Madison things got worse and the United States finally went to war with England (1812-1815) ostensibly over the issue of maritime rights. Maritime and Anglophile Boston, forty years earlier a hotbed of Independence, was mostly cool or hostile to the "Second War of Independence." Boston Federalists came to believe that the Southern-dominated national government was bent on ruining New England. They sank into bitter sectionalism, talked loudly of states' rights, and some whispered threats of secession. By 1822 the Commonwealth four times cast a majority of votes for Republican candidates for governor (1807, 1808, 1811, 1812), but the town of Boston never did. The Federalist majority in Boston became weaker during the "Era of Good Feelings" as partisan passions ebbed after 1815, but even when the Republicans finally conquered the state in 1823 and 1824, Boston returned slim Federalist majorities.[5]

Opposition to an outside power (Washington) helped to solidify the majority behind the local elite. As tensions eased, the Federalist leaders enjoyed other advantages which helped them maintain majorities in Boston. They had begun with an array of social institutions and allies: most of the Congregational clergy, the professions, the judiciary, and most federal, state, and local office holders, all of whom together made up a small army. With a large part of the social establishment at their disposal, at least at the beginning, Federal leaders did not need an organized political party. The Republican dissidents who challenged them needed organization more, but the entire generation did not think or act in terms of the mechanical, permanent institutions which Whigs and Democrats later developed. So political party leadership corresponded closely to economic, social and cultural leadership. Boston's top Federalist leaders (and a few Republicans) exercised great personal authority in town meetings, debates, crises and elections, not because at some point they organized a "State Central Committee" (which they did, secretly), but because they and their families were *who* they were. Even in the early 1830s John Quincy Adams referred to Boston's "aristocracy." He spoke not, of course, about a hereditary caste, but nevertheless of a known and visible group, possessing "wealth, talent and respectability," who had acquired learning, cultivation and the patrician manner, and who mingled with the middle and lower middle classes for public business until well into the nineteenth century.

But Boston was changing and comfortable relations across the hierarchy of class and status were decreasing. In part this resulted from physical growth and improvements. Originally a peninsula of only 500 acres connected with the mainland by a narrow neck of land, Boston had been regarded for over a century and a half as a "tight little island."

From the 1780s to 1822 the physical setting changed dramatically.[6] Population began rising at decadal rates of 40 to 50 percent; the 43,000 of 1820 by 1826 had grown to over 58,000. By 1822 five bridges spread out from the peninsula like the fingers spreading from a fist. Boston's three hills fell to pick and shovel and were dragged away by men and horses to make land out of water.

This was Prospero's Boston, with square miles of saltwater changed to glittering real estate. The frustration with Jeffersonian commercial policy and the cries of pain because of "economic ruin" caused by embargoes and war with England can hide the fact that this was a time of great prosperity. This was Bulfinch's Boston, with stately and elegant private mansions, churches, public buildings, and especially commercial developments rising throughout the town. In 1807-9 the rejuvenated India and Long wharves began operating, and when Central Wharf was completed in 1816 it was the jewel of the Atlantic coast: four stories high, with 54 stores and a special hall in the center over which was an observatory. A contemporary said that it was "for extent, convenience, and elegance . . . not exceeded by any in the commercial world." But the wonder of the day preceded this by eight years. The Exchange Coffee House was an unprecedented seven stories, making it "an immense pile" larger than any in the United States.[7] The spirit of Improvements was transforming Boston. It was one of the major reasons the Federal elite wanted to change from a town to a city organization, to have a stronger government more efficiently promoting development.

From Town to City

In his 1852 classic history of the early city Josiah Quincy said that one reason Boston needed to become a city in 1822 was that "seven thousand qualified voters" could no longer conduct town affairs by assembling in Faneuil Hall.[8] Though repeated by generations of historians, the statement is more myth than fact. While seven thousand voters might legally have attended town meetings in Faneuil, in practice they never did, nor did large numbers routinely assemble to discuss local questions. Indeed, participation in town affairs was usually low, especially compared to voting in state elections. As many as five and six thousand did troop to Faneuil Hall to cast ballots for state and federal officials, but this was far above the norm for town affairs.[9] Significantly, Federalist notables such as Harrison Gray Otis wanted desperately to keep voters coming only to Faneuil Hall for state and federal balloting, and accepted a provision for ward elections of such officers only when the active townspeople of the middling class rebelled and made it a condition for acceptance of the city charter.

Before 1822 the greatest number to vote was 5700, in the highly tense and hard fought state election of 1812. On the same day only some 3960 cast ballots for Presidential electors and a few weeks later less than 1600 voted for state representatives. Usually the total vote for representatives was even less than that. In 1824 the 1812 high turnout was exceeded when 6418 men voted in the last governor's election fully contested along Federal–Republican lines. Since population had increased greatly, however, the actual turnout (i.e., percent of eligibles) was probably greater in 1812. Indeed, from that standpoint, only in the years from roughly 1805 to 1815 was turnout impressive and probably in the range of 60 to 70 percent.

But the numbers participating in routine town affairs were much lower, often numbering 150 to 250. In 1815 a hotly debated plan to become a city was rejected by a not-routine vote of 951 to 920. In an October, 1812, town meeting, on the other hand, a measure involving the emotional issue of imprisonment for debt was narrowly defeated by a vote of 79 to 75. About 1820, however, dissatisfaction among the citizenry over the administration of justice, taxes, and other matters, brought unusually higher votes: 2037 for County Treasurer,[10] 2498 for state representatives, and in a special election for four vacancies on the school committee, 1582, though no choice resulted. Then during the city vs. town debates of 1821-22, participation in formal voting on a series of referenda was fairly high, at least by town standards, and meetings were crowded spectacles. It is still unlikely, however, that three or four thousand citizens crammed into the hall for the lengthy debates, and even the numbers casting ballots on controversial referenda remained well below those voting in hotly contested state elections.

The transition of 1821-22 was the immediate backdrop for a populist movement known as the Middling Interest, which emerged briefly in Boston and hastened the exit of Federal and Republican politics. The Middling Interest was a restrained middle-class sort of populism, but it anticipated social movements which flourished in the next several years. It also challenged the domination of Boston by a clique of high-toned Federalists, and gave vent to the resentment and aspirations of usually deferential middle- and lower-middle-class citizens. Of course Jeffersonian Republicans had mounted similar challenges and vented like frustrations before—this time the protest came from within Federal ranks and from men who had usually followered where T. H. Perkins, H. G. Otis, William Sullivan, and others had led. Though Republicans jumped on the bandwagon, the Middling Interest was a Federalist splinter group tired of the old Federal slogans. Among the middling classes it was a genuine grass-roots protest against "party" and against elite domination.

Up to 1822 Boston town meetings were run by the aristocratic Federalists with cooperation from a broadly based oligarchy reaching well down into the middle classes. The elite did not always get its way, and had failed on several occasions (1784, 1792, 1804, 1815) to convince the citizenry to adopt a city plan. (This veto power, in effect, which the middle classes sometimes wielded might be considered an important "democratic" element in the deferential-participant mix.) For various reasons many citizens still opposed changing to a city, and distrusted the proponents. Evidence could not be ignored, however, that the easy familiarity and cooperative spirit of the old town had deteriorated. Peace officers, for example, no longer dared to call on citizens for aid in making arrests, and firewards found it difficult to organize bystanders into traditional bucket brigades.[11] The decline of community spirit, however, did not create sentiment to organize a city government. The most important impetus came from abuses in the administration of justice and taxes, which resulted in part from an archaic county system over which Boston's citizens had little control.[12] Indeed, the most popular reform proposed by the city promoters in 1821-22 called for abolishing the county court of sessions and replacing it with a municipal police court, and for making the county treasurer the town treasurer. The voters approved this measure by 4557 to 257, while the charter had tougher going.

The charter controversy was not a party matter between Federalists and Republicans. The city proponents had always included leading Republicans on any committee which drew up city plans, and Republicans, like Federalists, had been divided on the issue. In general, town politics before and after 1822 remained far less influenced by party considerations than state and national elections, though the allegiances (or neutrality) of men influential in town meetings were generally known. Republican leaders, furthermore, led in calls for modification of the plan of 1821-22, and their support was gradually secured through several formal and informal compromises.

Opposition to the town's becoming a city sprang from inertia, and a vaguely defined though deeply held attachment to traditional ways of doing things. Average and ''middling'' men feared that innovation would deprive them of their accustomed rights and liberties. This was not just negativism, and many in Boston besides opponents of the charter still clung to an ideal of their community that was no longer a reality (though their faith might yet produce works). While the Middling Interest and those opposed to city incorporation were not necessarily the same groups, the doubts expressed by city opponents received vivid illustration in the events of early 1822 which led to the Middling Interest revolt.[13]

After three days of intense but orderly debate in packed meetings at Faneuil Hall, the town insisted that the charter as well as several controversial items be submitted to a general vote. One of the latter was the provision to elect state and federal officers in wards and not at Faneuil Hall. This proposal had come from the floor and had been pressed by Republicans who indicated they would throw their weight against the charter without it. Republicans also received private assurances that they would be given a share of city councillors and aldermen each year. Though the Federalist elite did not want ward elections, the measure and the charter both passed easily at the first balloting.[14]

The state legislature passed the new charter, but left out ward voting. Bostonians had elected some city officials by ward since 1799, and the legislature's action outraged many citizens and led to demands to resubmit the charter and ward voting to another referendum. Some moderate Federalists now warned that the legislature's action threatened acceptance of the charter. Both charter and ward voting prevailed again by healthy majorities, however, with support for ward elections increasing in the interim.[15]

The General Court had ignored the town's wishes on another matter which created an even greater storm of protest. During the past year a loose coalition of middle-class entrepreneurs and artisans had pushed for repeal of an 1803 law which prevented wooden buildings from being built over ten feet in height. The law had come into being after long and disastrous experience with fires, which had plagued Boston throughout its history. There had been major fires in 1787 and 1794 (about 100 buildings) and lesser blazes in 1801 and 1802. Tall wooden buildings not only burned easily, but the taller they were the more they spread the conflagration by transmitting flying sparks. They also created difficulties and hazards for firemen attempting to pull them down. Fire from brick buildings, on the other hand, issued mainly from windows to the immediate vicinity. But many middle-class Bostonians now thought the 1803 law oppressive. Some artisans simply wished for larger homes out of cheaper materials, while some master carpenters (or contractors) and entrepreneurs wanted to develop row houses. They proposed a substitute for the 1803 law which would control the height of new buildings and would incorporate some safeguards. While those who wanted to keep the 1803 regulation were relatively quiet, the town's representatives in the legislature failed to get the 1803 law repealed, even though the town by vote had clearly expressed its wishes. The sense of betrayal felt by many, especially Federalists, was made more acute by the current debates over the city charter.[16]

All indications are that leading Federalists used their influence in the legislature to bury ward voting and the ten footer repeal, not expecting serious reaction. In this they acted as generals who calculated without their army. Most of those supporting the ten footer repeal were Federalists, and they carried their protest not only into city politics but also probably contributed to the Federalists' demise in the state in 1823 and 1824.

On March 7, 1822 the town voted 2837 to 547 to revise the wooden buildings law. On March 11 a meeting of "citizens from all wards" ignored the traditional leadership and nominated a ticket of independent Federalists and Repubicans for state senators to oppose any list put forward under the auspices of the Federal Central Committee. The organizers were men from the "middling" ranks while their candidates were drawn from the pool of substantial men typically prominent in the town's politics–men, in short, from the oligarchy just below the level of the "aristocrats." The March 11 meeting passed two resolutions which came to be the two main principles of the Middling Interest: 1) Government was for the common good and not for the profit or interest of "any one man, family, or class of men," and thus none had any special or "exclusive privileges distinct from those of the community"; and 2) history showed that all men were "in danger of being led by party names to act contrary to their own true interests—names which might have originally arisen from a difference of opinion with equally patriotic motives, but which are often kept up ... long after that difference ... has ceased among the great body of the people." The protesters soon came to call themselves the Middling Interest, a name suggestive of both their social position and their desire to occupy a centrist position above party and appealing to both Federalists and Republicans. "Party spirit," they said, was a device used by the overbearing few to control the many.[17]

The same themes dominated an anonymous pamphlet which could be regarded as the manifesto of this grass-roots political revolt: *An Exposition of the Principles and Views of the Middling Interest.* This brief tract located the origin of the movement clearly in the wooden buildings and ward voting issues, but it also defined the fundamental question as nothing less than majority rule. The Middling Interest expected "from our constitutional agents some deference to the known will of the majority, and we deprecate the secret influence of a FEW." For several years now, it said, the truly patriotic men of both parties had grown dissatisfied "at the unnecessry excitement of the people, and the wanton violence of party spirit." Men of the Middling Interest supported good measures "by whomsoever adopted, without regard to any old party name." Moreover, they recognized that party spirit often served only to support the overbearing domination" of those who used it to control the freedom of opinion and independent suffrages of others.[18]

The Middling Interest's candidates for state senate did not win election, but they did get a respectable vote. As soon as the state election ended, the Middling Interest turned its attention to that for the new city government. The Federal elite planned to elect Otis, then serving as a

United States Senator, as Boston's first mayor. The Middling Interest, however, decided to back Josiah Quincy, an arch-Federalist famous for his opposition to the War of 1812 and to all things Jeffersonian. Indeed, Quincy's extreme views had made him something of an embarrassment to the Federalists in the Era of Good Feelings, and in 1820 he had been rebuffed by the Central Committee who dropped him from the state senatorial ticket. Moreover, Quincy had opposed incorporation in 1815 and 1821 before going along with it and helping to write the new charter, all of which made him an ideal candidate for the Middling Interest. Quincy had also become a leading expert on poverty and other city problems, but more important was his availability and, in the words of his recent biographer, the Middling Interest's need for "a well-known figure, but one neither politically beholden to the Otises, Sullivans, Tudors, and Perkinses, nor terrified by the social consequences of cross- ing them." In early March a delegation of Boston Federalists led by a carpenter paid a visit to Quincy at home and invited him to stand for mayor.[19] By early April there were two different candidates for mayor before the public, the regular Federalist nominee, Otis, and the Middling Interest candidate, Quincy. Appeals from Otis to party loyalty served only to anger the insurgents. But the election ended in a stalemate, with neither Quincy nor Otis winning a majority because a small group of Republicans refused to support either, though the Republican papers generally supported Quincy and enthusiastically made the cause of the Middling Interest their own. Several days later, in separate meetings, the regulars and insurgents both agreed on the popular John Phillips, a non-partisan figure prominent in community affairs. In the May election for state representatives, finally, the Middling Interest elected, after two trials, eight of twenty-five candidates in opposition to the regular Fed- eralist ticket.[20]

Besides winning repeal of the wooden building law, the movement also helped change the climate of Boston so that the rights of the middling and artisan classes became openly discussed and more freely asserted than ever before. Newspapers now appeared which cried out boldly against imprisonment for debt as oppressive to the poor (while rich bankrupts never went to jail) and even agitated for the rights of truckmen, laborers who carried heavy loads about the city in two- wheeled carts.[21] Moreover, Boston voters remained restless. Otis was now the Federal candidate for governor and some resentment may have lingered from the year before. He carried Boston by one of the slimmest majorities ever given to a Federalist gubernatorial candidate (2835 to 2727), and not all of the Federal senate candidates won election.[22]

In the 1823 city election Republicans put together a "Union" ticket behind George Blake, a Republican lawyer, but the Federalist candidate was now Josiah Quincy. While the Federalists' top brass still condemned Quincy's treachery of the year before, they needed him. Phillips had retired and Otis, running for governor, wanted no feud with Quincy. With the high Federalists doing nothing to help or oppose him, Quincy won, 2495 to 2182, while at the ward level Federalists and Middling Interest men mostly rejoined forces.[23] Partisan appeals had always been weaker in local politics and in the wake of the Middling revolt they were feebler still. In 1823 the Republicans defeated the Federalists in the state election, and after one more old style party contest in 1824, again won by the Republicans, party lines began to dissolve and the Federalists disappeared as a statewide political entry.

The Middling Interest insurgency gave an early clue that the partisanship of the Federal-Republican period was on the way out. Many voters presumably had lost interest in continuing debates over the 1807 Embargo, the 1812 War, or even more, Jefferson's "atheism." The episode gave vent to powerful social tensions and class resentments, not of poor against rich, but within the upper half or two-thirds of society. The ten footer and ward voting issues had united Federalist mechanics, artisans and shopkeepers with Republican lawyers, merchants, carpenters and others in opposing the elite because it directly affected their pockets and their self-esteem as citizens. Besides heralding the dissolution of Federalism and of party lines, the Middling Interest showed the potential for channeling middle- and lower-middle-class resentments and aspirations into anti-elitist and anti-party politics.

In the city elections deciding on the charter and mayoralty, some four to five thousand citizens voted. By contrast more than 5500 Boston men in 1823 and over 6400 in 1824 voted in the gubernatorial elections (though attention to state elections soon declined sharply). Perhaps the figure of 6400 was what Quincy had in mind when he spoke of seven thousand voters. In fact the potential electorate of taxpaying adults must have been larger than 7000. In 1820 there were by conservative estimate some 10,500 adult males 21 years or older. After he became mayor, Quincy revised the assessors' lists himself and determined the members paying any tax, even a poll tax, who were thus qualified to vote. The number in 1827 amounted to 12,000.[24] Therefore, as many as three to six thousand did not vote in gubernatorial elections and an additional two thousand or more never had anything to do with town affairs. Thousands of the young, the transient, and the poor participated little in elections or referenda, let alone town meetings. Those voting and campaigning for various men or causes came predominantly from the upper levels of the lower class and from the middling classes.

Thus, as the town became a city, its middle classes asserted themselves through political action designed for no more radical purposes than to assert majority rule against an elite accustomed to leading by nods and gestures, by courtly speeches and partisan oratory. Economic interest joined with class resentment and frustration with party loyalties that had outlived their day. The Middling Interest revolt also came from men who normally had been deferential. Soon, other groups in the middling, and even in the lower ranks, would also be asserting themselves and appropriating some of the same rhetoric of 1822-23.

Early City Politics

After the spring of 1824 city politics enjoyed more attention, especially with Josiah Quincy bringing energy and activism to the office that began Boston's transition to a city in more than name. The Market he built still stands as a symbol of the commercial growth which Quincy aided by construction projects, improved sanitation, attacks on vice and crime, and revamping inefficiently organized city services, particularly those dealing with fires and the poor. Under Quincy city expenditures went from $187,000 in 1821, the last year of the town, to $376,126 in 1826, not counting over $600,000 spent in the latter year on Quincy Market—which eventually paid for itself. Quincy was, in short, exactly the type of mayor which the city proponents of 1821-22 had wanted. Ironically, he alienated many groups similar to those who had opposed leaving behind the old town ways. He stripped the overseers of the poor of their power over "outdoor relief" and emphasized reformation of the poor. He battled with the fire companies, manned by societies of young men who competed for prizes in putting out fires and who often turned relief efforts into rowdy contests and brawls. At the end of his struggle to make fire fighting more efficient, Quincy had turned scores of young men into a political interest group against him, though the need for better means of putting out fires continued into the late 1830s.[25]

The events of the reign of "The Great Mayor" (1823-1828) are too well known to repeat here. For the purposes of this essay, Quincy's relations with the firemen and other interest groups are worth noticing because they throw light on Boston's changing society and politics.

Party considerations of any kind were largely irrelevant. Interest groups formed and reformed on particular issues, but had little permanence—except, perhaps, for the "grocers," a term covering many different kinds of sellers of ardent spirits. Quincy was "modernizing" Boston, helping to drag the town into a city, but the process remained incomplete long after he left office. Quincy was also highly traditional in many ways and relied on a mixture of innovation and older forms of influence, not the least of which was his own personal prestige and energy. While broadly interpreting the charter to give the mayor as much power as possible, Quincy recognized the utility of Section 25 of the charter, which still allowed for general meetings at Faneuil Hall. Though the impression persisted that votes at such meetings were legally binding, in reality they were only advisory. But the section had been written in to ease the transition and Quincy thought such meetings a good thing and encouraged them.[26]

Recognizing that the old cooperative spirit was gone and that essential services could no longer depend on citizen voluntarism, Quincy thus promoted professionalization of the police and fire services. At the same time he injected himself as public persona in the manner of the Federal notable to help make things work. But society was in transition, and his personal authority, which depended in part on continuing deference, had its limits. When Quincy decided to assault the Combat Zone of his day, a particularly lawless section of town, he was prestigious and popular enough with the burly truckmen to call upon them for aid in forming a posse. His son, in his biography of the mayor, called the truckmen "respectable."[27] What clearly mattered was that they were "respectful," that is, friendly (his policies helped them) and deferential to Quincy. The mayor's difficulties with the young firemen, however, with whose interests he clashed, also showed that deference had its limits in Quincy's Boston. And those limits were closing in quickly.

Yet the spirit of the Federal town passed slowly and still clung to the mayor's office. Quincy was elected five times, and after him, Otis served two terms. Thus, Boston's first three mayors were all men prominent in the life of Federal Boston, and two of them, Quincy and Otis, were names synonymous with New England Federalism. Mayor Charles

Wells (1831-1832) was different, younger and middle class. But then with Theodore Lyman, Jr. (1833-1834), and Samuel T. Armstrong (1835), Boston again had mayors similar in social character to Otis and Quincy.

Political parties did not intrude upon Quincy's mayoralty, and elections turned on his personality and policies. In 1824 and in two elections in 1825 (the time of election was changed to December) he faced little opposition. In 1826 his opponent of 1823 ran again and while excitement was high and the total vote in a mayoral contest the highest ever (5049), Quincy won handily. Only 2629 bothered to vote in 1827, but in 1828 Quincy's opponents, an aggregate of offended interest groups, sprang up on every side. Several different candidates ran poorly against him but in two trials succeeded in denying him a majority (the total rose from 4082 to 5253 in the two elections). So Quincy withdrew and the voters settled on the old war-horse Otis, who won re-election the next year with 79 percent of the votes cast (total of 3597). Though a "National Republican convention" nominated Otis for re-election in 1830, party was not a factor in these elections.[28]

Bridges and Railroads

While city politics remained non-partisan and vaguely Federal, a more complex pattern developed in state politics. Federalists and Republicans merged into a broad "union" coalition behind President John Quincy Adams and Governor Levi Lincoln, Jr. In 1825 both Federal and Republican caucuses backed Lincoln, a Republican, and he thereafter won re-election without much opposition. Boston, however, was a hatchery of schemes and rivalries, mostly coming from diehard Federals or "exclusive" Republicans who did not accept "union." Though citizen interest was unusually low, Boston elections for the state legislature were lively affairs displaying a Byzantine factionalism with a bewildering array of pure and hybrid tickets presented to voters. Those who did vote commonly split their tickets. In 1826 bitter Federalists led a revolt against Lincoln that gathered support only in the western part of the state.[29] In 1827 mostly dissident Republicans were involved in another factional outburst. This arose from a controversy over a "free bridge" between Boston and Charlestown. It led to the formation of a Free Bridge Party whose support was limited primarily to Middlesex County and Boston. It was significant for many reasons, leading to the famous Charles River Bridge decision of the Supreme Court. In the 1820s the controversy stood part way between the Middling Interest and more disruptive social movements yet to come.

Its origins lay in Boston's geography and in the aspirations of entrepreneurs, politicians, and lesser businessmen outside the old elite. Principal among these was the faction of anti-union Republicans whose organ was the Boston *American Statesman*, owned by David Henshaw, who had made money in wholesale drugs and now aimed at power and money through politics. The free bridge cause was a way station for Henshaw on his road to back Jackson in 1828 and eventually to become boss of the Jackson Democratic party in Boston in the 1830s. The *Statesman* had supported Crawford against Adams in 1824 and had made its trademark a strident anti-Federalism. Such was the magnetism of "union," however, that by 1826 even the *Statesman* was allied with Adams and Lincoln.

Meanwhile, the Adams-Lincoln Republicans increasingly reflected the views of the manufacturing elite which was building a powerful economic empire in cotton textiles, banking, insurance, and, a bit later, railroads. This elite was not new, for it had grown out of the old commercial elite and it contained men who valued wealth, talent, and respectability in a manner similar to the older Federalists. They could romantically idolize a Daniel Webster, who had risen from humble beginnings, but to them, men such as Henshaw, whose drug business had an air of disreputability about it, were untrustworthy upstarts and not their social or political equals. Henshaw and his associates entertained different views, however, and soon defied the elite and their "unionist" protectors on a matter that affected their purses and pride.[30]

In 1786 Boston merchants and investors had built the first bridge, the Charles River Bridge, across the many waters around the peninsula. The legislature chartered the bridge company and set its toll rates and rules of maintenance. Saving time and freight costs for merchants, farmers, and others of Charlestown and the near hinterland, the bridge enjoyed broad popular approval. To its proprietors it quickly paid huge profits, and other bridges soon followed.[31]

Throughout the Federal period the commercial elite dominated the planning and financing of such large projects of private enterprise which had a public bearing. The next four bridges (1793, 1805, 1809, 1821) were all ventures of the established elite and, as it developed out of that group, the merchant-manufacturing elite. They sought profits from tolls and from real estate speculation tied to the bridge's route.[32] It was not surprising that in the early 1820s, with old inhibitions crumbling and with the spirit of "improvements" abroad like a fever, new capitalists not sanctioned by family status or connections with the "aristocracy" should also try to make money from similar schemes.

In 1823 a group of Charlestown merchants petitioned the legislature to build a bridge over the Charles. It would collect tolls for no more than six years or until their expenses at 5 percent interest were recovered, and then the new bridge would be free. This venture thus aimed at returns from lower transportation costs and from higher real estate values.[33] And it was launched by men who must be considered prominent members of the economic and political elite of Charlestown—a group peripheral to the Boston elite and seeking to unshackle its own fortunes from Brahmin control of the main bridge to their town.

Though the legislature ignored this petition it soon received another from a Boston group, headed by David Henshaw, to build a similar free bridge to South Boston. The promoters sought the same object as the Tudors and Otises who had built the old South Boston bridge, to make money from real estate development in sparsely settled South Boston. The old bridge was vulnerable, however, because the need for a different bridge had been debated since its construction, and because it had made no money but had become a "fashionable promenade" with an appealing view of the town. On March 15, 1824, a city meeting voted 2847 to 779 in favor of a free bridge or dam to South Boston and "instructed" the city government (in the manner of the Middling Interest) to press the legislature for a charter. When the legislature hesitated Henshaw mounted a newspaper and pamphlet campaign which expanded the egalitarian appeal of the Middling Interest to a denunciation of monopoly and a celebration of competition. The proprietors of the old bridge did not put up prolonged resistance and by 1826 the South Boston Free Bridge won its charter.[34]

The Charlestown petitioners, however, would kill a goose that laid a golden egg. The owners of the goose, quite understandably, resisted furiously and the controversy raged inside and outside the legislature. But in March 1827 the legislature voted to charter the Warren Bridge Corporation, fixing its terminus on the Charlestown side a mere 260 feet from that of the old bridge. The proprietors cried out that this action endangered the security of all property and undermined basic property rights. To their aid at the eleventh hour came Levi Lincoln, Jr., casting

the first veto ever by a Massachusetts governor to stay the foul deed.[35]
To the polls then went insurgent Republicans (and Federalists) in
Charlestown, Boston, and the Middlesex County inner periphery. Voting for a man who refused their nomination, the Free Bridgers sent
Lincoln a message in the April state election, turning 57 percent of
Middlesex's vote against him, 28 percent in Boston (1237 votes), and
lesser amounts elsewhere. William Jarvis, their non-candidate, got under 20 percent statewide, but the next year the legislature again chartered
the Warren Bridge, and Lincoln, who much relished his role as an all-
popular consensus governor, did not oppose it.[36]

The controversy marked a stage in the transition to two Republican
factions—Adams men and Jacksonians—that would contest the 1828
Presidential election and then would develop into the loosely organized
National Republican and Jackson Republican or Democratic parties. In
1827 four and then five tickets appeared in Boston's elections for state
representatives (in two trials). Henshaw and several of his South Boston
Bridge associates appeared as candidates on the Free Bridge ticket and
by July Henshaw was running for Congress on an anti-tariff platform,
trying to cultivate free trade merchants and artisans opposed to the
manufacturing interest and getting in line nationally with the Calhounites
coalescing behind Jackson. By then the "unionists" had formed a Suffolk Republican Administration Committee and were holding up Adams,
Lincoln, and the defense of property as their standards.[37]

Despite the rhetoric about property rights, the Free Bridgers and the
elite did not really differ on basics of political economy. They certainly
did not disagree on economic development: both favored it. The bridge
conflicts simply but pointedly raised the question of under whose auspices development would occur, making it then anything but simple
and requiring the arbitration of all the courts of the land. Depending
on circumstances, both sides showed themselves willing to set aside
traditional definitions of property which stood in the way of freeing
their capital to maximize its potential. The underlying consensus on
development surfaced dramatically a short time later when railroad fever
swept Boston. From 1827 to 1830 Boston's economic and political
leaders, jealously watching the growth of New York City, became
convinced that the key to Boston's prosperity lay in a railroad connection
to the West which would link with the Erie Canal at Albany. Republicans
and former Federalists of all factions joined in the enthusiasm and
focused first on urging the legislature to build a state railroad, much as

New York had built the Erie. In February 1829 the citizens voted 3055 to 59 to authorize the city to purchase stock in such a road. But in the legislature all the peripheral regions of the state ganged up against Boston and other towns directly on such a line (Worcester, Springfield, Pittsfield) and refused to act. In 1830 both sides concentrated on sending representatives to the legislature and the May elections aroused unusual interest. Boston closed ranks on this issue and sent delegations strongly pro-railroad. But as sectional particularism proved too much to over-come, the merchant-manufacturers wanting railroads for their inland factories decided to begin on their own with shorter lines. In 1830 and 1831 the legislature granted them charters for a line from Boston to Lowell and another from Boston to Worcester. The charters showed that investors had learned well the lessons of the free bridges. The grants "paid lip service to public rights but actually put tremendous power into the hands of investors," giving them almost complete control over their property and routes, and protecting them from possible competi-tors. The views of the radical critics of "monopolies" regarding these charters have escaped historians' notice. So too have the views on property rights of the owners of the Middlesex Canal, alongside which the legislature permitted the manufacturers to build the Lowell Railroad.[38]

The campaign for a railroad to Albany helped revive interest in state elections, particularly for state senators and representatives. In Boston it forged a consensus amid competing political factions and entrepre-neurial interests, and, indeed, among most attentive social classes and groups. This short-lived harmony fittingly climaxed the early years of the city through which lingered the ethos of the Federal town.

The Rise of Organized Parties

Wooden ships had carried Boston into the nineteenth century as a rich town with capital resources, and in the 1830s the various enterprises connected with maritime trade were larger than ever, from the shipyards that built the vessels to the State Street companies that insured them. By then Boston merchants had created additional wealth from large-scale manufacturing, but the shadows of their huge brick factories did not darken Boston's streets, rather those of such places as Lowell, Waltham, and Springfield. As a leading producer of consumer goods and as a cultural center for New England and the United States, Boston was no factory town, but in many ways remained an eighteenth-century urban seaport and commercial entrepot.[39]

But if wooden ships and small-scale industry persisted, much else had changed. While rich patricians felt deeply their community responsibility and diverted impressive amounts of their treasure to improve the quality of life, the city's size, heterogeneity and mushrooming population growth did not come without cost. In the 1830s Boston politics lost most of the remaining attributes of the Federal town. Community cohesion weakened as class lines hardened and social distance lengthened between the rich and the middle and lower classes. The town and early city had known religious disputation and class resentment, but a new ugliness entered city life in the form of mob violence. Mobs had been active during the Revolution, but a different mix of passions and interests drove the mobs that burned a Charlestown convent-school in 1834 and that fought a pitched battle with Irish Catholics in Broad Street in 1837. These outbreaks quickened the professionalizing of the police and fire departments begun under Quincy, but they also exposed deep social divisions, not only among lower-class Catholics and Protestants, but also among upper- and lower-class Protestant natives.[40] These were but some of the signs pointing to the passing of the social context which had supported deferential-participant politics.

In 1835 still another kind of mob nearly lynched the abolitionist Garrison. Though this was the famous "broad cloth mob" led by gentlemen of property and standing and soldiered by counting house clerks, appeals to its sense of civility had gone unheeded. Mayor Lyman tried, in the manner of Quincy or Otis, to stop the mob by placing himself in its path. Though he helped rescue Garrison by fooling the mob, he and other "good men" could not stop the mob from surging at will through the streets and the city's offices.[41] More than five years before, even Mayor Otis had failed to restore order to a Faneuil Hall meeting of Antimasons which middle-class Freemasons had harassed and disrupted.

The controversy between Masons and their critics, indeed, was forming even during the fleeting consensus which had united Boston on railroads. Antimasonry originated in western New York when dozens of Masons had engaged in vigilante actions (including kidnapping and probable murder) and for the most part had escaped punishment through the complicity of law enforcement officials. Shock at these Masonic "outrages" particularly affected religious folk who already distrusted

Masonry's secrecy, pretentious titles, and impious oaths and who believed it anti-Christian, anti-republican, and immoral in all its tendencies. Cries for the fraternity's abolition spread from New York throughout the North, and in Massachusetts Antimasonry attracted pious evangelicals and especially Orthodox Congregationalists, already convulsed against Unitarian domination of a religious establishment that was once their own. To many Massachusetts Antimasons of whatever denomination, Masonry seemed to be a government within a government, enjoying special privileges, monopolizing public offices, and making a mockery of equal opportunity. Boston's Antimasonic leaders sprang from those solid middle classes marked by devotion to moral and material improvement of all kinds. The Masons tended to enjoy support among the leadership of the dominant National Republican Party, and the political elite either tolerated or protected the fraternity while disliking the "fanatics" crusading against it. Thus the attack on Masonry also became in part an assault against the political establishment.[42]

State and national politics bore the brunt of the Antimasonic political thrust, and, with former President John Quincy Adams as their gubernatorial candidate, in 1833 Antimasons garnered 30 percent of the state vote. In Boston, however, Antimasonry was relatively weak at the polls and intruded only slightly into city politics, though Boston Antimasonry provided the state movement with most of its leaders, money, and printed materials. Yet its total impact on Boston's public life went further: for five years the Antimasons and Masons carried on rancorous disputes in public forums, in churches, courtrooms, political parties, places of business, and in the streets. All of this helped to chip away at Boston's civility and inbred tolerance; and beyond the number of actual Antimasons, the movement must have added to distrust of government and authority spreading as well from other sources.[43]

At the same time that Antimasonry grew among the middle classes, lower-middle-class artisans and mechanics and working-class journeymen and apprentices also began a protest movement. From 1830 to 1835 Boston experienced several strikes and the growth of a Trades Union movement. While Antimasonry fed on the religious and moral evangelism of an aspiring middle class, this Working Men's movement aimed for a better material life for ordinary workers. Though a Working Men's Party entered the state elections of 1833 and 1834, activist workers (relatively few of the whole) pursued their goals—and lost their fight—largely outside of politics. Neither the movement nor the party had any discernible impact on city elections, and in the governor's elections of 1833 and 1834 the "Workies" polled only 9 and 5 percent of Boston's vote. Yet the movement bore witness to the disintegration of traditional economic relations and to the great disparities in wealth now so obviously existing in Boston. And defiance from young workers near the bottom of the social status hierarchy must have contributed to the sense of things coming apart in the early and mid-1830s.

Amid the centrifugal tendencies of 1830-1835 there also emerged powerful counter-trends toward order in political life. One of these came from within: as an active city government grew, an incipient bureaucracy spread from—where else?—the top and center. Another ordering force came essentially from outside: from the major political parties which did not much affect city politics until the late 1830s.

Political parties had been forming slowly in the struggles over state issues, with the minority Jacksonians aided by federal patronage. Suddenly, for the first time since the War of 1812, great numbers of citizens again took an interest in national politics, drawn by another war—this time President Andrew Jackson's "war" against the Bank of the United States. The city's National Republican leaders used the financial distress caused apparently by Jackson's policies to rally support for a new party, the Whig, protested Jackson's tyrannical removal of government deposits from the Bank, and called for a sound currency and restoration of the Bank or some central banking institution. Boston's middle classes and workers joined in the protests by the hundreds. In the fall of 1834, with the Antimasons making a last and poor showing in a state election, both the new Whig party and the Democratic party gained in voters and expanded their support. Bostonians flocked to polling places casting an unprecedented total of almost 8500 ballots in gubernatorial voting, while in 1836 just over 7600 voted for governor and just slightly more for Presidential electors.[44]

Yet the dramatic arrival of Whig-Democratic competition developed separately from city politics. Before 1835 party organizations were weak and loyalties and passions generated by state and national issues entered only momentarily into city affairs. After Quincy and Otis, mayoral elections continued to be a matter of struggles among personalities backed by interest groups and various factions of National Republicans. In 1831 three separate groups of Nationals nominated three different candidates for mayor. A coalition of grocers, Nationals, independents, and Jacksonians backed Theodore Lyman. It took two trials for Charles

Wells to beat Lyman 3316 to 2389, with 223 scattering.[45] In 1833 Lyman, a maverick who had backed Jackson in 1828, won easily over another National Republican in an election in which the National Republican ticket for Aldermen encountered no opposition. Though some historians have believed Lyman to be a Democrat, the fact is that in 1834 he was presented as part of a ticket of "Regular Whig nominations" for all city elective offices. This was the pre-dawn of party's intrusion into city elections with Lyman now uncontested, with 4261 of 4404 votes cast.[46]

The Whig and Democratic party organizations, built on the convention system, did not develop fully throughout Massachusetts until the late 1830s. They were vigorously gathering momentum, however, in 1834-35. Although party lines did not influence the Boston city election of 1834, in 1835 two organized parties nominated rival tickets for city officers.[47]

The Democratic opposition attracted only a fraction of the city's electorate, however, and the Whigs won the city elections of 1835 and 1836 by about three to one. Turnout for mayor remained well below that for governor. Yet from 1835 on the Whig and Democratic organizations imposed themselves more firmly on the city, at least on the annual nominations and elections for mayor, aldermen, and ward officers. By the late 1830s party organizations permeated city politics more than ever before. They hardly controlled all areas of city politics, but parties now existed as institutions with a life and rationale of their own. They differed fundamentally from the immature parties of the Federal era, and constituted a much different way of mobilizing popular participation in city affairs.

Party organizations now channeled the voting of a much larger electorate, and did so in all arenas: federal, state, and local. From the mid-1830s to the mid-1850s the Whig party dominated Boston and Massachusetts, though the Democratic party remained a vital force at the polls. In 1850-51 the anti-slavery Free Soil Party, containing many Whig defectors, combined with the Democrats in a Coalition which temporarily ousted the Whigs from power. In 1852 and 1853 the Coalition floundered and the Whigs reasserted their hegemony, but in the mid-1850s both the Whigs and the party system itself came under attack in a populist upheaval of unprecedented proportions. Social tensions at home and national political controversy over slavery extension brought about a realignment of parties in the 1850s in which the Whig Party sank from sight. But the new Republican Party took its place as the state and Boston's majority party, and by the late 1850s political party organizations once again became the controlling structures for the political life of the city.

In many places throughout the United States, the rise of political parties brought about a decrease in upper-class participation in public life, and in electoral politics especially. Elites of the Federal-Republican era withdrew in disgust from the hurly-burly of mass mobilization and the unrestrained invective of partisan politics. No-longer deferential voters now rejected men who appeared to be too much "gentlemen of taste and refinement," lacking the common touch.

These changes came to Boston, of course, and by the 1840s the social status of men elected to the principal city offices already had slipped perceptibly. Yet the elite of the Federal-Republican era, as Frederic Cople Jaher shows in the next essay, remained very active in public affairs generally, and in fact retained a dominant role in the city's life.

Notes

1. For an elaboration of this theme see Ronald P. Formisano, "Deferential-Participant Politics: The Early Republic's Political Culture, 1789-1840," *American Political Science Review* 68 (June 1974): 473-87.

2. J. R. Pole, *Political Representation in England and the Origins of the American Republic* (New York: Macmillan, 1966), pp. 44-46; also, John B. Kirby, "Early American Politics—the Search for Ideology: An Historiographical Critique of the Concept of 'Deference,' " *Journal of Politics* 32 (November 1970): 827.

3. Boston's seafaring glory is described in Samuel Eliot Morison, *The Maritime History of Massachusetts, 1783-1860* (Boston: Houghton Mifflin Company, 1921), pp. 225-52; Paul Goodman, "Ethics and Enterprise: The Values of the Boston Elite, 1800-1860," *American Quarterly* 18 (Fall 1966): 437-51.

4. For the general political situation: Paul Goodman, *The Democratic-Republicans of Massachusetts: Politics in a Young Republic* (Cambridge, Mass.: Harvard University Press, 1964); James M. Banner, Jr., *To the Hartford Convention: The Federalists and the Origins of Party Politics in Massachusetts, 1789-1815* (New York: Alfred A. Knopf, 1970); George Athan Billias, *Elbridge Gerry: Founding Father and Republican Statesman* (New York: McGraw Hill, 1976); and still valuable Anson Ely Morse, *The Federalist Party in Massachusetts to the Year 1800* (Princeton: Princeton University Press, 1909).

5. Election returns for gubernatorial and Presidential elections (1800-1840) came from the manuscript returns at the Massachusetts State Archives, Boston.

6. Walter Muir Whitehill, *Boston: A Topographical History*, 2nd ed. (Cambridge, Mass.: Harvard University Press, 1968), pp. 47-91.

7. Caleb H. Snow, *A History of Boston* (Boston, 1825), pp. 327, 329, 330-35.

8. Josiah Quincy, *A Municipal History of the Town and City of Boston, 1630-1830* (Boston: C. C. Little and J. Brown, 1852), p. 28.

9. These statements and those below regarding elections are based on the manuscript returns for state and federal elections, and on the numbers given as voting for town officers in *Boston Town Records, 1796 to 1813*, Vol. 35, and *Boston Town Records, 1814-1822*, vol. 37, *Records Relating to the Early History of Boston* (Boston, 1906). Returns for city elections from 1822 were compiled from various newspapers. For assistance in assembling the latter I am indebted to Constance K. Burns and Ann M. Grenell.

10. Voting for country treasurer often was done after most other city officers were elected, and votes cast ranged from approximately 150 to 250. One might guess that after electing 110 other town officers interest had waned and the numbers present were lower than at the start of the meeting—yet they do give some indication of interest levels. Another credible rationale for changing to a city involved the number of town officers chosen. At one time they were probably known to most voters but that could no longer be the case in the 1820s.

11. Roger Lane, *Policing the City: Boston 1822-1885* (Cambridge, Mass.: Harvard University Press, 1967), p. 12-13; John Koren, *Boston, 1822 to 1922: The Story of its Government and Principal Activities During One Hundred Years* (Boston: City of Boston, 1922), pp. 7-8. An anonymous gadfly also commented on the decline of community spirit: *Selections from the Chronicles of Boston* (Boston?, 1822), Widener Library, Harvard University. Also, Edward Lewis Ballantyne, ''The Incorporation of Boston 1784-1822'' (honors thesis, Harvard College, 1955), pp. 53-56.

12. Carl Wilhelm Ernst, *Constitutional History of Boston, Massachusetts: An Essay* (Boston, n.pub., 189?), pp. 73, 74.

13. For debates over the change: Boston *Palladium*, Feb. 26, Mar. 1, 1822: [William Emmons], *Mr. Emmons' Speech, Delivered at the Grand Caucus, Held in Faneuil Hall, On the Evening of the Third of March, 1822, Upon the Acceptance of the City Charter* (Boston, 1822); Snow, *Boston*, pp. 363-64, 366.

14. *Palladium*, Jan. 1, 4, 8, 1822. Federal opposition to ward voting: ''A North End Mechanic,'' Boston *Columbian Centinel*, Jan. 5, 1822; other Federalists said the measure needed to pass or the charter would fail, *Palladium*, Mar. 1, 1822.

15. On January 7 the town approved the charter 2805 to 2006 and ward elections 2611 to 2196. On March 4 it passed the charter 2797 to 1881 and ward elections 2813 to 1887, *Palladium*, Jan. 8, Feb. 15, Mar. 5, 1822.

16. Petitions to town meeting before and after the legislature's action: *Palladium*, Jan. 15, Mar. 5, 1822; arguments against wooden buildings, *Palladium*, Jan. 25, 1822, and esp. "Z" in Boston *Patriot*, Mar. 5, 1832. The 1803 law and earlier fires are treated in Snow, *Boston*, pp. 322, 325, and Whitehill, *Boston: A Topographical History*, p. 50.

17. *Palladium*, Mar. 15, 1822; Robert A. McCaughey, *Josiah Quincy, 1772-1864: The Last Federalist* (Cambridge: Mass.: Harvard University Press, 1974), p. 102.

18. *An Exposition of the Principles and Views of the Middling Interest: In the City of Boston* (Boston, 1822), quotations pp. 4, 5, 7. A subsequent *Defense of the Exposition of the Middling Interest . . .* (Boston, 1822), devoted itself to justifying the right of Bostonians to instruct their legislative representatives and also undergirded its argument with the same themes: the adherents of "the few" denied the right of instruction "because they believe the people must be managed, and that THE FEW are better able to direct public affairs;" people were now beginning to bring more knowledge and common sense to bear on politics and were interested in knowing the truth, "moreso, than in favoring any party or set of men," pp. 3, 4.

19. McCaughey, *Josiah Quincy*, pp. 89-91, 93-94, 103-04; Thomas H. Perkins to Harrison Gray Otis, Boston, 5 April 1822, Otis Papers, Massachusetts Historical Society.

20. McCaughey, *Josiah Quincy*, pp. 104-05; Speech Before a Federalist Caucus, Spring (no date) of 1822, Otis Papers; *Palladium*, Apr. 9, 16, 1822. The Middling Interest nominated its own slate of candidates for sixteen ward officers in Ward Seven, and probably in other wards as well. In Seven most but not all were elected, indicating compromise tickets at the ward level, *Palladium*, Apr. 5, 9, 1822.

21. In July *The Bostonian and Mechanics' Journal* appeared to champion the rights of "mechanics," a term encompassing a variety of skilled craftsmen and small businessmen. Later it usually backed Republican candidates for Congress, Nov. 2, 1822, June 28, 1823; also Boston *Evening Gazette*, Oct. 26, 1822.

22. *Palladium*, Apr. 8, 15, May 13, 16, 1823; *Bostonian*, Feb. 8, Apr. 5, 12, May 3, 1822; E. Starkweather to H. G. Otis, 29 Jan. 1823, Otis Papers.

23. *Palladium*, Apr. 15, 18, 1823; *Evening Gazette*, Apr. 12, 1823; *Bostonian*, Apr. 19, 1823.

24. Quincy, *Municipal History*, pp. 237-38.

25. McCaughey, *Josiah Quincy*, pp. 106-13; Lane, *Policing the City*, pp. 14-25; Charles Phillips Huse, *The Financial History of Boston: From May 1,*

1822 to January 31, 1909 (Cambridge, Mass.: Harvard University Press, 1916), p. 13.

26. Ernst, *Constitutional History*, p. 111.

27. Edmund Quincy, *Life of Josiah Quincy* (Boston: Ticknor and Fields, 1868), p. 397; Lane, *Policing the City*, p. 24; McCaughey, *Josiah Quincy*, pp. 112, 118-19.

28. McCaughey, *Josiah Quincy*, pp. 127-31; Boston *Columbian Centinel*, Dec. 12, 1827, Dec. 10, 17, 1828, Dec. 6, 16, 1829; Boston *Evening Transcript*, Dec. 14, 1830; Samuel Eliot Morison, *The Life and Letters of Harrison Gray Otis, Federalist, 1765-1848* (Boston: Houghton Mifflin Company, 1913), II, 287.

29. Shaw Livermore, Jr., *The Twilight of Federalism: The Disintegration of the Federalist Party, 1815-1830*. (Princeton: Princeton University Press, 1962), pp. 190-92, 227; Boston *Patriot*, Apr. 8, 1826; *Palladium*, Mar. 31, Apr. 4, 1826; Newburyport *Northern Chronicle*, Mar. 3, 17,1825; Robert C. Winthrop, *Memoir of the Hon. Nathan Appleton, LL.D.* (Boston, 1861), p. 31.

30. Boston *Statesman*, 1825-1826, *passim*. On the Boston elite there are many sources, including Robert F. Dalzell, Jr., ''The Rise of the Waltham-Lowell System and Some Thoughts on the Political Economy of Modernization in Ante-Bellum Massachusetts,'' *Perspectives in American History*, 9 (1975): 227-68; and Frederick Cople Jaher, ''The Boston Brahmins in the Age of Industrial Capitalism,'' in Jaher, ed., *The Age of Industrialism in America: Essays in Social Structure and Cultural Values* (New York: The Free Press, 1968), pp. 188-262.

31. This account is based heavily on Whitehill, *Boston: A Topographical History*, pp. 47-91, which is indispensable for understanding the background of the bridge controversy, though it contains, ironically, almost nothing about the Warren Bridge matter.

32. Stanley I. Kutler, *Privilege and Creative Destruction: The Charles River Bridge Case* (Philadelphia: J. B. Lippincott, 1971), pp. 19-20; Whitehill, pp. 51-52, 76, 78, 85-88, 90-91; Snow, *History of Boston*, pp. 327, 329, 330, 332-35.

33. The Warren Bridge incorporators included Nathan Tufts, John Cofran, Nathaniel Austin, and Ebenezer Breed, *Laws of the Commonwealth of Massachusetts, 1825-1828* (Boston, 1828), X, 851, 852, 855. Earlier interpretations of this affair have neglected the business interests and social standing of these men. For information on some of them: Timothy F. Sawyer, *Old Charlestown: Historical, Biographical, Reminiscent* (Boston: James H. West, 1902), pp. 107, 167-68, 173, 175-78, 217, 219, 220-22, 226, 227, 371, 957-67; Thomas Bellows Wyman, *The Genealogies and Estates of Charlestown, In the County of Middlesex and Commonwealth of Massachusetts, 1629-1818* (Boston: David Clapp and Son, 1879), II, K-Z, 870; *A Century of Banking in Historic Charlestown, 1825-1925* (Boston, 1925), pp. 7, 8, 17, 19, 21.

34. [David Henshaw], *An Appeal to the Good Sense of the Legislature* (Boston, 1825), pp. 4, 19-20; Darling, *Political Changes*, p. 49; Whitehill, *Boston*, p. 78; Samuel H. Riddell, "Mr. Charles Ewer," *Memorial Biographies of the New England Historic Genealogical Society, 1853-1855* (Boston, 1881), II, 116.

35. *Review of the Case of the Free Bridge, Between Boston and Charlestown* (Boston, 1827); Kutler, *Privilege and Creative Destruction*, pp. 19-25, 27; *Boston Patriot*, Apr. 3, 1827; Oscar Handlin and Mary Flug Handlin, *Commonwealth: A Study of the Role of Government in the American Economy: Massachusetts, 1774-1861* (Cambridge, Mass.: Harvard University Press, 1969, rev. ed.; first ed., 1947), p. 150. The House voted to override Lincoln's veto but the Senate fell short of a two-thirds majority.

36. Huge majorities were given to Jarvis in Charlestown and towns in its vicinity. In Boston factionalism was still rampant: *Palladium*, Mar. 27, Apr. 3, 1827; *Statesman*, Mar. 10, 15, 22, 27, 31, 1827; Boston *Courier*, Mar. 26, 29, Apr. 2, 1827.

37. *Patriot*, May 8, 16, 18, 1827; *Courier*, May 9, 1827; *Statesman*, May 10, 12, 14, 17, 19, 1827. Regarding Henshaw's Congressional run: "Member of Congress," July 24, 1827, Broadsides, Rare Book Room, Boston Public Library. On the emerging Union party, David Lee Child, Boston, 24 May 1827, to Levi Lincoln, Lincoln Papers, Massachusetts Historical Society; *Palladium*, Apr. 20, 24, May 15, 18, 1827.

38. Quotation from Stephen Salsbury, *The State, the Investor, and the Railroad: The Boston & Albany, 1825-1867* (Cambridge, Mass.: Harvard University Press, 1967), pp. 80-81, and 31-81 *passim*. Salsbury judged the Bridge episode to have been a long run blessing in disguise for potential railroad investors. On the consensus in Boston on state aid, Handlin and Handlin, *Commonwealth*, pp. 172-73. Mayor Harrison Gray Otis was a strong proponent of railroads, Quincy, *Municipal History*, pp. 284-86, and most of Boston's papers had railroad fever, e.g., *Centinel*, Feb. 7, 11, 14, 21, 25, Mar. 7, 21, 1829.

39. Richard D. Brown, *Massachusetts: A History* (New York: W. W. Norton & Company, Inc., 1978), pp. 147-49.

40. Theodore M. Hammett, "Two Mobs of Jacksonian Boston: Ideology and Interest," *Journal of American History* 62 (March 1976): 549-56; Lane, *Policing the City*, pp. 26-38.

41. Lane, p. 32; Theodore Lyman, *Papers Relating to the Garrison Mob* (Cambridge, Mass.: Welch., Bigelow, 1870).

42. For the origins of Antimasonry: Ronald P. Formisano and Kathleen Smith Kutolowski, "Antimasonry and Masonry: The Genesis of Protest, 1826-1827," *American Quarterly* 29 (Summer 1977): 139-65. Statements about the social attributes of Antimasons and Masons are based on collective biographical study reported in Formisano, "Antimasons and Masons: Massachusetts and Western

New York,'' Paper prepared for the Annual Meeting of the American Historical Association, San Francisco, December, 1978.

43. Ronald P. Formisano, *The Transformation of Political Culture: Massachusetts Parties 1790s-1840s* (New York: Oxford University Press, 1983), pp. 197-244.

44. Arthur B. Darling, *Political Changes in Massachusetts, 1824-1848* (New Haven: Yale University Press, 1925), pp. 127-29, 130-43, 190-91, 199-201; Manuscript Election Returns, Massachusetts State Archives.

45. *Evening Transcript*, Dec. 5, 9, 13, 20, 23, 1831. Wells won re-election without significant opposition, receiving 2918 of 3699 votes cast, *Transcript*, Dec. 11, 1832; also, Boston *Daily Advertiser*, Dec. 5, 8, 11, 1832.

46. *Advertiser*, Dec. 2, 4, 9, 11, 1833; and Dec. 8, 9, 10, 12, 1834.

47. *Advertiser*, Dec. 7, 12, 14, 1835, for Whig nominations of Mayor, Aldermen, and ward officers; for nominations and election results the next year, *Advertiser*, Dec. 10, 12, 14, 1836.

3

The Politics of the Boston Brahmins: 1800-1860

FREDERIC COPLE JAHER

During the early national period urban patriciates dominated the commercial, political and cultural life of Philadelphia, New York, New Haven, Connecticut, Salem and Newburyport, Massachusetts (along with low country planters), Charleston, South Carolina, and other old East Coast cities. The persistence and accomplishments of these groups varied in different places, but the most notable and long lived of this species of urban gentry appeared in Boston. From the 1780s to the Great Depression the Boston Brahmins wielded considerable influence in the most important public and private activities in the city. At times, especially between 1800-60, this multi-functional upper-class, by dominating the foremost local business establishments, political organizations and cultural and philanthropic institutions, assumed the role of a ruling elite.

The Brahmin community had variegated roots. A few members of the Puritan oligarchy, Endicotts, Winthrops and Saltonstalls, reappeared in the nineteenth century upper order, thus bridging the gap between Boston's oldest elite and its post-Revolutionary successor. Another source of continuity came from survivals of the provincial government-mercantile enclave, Amorys, Quincys and Otises. The struggle for independence also created openings in the highest rank in Boston for men from humbler local elites in New England and even more obscure antecedents. Family

Chapter 3, "The Politics of the Boston Brahmins: 1800-1860," by Frederic Cople Jaher appeared previously as Chapter 2, "Boston," in THE URBAN ESTABLISHMENT: UPPER STRATA IN BOSTON, NEW YORK, CHARLESTON, CHICAGO, AND LOS ANGELES, by Frederic C. Jaher (© 1982 by the Board of Trustees of the University of Illinois). This work is used with the permission of the University of Illinois Press, Urbana, Illinois.

fortunes were made in trade, piracy and speculating during the Revolution, and in pioneering post war commerce with China, India and the South Sea Islands. The Higginsons of Salem, the Danas of Cambridge and the Jacksons of Newburyport had ranked among the first families of their home towns for several generations. Other prominent Bostonians had respectable and even substantial backgrounds of more recent advent. The Lees of Salem and the Lowells and Tracys of Newburyport achieved business success a generation or two before independence. But many self-made men reached the top in the late eighteenth century. The fathers of William Sturgis, William Gray and Samuel Eliot, founders of great overseas trading houses, were respectively a sea captain, a master shoemaker, and an impecunious printer and bookseller. Boston's richest capitalist, Peter Chardon Brooks, was the son of a poor minister. The Appleton and Lawrence brothers, incorporated in the enclave in the next generation, were children of respectable farmers from New Ipswich and Groton. By the 1820s the Brahmin enclave, composed eventually of some forty inter-related families, was substantially established.[1]

Leading Bostonians often came from small towns, villages and farms; a migration from the country to the city, from the periphery to the center, that frequently occurred in other urban elites. Such movement indicated a willingness to cut roots and break with traditions, a personality trait suited to the acquisition of wealth, power and prestige in an era and a place of rapid economic and political change. As the group consolidated, differences in social and economic origins gave way to shared interests, activities and intermarriage, and newcomers merged with the old guard.

The Brahmins were not exclusively a political elite. Control over municipal government was a facet of the comprehensive leadership that the group exerted in Boston and was used to protect its dominance over other aspects of urban life and, in turn, the other dimensions of its sovereignty enhanced its political power. Multi-dimensional hegemony made the Brahmins an upper-class, and thus distinguished the enclave from more narrowly based political, economic or social elites that characterized the fragmented power structure of other cities.

In its formative phase the economic base of the Boston patriciate consisted of the great overseas trading houses, e.g., Russell & Co., J. & T. H. Perkins, and later, Bryant & Sturgis. The need for capital and the quest for wealth drew eminent merchants into other enterprises to solidify and expand their commercial position. The Massachusetts First

National Bank of Boston (1784), until 1815 the largest bank in New England, was organized, directed and owned by Brahmin traders. This institution served the maritime elite as a source of funds and profits, a mechanism of exchange and a force to stabilize the supply and value of credit and currency. The other major banks in Boston, including the local branches of the first and second Banks of the United States, were similarly dominated by Brahmin merchants and their kin. While gaining control of foreign trade and banking the commercial elite, along with its relatives and other allies well placed in the state and municipal governments, became large urban land owners, improvers and speculators. Around the turn of the century the Mt. Vernon Proprietors, a syndicate of prominent merchants and their associates, began to develop Beacon Hill, a real estate venture of unprecedented magnitude. Until the 1860s Brahmins conceived, financed and directed the development of Beacon Hill, Back Bay and large parts of South Boston and the waterfront, the city's largest antebellum undertakings.[2]

These initiatives reflected the juncture of political and economic power and blended private gain with class interests and the public good. Banks, bridges, improved wharfage, widened streets, better markets and building construction facilitated transportation and trade, provided employment and upgraded land values. These achievements and their consequences served the interests of the upper class while benefiting the entire community. Thus the largest speculators, when in public office, sometimes accomplished highly useful projects. Mayors Josiah Quincy and Harrison Gray Otis cleaned up Boston Common, and Quincy widened Fanueil Hall Market and helped establish the Public Gardens. Their efforts contributed to the transformation of the Yankee town into a sophisticated city.[3]

Land speculation contributed to Brahmin wealth and, as another field of cooperative endeavor, united the upper-class. Real estate investment particularly promoted group cohesion when it created patrician residential areas. The Proprietors, by developing Beacon Hill as an exclusive neighborhood, exemplified elite enterprise enhancing upper-class integration. Beginning in 1796, Brahmins bought up land and built family mansions on Beacon Hill. To this day parts of the Hill remain an upper-class district and descendants of the original investors live in some of the old houses. Distinctive ethnic and social enclaves seek their own turf and the Boston gentry were no exception to this dwelling pattern. Residential proximity and retention of ancestral homes became a class emblem both for the elite and for outsiders. Arrivistes moved there to legitimize their acquired status and joined oldtimers in fighting to save the historical, genealogical and esthetic integrity of the neighborhood. Despite its location near the business center they successfully resisted rezoning even though the introduction of hotels, apartment houses and commercial structures would raise property values. Cultural and class solidity preempted the profit motive and preserved Beacon Hill as an expression of Brahmin Boston.[4]

Brahmin ascendancy encompassed the prestigious professions as well as politics and business. Prominent in the legal, medical, religious and educational elites, the enclave commanded skills that extended its power and wealth, celebrated its position through manipulation of ritual and symbol, affirmed its leadership by shaping community values and initiating civic welfare and cultural projects, and protected itself by recruiting new blood. Lawyers participated in the formulation and implementation of constitutions, articles of incorporation and other important pieces of legislation, and in the litigation and adjudication of vital issues. Heavily involved in these matters, the patriciate was well represented at the bench and the bar. Harrison Gray Otis resuscitated his family's failing fortune through successful practice in admiralty and maritime litigation. Upper-class legal dynasties that lasted over a century, the Lowells, Danas and Paines, originated in the 1790s and early 1800s and matched in repute their kin among the pre-eminent maritime clans.[5]

Medicine also attracted men from distinguished families. This vocation made its greatest contribution to urban upper-class leadership by aiding the sickly poor, a mission which brought together Brahmin physicians and their relatives among the economic and political elite. The founding of Massachusetts General Hospital (1821) exemplified the spirit of Brahmin civic obligation. Boston lacked facilities for the general treatment of disease and the indigent were woefully deprived of medical care. Massachusetts General, staffed, financed and run by upper-class doctors and trustees, ministered to the ill and underprivileged.[6]

Professional activities in religion and education further buttressed Brahmin hegemony. Upper-classes throughout history sought control over thought and culture to spread their dominion. Churches and schools traditionally cultivated the conceptions, inspired the beliefs, and advocated the arguments that legitimize the authority of the reigning strata. In antebellum Boston, Unitarianism and Harvard became the cultural arm of the mercantile-Federalist establishment, the vehicles for disseminating its ideas and values.

After the Revolution the Brahmins embraced Unitarianism. Liberal Christian ministers saved the souls of the upper class at King's Chapel and the Brattle and Federal Street Churches; Unitarian scholars informed the community and deepened their wisdom at Harvard and The Boston Athenaeum and through *The North American Review*. Staunchly Federalist in politics, faithful defenders and close associates of the patriciate, Unitarian pastors, professors and pundits stood guard over the cultural bailiwick of Brahmin Boston.[7] By 1805 Harvard was a Unitarian stronghold. The educational citadel of proper Boston was also a bastion of Federalism because, in the words of its official historian, "Harvard in politics has always reflected the sentiments of the ruling economic class in Boston." Since colonial times the College had been attended, supported, directed and often staffed by the establishment. Undergraduate life, where a smattering of the classes combined with good fellowship among peers, created a comprehensive class atmosphere in which morals were taught, manners polished and connections made. For those with assured places in society Harvard was a relaxed stage of passage from childhood to the family firm or some other upper class calling.[8] For outsiders a Harvard degree might facilitate entry into the urban gentry. Two years after graduation, Edward Everett, son of a poor clergyman, became minister of Boston's elite Brattle Street Church. He later married Peter Chardon Brooks' daughter and was a Massachusetts Governor, United States Senator, Secretary of State and president of his alma mater.[9]

Supplementing Harvard and Unitarianism as instruments of cultural leadership, the Brahmins founded societies and journals which helped determine the direction of respectable scholarship and literature. The Massachusetts Historical Society (1791), The Boston Athenaeum (1807) and *The North American Review* (1815), products of the formative period of the patriciate, became permanent monuments of upper class intellectuality. Their overlapping memberships and sources of support comprised the interlocking cultural complex of Harvard, Liberal Christianity and Brahmin business and political figures.[10] The upper class professors, ministers, benefactors, administrators and authors active in these institutions ushered in the renaissance that made Boston the "Athens" of nineteenth-century promotion, individual, family and group advancement, moral inspiration, and intellectual refinement. The upper class derived from Boston's national reputation much of its sense of status and accomplishment as a ruling enclave. As the richest and most powerful group in Boston the Brahmins assumed a proprietorial attitude toward the city. Identifying themselves with the destiny of the town, they conceived of their cultural attainments and institutions as a weapon in the interurban competition among the Atlantic seaboard metropolises. Thus in 1815 William Tudor, a founder of The Athenaeum and first editor of *The North American Review*, tried to organize a "Fine Arts" museum to "give us the start of New York & Philadelphia" and make Boston "the capital of arts & sciences."[11]

Brahmin civic consciousness involved philanthropic as well as cultural activity. Voluntary association functioned expressively and instrumentally to perpetuate patrician hegemony. Cultural institutions usually emphasized the former role by articulating and inculcating Brahmin values to foster elite cohesion and legitimize elite leadership. Charitable agencies tended to emphasize the latter role by using proper Boston money and influence to create rewards and punishments that would encourage the underprivileged to accept the virtues of the established order.

With the noteworthy exception of Massachusetts General Hospital, the upper-class, before 1830, mainly patronized Harvard and kindred religious and intellectual institutions. Other aspects of the city life were deemed the province of the family or the government. The Brahmin concept of social responsibility broadened in the 1820s when the establishment discovered the existence of large numbers of poor and began to doubt the adequacy of traditional benevolence. Destitution, argued contemporary observers, led to delinquency, and enflamed by Jacksonian democracy, the immigrant influx, local riots, and rising rates of drunkenness, pauperism and arrests for assault and battery, could kindle a social conflagration that might consume the propertied. Fears of class conflict mixed with the higher morality of human sympathy and *noblesse oblige* stimulated public and private efforts to reform the poor and improve the quality of relief. Mayor Josiah Quincy, who had chaired the 1821 General Court Committee on Pauper Laws which gave the first widespread publicity to the problem of poverty, reorganized the administration of municipal assistance to the needy. Spurred by self-interest and altruism, the Harvard-Unitarian-business-Federal-Whig establishment dominated organized private charity. Whig statesmen Robert C. Winthrop and Samuel Atkins Eliot, for example, presided over several important benevolent agencies and headed the Boston Provident Association, founded in 1851 to coordinate the city's numerous charity organizations.[12]

Individually and as a group the Brahmins were the greatest donors in Boston. Between 1800-30, according to Quincy, contributions for charitable, moral, religious and cultural activities totalled $1,801,273. Upper class institutions received the lion's share of Bostonian largesse. Massachusetts General ($354,000) was the most heavily endowed, followed by Harvard ($222,696). The treasuries of these and other patrician favorites account for over half the expenditure during the three decades. In the next fifteen years, according to another estimator (probably S. A. Eliot), Bostonians spent $2,938,020 on various welfare and uplift causes. Organizations controlled by the Brahmins, such as The Lowell Institute ($245,000), Massachusetts General ($286,513) and Harvard ($83,755), again account for over half of the total donation in this period.[13]

This brief survey of upper class economic, cultural and philanthropic endeavor illuminates the perspective of the local political elite—Proper Bostonians or their auxiliaries—who held government office, served as party chieftains or otherwise wielded political power during the years of Brahmin supremacy. These figures thought of themselves as public spirited, informed and privileged gentlemen who represented, through kinship, common interests and shared values, a network of commercial enterprises, cultural and charitable activities, genteel families and social values, and community obligations and civic pride. Brahmin politicians had many roles, as reflected in the careers of Whig leader and United States Senator and Congressman Robert C. Winthrop and Congressmen and Boston Mayors Josiah Quincy and Samuel A. Eliot. Winthrop was president of The Children's Hospital of Boston, chairman of The Board of Overseers of the Poor in Boston, head of The Boston Provident Association, The Massachusetts Bible Society, The Massachusetts Historical Society and The Board of Commissioners charged with building the Boston Public Library. Quincy, nephew of a patrician Boston merchant and president of the Massachusetts First National Bank, was a trustee of Massachusetts General Hospital, treasurer of the Historical Society and president of Harvard and The Athenaeum. Textile manufacturing executive Eliot headed the Prison Discipline Society, The Boston Provident Association and The Boston Academy of Music, and served on the board of Massachusetts General and as warden of King's

Chapel. Their careers were not unique among the Boston gentry. Abbott Lawrence, another Whig chieftain, Congressman and textile magnate, Edward Everett and many others had similarly diverse but interrelated posts of leadership in upper-class institutions.[14] Political activity was the major public role of Winthrop and H.G. Otis. For Eliot, Quincy and Lawrence, it was one of many activities undertaken on behalf of their class, their community, their business interests and their own self-fulfillment.

The multi-dimensional structure of Brahmin hegemony did not preclude ambition for material gain and political place; nor did it prevent rifts in the ruling enclave. The interrelated and comprehensive nature of Brahmin leadership, however, created an outlook that restrained the disintegrative tendencies of unbounded individualism and thus encouraged the patriciate to use political power to sustain class cohesion and to make Boston the best governed antebellum American metropolis. If the proprietorial posture of the Brahmins toward Boston impelled them to act on behalf of the public good it also impelled them to identify that good with their individual and class interests. Bostonians of other strata and ethnic origin would discover that their versions of effective government and civic welfare and their aspirations to acquire and distribute the assets of power, wealth and status would be opposed by an upper class determined to preserve its hegemony over the urban community.

Brahmin influence permeated every layer and branch of government. Boston was the center of New England Federalism and the party directorate, the Essex Junto, came mostly from kinship linked mercantile clans whose eminence dated from the Revolution or earlier times. Among this group were two United States Senators (George Cabot and H. G. Otis), six Congressmen (Otis, Francis Dana, Jonathan Jackson, Josiah Quincy, John Lowell and Stephen Higginson), one Federal Judge (Lowell), one Minister to Russia (Dana), one Chief Justice of the Commonwealth (Dana) and two Boston Mayors (Otis and Quincy). Numerous relatives of these statesmen served as Boston Mayors and Councillors, as state legislators and as judges. Primarily Federalist, upper class Boston also contained opposition leaders; Russell Sturgis, John Quincy Adams, William Gray, and the Salem Crowninshields, the pre-eminent Democratic-Republican family in Massachusetts, had marital and commercial ties with the patriciate.[15]

Office holding elevated Brahmin status through the highly visible symbols and rituals of the political process. Although public officials and political leaders do not always control decision-making, the Boston political and economic elites merged and government service advanced class power as well as class or individual honor. Junto members in the national government effectively promoted maritime enterprise. They secured advantageous tariffs, drawbacks on products imported and exported by Massachusetts traders, and tonnage duties which discriminated in favor of Bay State shipping. Alexander Hamilton, a close friend of the junto, played the key role in furthering mercantile interests. His financial strategy also increased the value of public securities, held in large amounts by the merchants, assisted patrician banking institutions, and provided the commercial elite with stable and substantial sources of credit. According to Samuel Eliot Morison, "No section or interest in the United States was so favored by Washington's and Adams's administrations as maritime Massachusetts."[16]

Overseas trade could best be protected at the national level, but other Brahmin objectives required the support of the state government. Here, too, patrician political leaders capably guarded group interests. The initial triumph of the mercantile–Federalist enclave was the state constitution of 1780. Delegations from the port towns of Boston, Salem, Newburyport, and Beverly included prominent merchants and lawyers. They brought forth a conservative document that protected commerce.[17] In 1786 the patriciate again defeated the agrarian debtor group from western Massachusetts by helping to suppress Shays's Rebellion. Governor James Bowdoin, offspring of an aristocratic colonial family of Boston merchants, acted vigorously to crush the insurgents. He sent out an expeditionary force chiefly financed by himself and other maritime titans. Younger members of the gentry contributed by officering an infantry company raised in Boston.[18] Fearing agrarian uprisings, debtor depredations, and business disasters, the Boston elite enthusiastically backed the United States Constitution. During the bitter struggle over ratification they played a pivotal part in obtaining the necessary votes for acceptance.[19] In these contests the maritime elite bested its most formidable foe, the agrarian enclave. Federalist–mercantile primacy, once established, became a versatile and influential force in advancing the interests of proper Boston.

In banking, political connections were almost as important as financial assets. Charters had to be secured from the state legislature and possibly defended against rivals. If subsequent incorporators were relatives or associates of the proprietors of constituted financial organizations, they advanced a common interest by expanding available resources and services. But newcomers might be competitors who could divert profits, unsettle business conditions, or challenge the established group. Politics also played a significant role because banks were considered quasi-public institutions and their presidents semi-government officials. This relationship was underscored by governments keeping public funds in private financial institutions or using them as fiscal agents. Such practices expanded a bank's resources and political leverage was crucial in obtaining these privileges. As a consequence of the interaction between public bodies and the banks, directors and officers were frequently chosen for their government influence. America's first great banker, Philadelphia aristocrat Thomas Willing, President of the Bank of North America and later of the BUS, was a friend of George Washington and a partner of Robert Morris, the prominent financier and Washington's first choice for Secretary of the Treasury. The chief executives of the Boston banks were similarly well connected. Bowdoin was the first president of the Massachusetts Bank, his successor served in the legislature, and Federalist leaders Higginson and Lowell were among the founding directors. Through the influence of its organizers and officers the bank became the fiscal agent of the Commonwealth: it issued notes with the state seal, the government punished counterfeiters of its currency, it held government deposits and made loans to the state. Chief executives of other banks were also politically active: William Gray, head of the State Bank of Boston and the Boston branch of the first BUS, served twenty years in the state House and Senate and refused an appointment as Secretary of the Navy. Bank directors and shareholders also often held office, or had familial and commercial ties with government officials.

Brahmin influence in the formulation and ratification of a city charter in 1821 equalled the enclave's role in the conception and adoption of the federal and state constitutions. Representatives of the maritime establishment dominated the committee that wrote this document.[20] The creation of the municipal government, albeit not without a struggle as described in the last chapter, and the numerous and important offices filled by patricians indicate their political importance in Boston. This power proved particularly useful in urban real estate operations, which necessitated involvement in local as well as state affairs. Building permits, incorporation charters, location of public improvements, low property assessments, rights of way, and purchase of property were secured by power in the Massachusetts and Boston governments. The Beacon Hill venture illustrates the relationship between private interests and political leverage. Mount Vernon proprietor Otis, who served on the legislative committee that sited the State House near Beacon Hill, had advance notice that the land values would rise in that area. Improvements in the Boston Common made under Mayors Otis and Quincy further increased the price of real estate in the section. In the 1820s and 30s Beacon Hill inhabitants defeated the zoning board's attempts to commercialize the neighborhood. Other Brahmin enterprises also benefitted from political influence. Otis's and Jonathan Mason's participation in the South Boston Bridge project (1805) entailed a legislative package that included the city's annexation of South Boston. Quincy bought a city wharf in 1852 and built warehouses on it.[21] Brahmin administrations also enhanced the interests of rich property holders through low tax rates and undervaluations of real and personal holdings.[22] Successes in these transactions disclose the ability of Brahmins to manipulate the government through office holding, organized resistance to competing groups and interests, or through other forms of leverage.

Intramural rivalries, e.g., the competition for public deposits among Brahmin financial institutions, did not disrupt the unified support of upper class Boston for Federalist political and economic policies.[23] During the heyday of Federalism the patriciate achieved an almost comprehensive degree of political consolidation; even Adams and Gray, the foremost Brahmin Democratic-Republican leaders, did not desert the Federalist Party until Jefferson's second presidential term.[24]

Soon after the Brahmins emerged as an upper class they felt threatened by Democratic–Republican victories and the damage wrought by Jefferson's Embargo and the War of 1812 upon Commonwealth and overseas commerce. This period of anxiety extended from the Virginia Dynasty's triumph in 1800 through the Democratic–Republican defeat of Otis in the Massachusetts gubernatorial election of 1823. The maritime based upper class outlasted these misfortunes only through the extraordinary energy and resourcefulness of its sons and the recruitment of new blood. The achievement of the younger generation transformed the group into an urban aristocracy and prolonged Brahmin predominance for many decades.

The stormy beginning of the nineteenth-century panicked the great overseas traders. Several failed and others suffered heavy losses.[25] Anxiety over vanishing profits turned conservative businessmen like Thomas Handasyd Perkins and Henry Lee into outraged, if temporary, disunionists and converted these self-confident merchants into intermittent harbingers of doom.[26] The younger generation of Brahmins met this threat to their economic base by turning from the sea to manufacturing. Ex-foreign traders Patrick Tracy Jackson and John Amory Lowell introduced modern mechanized textile production in this country and by the 1820s the Brahmins dominated the first great industry in America. During the 1830s and 40s members of this enclave also presided over the creation of the New England railroad system, which was an outgrowth of their need to move the products from their mills to the port of Boston. The interrelated Lowells, Jacksons, Lawrences, Appletons, Amorys, Dwights, Lymans and Coolidges, often called the Boston Associates, figured most prominently in cotton manufacturing and became the new economic core of blueblood Boston. In their prime the Associates controlled 20 percent of the national cotton spindleage, 30 percent of Massachusetts railroad mileage, 39 percent of Bay State insurance capital, and 40 percent of the city's banking resources.[27]

Absorbing the capital and talent of new men, like mill magnates Amos and Abbott Lawrence and Nathan Appleton, the Brahmins successfully mastered the challenge to their economic hegemony and were one of the rare mercantile upper classes that retained their standing by adapting to industrialism. The old patrician merchants initially reacted to the textile titans with the bitterness of a beleaguered elite and snubbed those manufacturers without blueblood credentials.[28] This rift was symbolized in the 1830 contest between Henry Lee and Nathan Appleton for a Boston congressional seat. Although the election took place when the breach was closing, it was a classic confrontation between the mill and the mast, between the archaic and progressive wings of proper Boston. The issue was the protective tariff and the outcome victory for the self-made factory owner. Friction between the mercantile and manufacturing elements of Brahminism, however, eventually subsided. Boston shipping recovered after 1819, the maritime gentry invested in textile mills, their offspring participated in cotton manufacturing and railroad enterprises and Lawrences and Appletons appeared on the boards of prestigious cultural, educational and charitable institutions and intermarried with the urban gentry.[29]

The Brahmin political situation for a generation after 1800 paralleled the course of the group's economic circumstances. An initial period of defeat and dismay produced rifts between older and younger patrician statesmen. But this division healed in the wake of recovery and reconstitution in the 1820s.

Political disasters accompanied the economic debacle of the early 1800s. The foreign policy of John Adams distressed the maritime elite and their discontent deepened into despair during the presidencies of Jefferson and James Madison. Old guard merchants and statesmen reacted to their loss of national influence by denouncing Democratic-Republican programs and popular rule. The patriciate blamed its displacement upon the insurgence of unrestrained democracy, which it thought could destroy the nation. Fearing for their property, disgruntled over business reverses, disgusted with government policies and outraged at losing national influence, Perkins, Quincy, Lowell, Cabot, Otis and other Brahmins were at the forefront of the opposition to the War of 1812. The main vehicle of their protest was the Hartford Convention (1814). Otis and Cabot were moderate Federalists who sought to deflect the anti-union sentiments of extremists like Lowell, but the Democratic–Republicans succeeded in weakening the Federalists as a national force by vilifying the Convention and its leaders as a secessionist cabal. The Federalists retained supremacy in Massachusetts until the party's defeat in the 1823 gubernatorial election. Its candidate, labeled as a Harvard–Unitarian aristocrat, even lost Essex Country. The death knell sounded a year later when John Quincy Adams, Democratic–Republican presidential nominee, took Boston.[30] The disappearance of Federalism, however, did not end Brahmin political power. A younger generation of upper-class Federalists (and some of their elders) showed the same resourcefulness as their entrepreneurial counterparts; the one switching to a new line of business, the other to the dominant political party.

A split—similar to that which surfaced between the old mercantile grandees and the younger members of the upper class who embraced industrialism—developed between older Federalists and their juniors who wished to continue their careers and preserve their power by joining or courting the Democratic–Republicans. Senior solons of the Essex Junto despaired over the triumph of the Jeffersonians and raged against defectors from their own ranks. Stephen Higginson believed that Otis "would sell any or all parties or persons in succession till he reaches the top." The Federalist knight-errant viewed J.Q. Adams in a similar light.[31] Those accused of opportunism thought little better of their elders. "Many of them," wrote Adams to Quincy, "are too much devoted to

personal and selfish views to make any sacrifice to party purposes."[32]
The cleavage divided upper-class Boston into defenders of the faith who
saw in flexibility betrayal and pragmatists who considered recalcitrance
a vice of Cronos rampaging Boston Federalism. Denunciations did not
deter desertion. "We are now all Republicans," observed Lee when
President James Monroe visited Massachusetts in 1817, "even the Essex
Junto."[33]

Trimming sail to survive the gale of democracy meant more than
switching party affiliation. Adjustments in attitudes, or at least in rhetoric, appeared among the younger politicians. In 1801 Otis "retire[d]
from" Congress to "remain a silent spectator of the follies and confusion, of the strife and licentiousness incident to all popular governments and to ours in a most eminent degree."[34] But he returned and
subsequently became a United States Senator and Boston Mayor. During
his later career Otis discovered, or at least stated, the virtues of popular
rule. Addressing the City Council in 1830, he rejoiced that "Many"
in the municipal government's "first ranks rose from humble beginnings
and hold out encouragement to others to follow their steps." This
felicitous condition of "equality" derives from the enfranchisement of
the "great majority," who "constantly" elect the "middling class as
respects wealth, the merchants and the working men ... to all offices
in state and city...."[35] An even more remarkable tribute to popular
sovereignty came from another Federalist. Quincy gracefully attributed
his defeat for reelection as mayor "to the sound principles of a republican constitution, by which the will of a majority [was] distinctly
expressed concerning the continuance in office of public servants."[36]
As David Hackett Fischer has observed, old school Federalist leaders
became increasingly aloof and bitter while younger members of the
party, with their careers before them, adapted to partisan tactics and
new political forces.[37]

The political pessimism of the early 1800s proved as inaccurate a
view of the future as were forebodings over the fate of Brahmin business.
Federalist defeats in national campaigns and in other states did not
prevent the party from usually winning Massachusetts state elections.
Commonwealth politics thus reinforced the strength of the urban patriciate. Many Brahmins were present in the delegations that Boston and
Salem sent to the Massachusetts Constitutional Convention of 1820-21
and they protected upper-class interests. The state senate remained ap-
portioned according to property, thus ensuring an over-representation

of Boston in that body, the judiciary retained its power and Unitarianism preserved its privileges when attempts to disestablish religion were defeated.[38] Gloomy predictions over the destiny of national affairs also never materialized. As the Jeffersonian spirit waned Brahmins found Republican policies more congenial. Higher tariffs, internal improvements and the rechartering of the National Bank enhanced the appeal of the party, especially for the growing industrial enclave in the upperclass.

Brahmin economic resurgence was linked with political power. Business required government nurture and upper class enterprises at first relied on the residue of proper Boston influence that survived the Democratic-Republican victories. As new beginnings matured into powerful corporations they interacted with political activity to enable the establishment to recover its primacy in the Commonwealth and increase its national influence. Similar to the development of mills, railroads and financial institutions, new men and new party organizations blended with the old guard to reassert upper class political supremacy. Massachusetts Whiggery, dominated by textile magnates and their allies, became the instrument of leadership.

Wealthy and well-born Bostonians achieved even greater political power in Boston than at the state level. The city had been a Federalist-mercantile stronghold and after the demise of the party rich businessmen and statesmen from distinguished families dominated local politics. The first three mayors, John Phillips, Quincy and Otis, and two of the next four, Theodore Lyman, Jr. and Samuel Atkins Eliot, were Brahmins. Between 1846 and 1851 proper Bostonians Josiah Quincy, Jr. and John Prescott Bigelow served in the office. Numerous members of the upper class were aldermen, common councillors and overseers of the poor. Between 1825 and 1850 three-fifths of the mayors and over one-third of the common council were merchants, though the proportion of maritime aldermen and councillors fell appreciably after the 1830s. Lawyers, with one-third of the mayors in these years, ranked next to merchants in occupations of chief executives. Attorneys also proliferated in the common council until the 1830s when they, too, declined in this body as patrician representation, measured by birth, wealth and vocational status, began to diminish in municipal affairs.[39]

The convergence of power, wealth and social elites may be demonstrated by calculating the percentages of government office holders and Brahmins among the wealthiest Bostonians on the city tax assessment lists of 1835 and 1860.[40] Merchants and lawyers, the highest frequency occupations of Brahmins (textile magnates were usually also merchants) and the highest frequency occupations of Boston mayors, aldermen and councillors, composed respectively 69 and 11 percent of the vocations of Bostonians assessed for at least $100,000 in personal property in 1830. Merchants comprised 66 percent and attorneys 10 percent of the Bostonians at that wealth level in 1850.[41] Fifty-two of the 79 Bostonians (65.8 percent) assessed for a minimum of $100,000 (actually $50,000 because the listing was for one-half the value of the property) were born, married into, or their children and grandchildren would unite with Brahmin families. These standards of affiliation are used because it is impossible to determine exactly when individuals or families moved into the upper order. Entry was usually a gradual process of multiplying business and family ties, inheritances, memberships in patrician institutions, etc. There were 130 Brahmins, 38.0 percent of the 342 Bostonians, rated as possessing at least $100,000 in personal property on the city assessment list of 1860.[42] The decline of Brahmin representation was caused by a sharp drop in textile profits after 1847 and by patrician reproduction and recruitment lagging behind economic expansion and the proliferation of personal fortunes in Boston.

The richest stratum possessed a large share of the personal (noncorporate) accumulations in Boston. The top 1 percent of the propertied in 1833 (those worth at least $75,000) owned one-third of the noncorporate holdings in the city; their 1848 counterparts (those assessed for at least $90,000) owned 37 percent of the noncorporate wealth. The top 1 percent increased its share of property ownership, a trend that began before the Revolution. (Salem, several other Massachusetts towns, New York, Philadelphia and Brooklyn had a similar proportion of maldistributed wealth and, like Boston, the inegalitarian trend grew throughout the antebellum era.[43]) Given its commanding position as proprietors, stockholders and officers in banks, railroads, textile mills, mercantile firms, real estate operations and insurance companies, the monied elite also controlled a large segment of Boston's corporate wealth.

Considerable fusion existed between the economic and social elites and between these groups and the political elite. Party leaders and high public officials, Otis, Quincy, Charles Francis Adams, Samuel Atkins Eliot, ranked among the wealthiest Bostonians. Twenty-four of the seventy-nine (30.4 percent) richest residents of 1835 were common councillors, aldermen, judges, mayors, state legislators, U.S. congressmen and senators and cabinet members. Eighty-one of the 342 most affluent city dwellers (23.7 percent) of 1860 held similar posts. Apart from the moderate decrease in the proportion of rich who filled public office, one major change occurred between earlier and later times. In 1835 seventeen office holders (21.5 percent) were Brahmins; twenty-five years later twenty-seven (7.9 percent) belonged to tthe enclave.[44] The upper-class component of rich officials fell sharply by 1860, a drop which reflected the waning political influence of proper Boston. The Whig collapse and the growing strength of the middle classes in city government accounts for this decline.

Manufacturers, railroad barons, and the new generation of bankers acquired political power in the same fashion and for the same purpose as did their mercantile forerunners. Between 1830 and 1860, when the second great era of blueblood office holding came to a close, textile magnates Appleton, his cousin William Appleton, Abbott Lawrence, Samuel Atkins Eliot, son of Samuel Eliot, and banker-railroad promotor Samuel Hooper, scion of a prominent shipping family, served in Congress. S.A. Eliot, Lawrence's brother-in-law John Prescott Bigelow, and Quincy's son, a railroad promoter, were mayors of Boston. Many patricians also sat in the state legislature and the city council.[45] Once again the upper order assumed leadership in business and politics.

Capitalists not only filled government posts, they also financed the Whig Party in Massachusetts and had marital and commercial ties with its stellar statesmen, Daniel Webster, Edward Everett, and Robert C. Winthrop. Webster's daughter married an Appleton, Everett wedded a Brooks, and Winthrop belonged by birth and marriage to the most distinguished clans in Massachusetts. Financial assistance and business affiliations solidified family connections. N. Appleton and Lawrence sold textile corporation stock to Webster and contributed to a fund to keep him in office. The great orator was counsel for the Boston & Lowell Railroad and the Boston Manufacturing Company and Everett held stock in the Western Railroad.[46]

The Whig Party between 1834-48, except for two years, controlled the governorship, and, excluding one year, both state houses. Every U.S. senator and twenty-seven of the thirty-one Commonwealth Congressmen were Whigs, and between 1836-48 the party won Bay State presidential contests.[47] During these years the overwhelming majority of rich Bostonians (86.5 percent of those worth at least $100,000 and 96.3 percent of the city's millionaires) were Whigs.[48] The party dominated Massachusetts and the Brahmins controlled the party. J.Q. Adams called Lawrence "perhaps the most leading man of Whig politics in Boston," Charles Francis Adams said that "Abbott Lawrence and Nathan Appleton" constituted "the ruling influence," and David Donald considers Appleton, Webster, Winthrop, and Rufus Choate "the real leaders of Massachusetts Whiggery."[49]

Whig chieftains labored to advance Brahmin business interests. National officeholders fought for a high tariff to protect cotton manufacturing against European competition. Webster, appearing before the Railroad Committee of the Massachusetts Legislature in 1845, successfully argued the Boston & Lowell's case against a rival's attempt to break its monopoly over the route between the city and the textile town. The Western, another line dominated by textile capitalists, received even greater favors from the General Court. State loans covered three-quarters of construction costs—no other road got as much public aid. Stockholder Everett played a crucial role in procuring public assistance. He was governor when the Western was built, and a commercial, political, and social intimate of Josiah Quincy, Jr., and Elias Hasket Derby, its main promoters.[50]

Whig supremacy in Massachusetts was shaken when the Party split into "Cotton" and "Conscience" factions over the annexation of Texas. Resistance to the extension of slavery created a rift within proper Boston as Cotton Whigs, led by the textile magnates and Webster, Winthrop and Everett, sought to maintain friendly relations with the Southern planters, suppliers of cotton to the New England mills. A minority of the upper class, opposing the spread of slavery, backed the Conscience faction, and a few Brahmins went even further and joined the abolitionists. The Conscience Whigs became Free Soilers in 1848 and Republicans in the 1850s. Charles Francis Adams, son of J.Q. Adams and son-in-law of Brooks, was one of the leaders of this movement and several bluebloods were among its supporters. Others of distinguished lineage, Edmund Quincy, Wendell Phillips, James Russell Lowell, and Thomas Wentworth Higginson, even more antagonistic to slavery, became abolitionists. The opposition, uniting with the Democrats in 1850, broke the string of Whig victories by preventing Winthrop from succeeding Webster in the Senate. Significantly, Brahmin Free Soilers and abolitionists mostly stemmed from colonial or mercantile origins rather than from textile families. Although they came from an older segment of the patriciate, the anti-slavery leaders were younger than most of the

Cotton Whig chieftains. They heralded, as had the defectors from Federalism, the emergence of another generation and a change in party affiliation from the establishment. Similar to the previous dispute between aging conservatives and new leaders, the struggle did not last long enough to threaten group cohesion. The Civil War healed the division and made Republicans of the vast majority of proper Boston. Ironically, intra-class partisan conflict weakened Brahmin political power—while demonstrating, in furnishing principals for both sides, the abundance of patrician leadership talent.[51]

The upper class relished its political and economic ascendancy in Massachusetts, but Boston was the citadel of Brahminism. Pride, place, proprietorship, and tradition, combined with power and prosperity, inspired a high order of civic responsibility and an impressive record of civic accomplishment accompanied, as usual, by indefatigable pursuit of self and class interests. For thirty years after the formation of the city government in 1822 the Brahmins ruled municipal affairs. Political leaders used their influence to promote personal concerns and the schemes of their associates. By the 1820s and 30s Appletons, Lawrences, and younger Lowells and Jacksons joined older entrepreneurs in urban real estate operations. The development of Back Bay, beginning in the 1860s, was the greatest project of the new generation.[52] Private interests spurred enlightened public policy. Wharves, markets, apartment and office buildings, railroad terminals, land development and elite neighborhoods appreciated in value through improvements in metropolitan life. The first Brahmin mayor, John Phillips, served a quiescent term, but his successors were more active. Josiah Quincy (1824-30), the greatest of the patrician mayors, established street cleaning and refuse removal procedures still in use sixty years later, began work on the public market, paved streets, cleaned up the Common, built schools, replaced volunteer firemen with a city fire department, centralized police and health agencies and supplanted the Overseers of the Poor and outdoor relief with a House of Industry under municipal government supervision.[53] Theodore Lyman established a state reform school, paved and repaired thoroughfares in the business section and built public schools. Samuel Atkins Eliot reorganized the police and fire departments, built a municipal office building, completed the public market, improved streets and constructed a hospital for the insane. Josiah Quincy, Jr. erected schools and a new jail, reformed the police, constructed a waterworks, also improved the streets and spent large sums on a park system.

John Prescott Bigelow, though dedicated to retrenchment of expenditures, built an almshouse and modernized the waterworks. According to Mayor Bigelow, New York, with three times the population, only doubled the annual government expenditures of Boston. Maintenance of a low tax rate while improving many aspects of urban life attests to the efficiency and honesty of the blueblood administrations.[54] During the first ten years of city government the tax rate was lower than in the previous decade and did not begin to climb dramatically until the 1850s.

The nature and limitations of these advances reveal the perspective of upper class rule. The main concerns of Brahmin municipal administration were to prevent disorder, improve the business district and adjacent exclusive neighborhoods and rationalize public services to maintain low taxes. Public policy, therefore, reflected the interests and values of proper Boston—the group whose members and representatives dominated local government. It was the Brahmins who had the most property to lose from lower class violence, deficient fire and police organizations and high taxes and the most to gain from a better business district, a House of Industry, a formidable jail house and a beautiful Common that would raise property values in Beacon Hill. Less privileged Bostonians participated marginally, if at all, in these urban benefits. The overcrowded, disease and death plagued slums did not stop growing and it is doubtful that the House of Industry, Quincy's monument to "scientific" charity, appealed more to its clients than the archaic, but kinder, system of outdoor relief. Nevertheless, Boston was a comparatively well governed city and the Brahmin policy of increasing public services while minimizing waste and corruption has led urban historian Constance McLaughlin Green to praise Boston as America's earliest and best provider of urban welfare.[55]

Notes

1. The best genealogical source for the Boston Brahmins is *The New England Historical and Genealogical Register*.

2. The best general works on the maritime elite are: Samuel Eliot Morison, *Maritime History of Massachusetts, 1783-1860* (Boston: Little Brown, 1921); Robert A. East, *Business Enterprise in the American Revolutionary Era* (New York: Columbia University Press, 1938), pp. 39-80, 180-263; Foster Rhea Dulles, *The Old China Trade* (Boston: Houghton Mifflin, 1930); N.a., *Professional and Industrial History of Massachusetts*, 3 vols. (Boston: The Boston History Company, 1894), I, pp. 69-155; Robert E. Peabody, *Merchant Ven-*

turers of Old Salem (Boston: Houghton Mifflin, 1912). For studies of individual merchants and firms see: Kenneth Wiggins Porter, *The Jacksons and the Lees*, 2 vols. (Cambridge: Harvard University Press, 1937); Edward Gray, *William Gray of Salem, Merchant* (Boston: Houghton Mifflin, 1915); Charles G. Loring, *Memoir of William Sturgis* (Boston: John Wilson and Son, 1894); Thomas G. Cary, *Memoir of Thomas Handasyd Perkins* (Boston: Little Brown, 1865); Carl Seaburg and Stanley Patterson, *Merchant Prince of Boston: Colonel T. H. Perkins, 1767-1854* (Cambridge: Harvard University Press, 1971); John T. Morse, Jr., *Memoir of Col. Henry Lee* (Boston: Little Brown, 1905). For published accounts by the merchants themselves see: Robert Bennet Forbes, *Personal Reminiscences* (Boston: Little Brown, 1878); Forbes, *Remarks on China and the China Trade* (Boston: Samuel N. Dickinson, 1844); Frances Rollins Morse (ed.), Henry and Mary Lee, *Letters and Journals* (Boston: privately printed, 1926). For manuscript sources see: The Perkins Papers, The Samuel Cabot Papers, the Patrick Tracy Jackson Letterbooks in the Massachusetts Historical Society (hereafter cited as MHS) and the Harvard Business School (hereafter cited as HBS). For Brahmin banking see: N.S.B. Gras, *The Massachusetts First National Bank of Boston, 1784-1934* (Cambridge: Harvard University Press, 1937); N.a., *The National Union Bank of Boston* (Boston: n.p., 1934); Amos W. Stetson, *An History of the Massachusetts Hospital Life Insurance Co.* (Cambridge: Harvard University Press, 1955). For Brahmin real estate operations see: Nathaniel B. Shurtleff, *A Topographical and Historical Description of Boston* (Boston: A. Williams & Co., 1871), pp. 385, 417-22; Nathaniel I. Bowditch, "Gleaner Articles", *Fifth Report of the Record Commissioners, 1880* (Boston: Rockwell and Churchill, 1884), pp. 77, 84, 100-01, 202-03; Walter Muir Whitehill, *Boston, A Topographical History* (Cambridge: Harvard University Press, 1959), pp. 48-49, 60-67, 76-78, 84-86, 95-98, 146-48; Harold and James Kirker, *Bullfinch's Boston, 1878-1917* (New York: Oxford University Press, 1965), pp. 142-64, 185-205; Walter Firey, *Land Use in Central Boston* (Cambridge: Harvard University Press, 1947), pp. 41-53, 65-70; Aileen Chamberlain, *Beacon Hill* (Boston: Houghton Mifflin, 1925), *passim*.

3. Shurtleff, *Topographical*, pp. 330, 338-39, 357; Whitehill, *Topographical History*, pp. 95-98.

4. Firey, *Land*, pp. 45-55, 87-135.

5. Ferris Greenslet, *The Lowells and Their Seven Worlds* (Boston: Houghton Mifflin, 1946), pp. 49, 54-55; S.E. Morison, *Harrison Gray Otis, 1765-1848, The Urbane Federalist* (Boston: Houghton Mifflin, 1969), pp. 51-55, 61-65, 218-19; S.E. Morison, *The Life and Letters of Harrison Gray Otis*, 2 vols. (Boston: Houghton Mifflin, 1913), I, pp. 27-29. William T. Davis, *Bench and Bar of the Commonwealth of Massachusetts*, 2 vols. (Boston: The Boston History Co., 1895), I, pp. 109-15; S.E. Morison, *Three Centuries of Harvard* (Cambridge: Harvard University Press, 1946), pp. 238-39; Arthur E. Suther-

land, *The Law at Harvard* (Cambridge: Harvard University Press, 1967), pp. 59, 77-78.

6. Walter L. Burrage, *A History of the Massachusetts Medical Society* (Norwich, Vt.: The Plimpton Press, 1923), pp. 16, 70-72, 462-63; Henry R. Viets, *A Brief History of Medicine in Massachusetts* (Boston: Houghton Mifflin, 1930), pp. 104-08, 127-35, 139-49; Nathan Ingersoll Bowditch, *A History of Massachusetts General Hospital* (Cambridge: John Wilson and Son, 1872), *passim*; James Jackson Putnam, *A Memoir of Dr. James Jackson* (Boston: Houghton Mifflin, 1905), *passim*.

7. Henry Wilder Foote, *Annals of King's Chapel*, 2 vols. (Boston: Little Brown, 1896), II, *passim*; Justin Winsor, *The Memorial History of Boston*, 4 vols. (Boston: Ticknor and Co., 1880), III, pp. 415-20, 476-82; Daniel Walker Howe, *The Unitarian Conscience: Harvard Moral Philosophy, 1805-1861* (Cambridge: Harvard University Press, 1970), pp. 6-12, 176, 310-12.

8. Morison, *Three Centuries*, pp. 181-91, 202-03, quote on p. 185; Howe, *Unitarian*, pp. 4-5; *Endowment Funds of Harvard University* (Cambridge: Harvard University Press, 1948); Samuel A. Eliot, *A Sketch of the History of Harvard College and of its Present State* (Boston: Little Brown, 1848); Josiah Quincy, *The History of Harvard University*, 2 vols. (Boston: Crosby, Nichols, Lee & Co., 1860); Andrew P. Peabody, *Harvard Reminiscences* (Boston: Ticknor and Co., 1888).

9. William R. Cutter, et al. (eds.), *Encyclopedia of Massachusetts Biography*, 12 vols. (New York, Boston, Chicago: The American Historical Society, 1916), I, pp. 266-68.

10. Stewart Mitchell, *Handbook of the Massachusetts Historical Society* (Boston: The Massachusetts Historical Society, 1949); Stephen T. Riley, *The Massachusetts Historical Society, 1791-1959* (Boston: The Massachusetts Historical Society, 1959); Josiah Quincy, *The History of the Boston Athenaeum* (Cambridge: Metcalf & Co., 1851); N.a., *The Influence and History of the Boston Athenaeum* (Boston: The Boston Anthenaeum, 1907). Howe, *Unitarian*, p. 176; Winsor, *Memorial*, III, p. 637.

11. William Tudor to Harrison Gray Otis, Sept. 2, 1815, *Harrison Gray Otis*, p. 235.

12. Josiah Quincy chaired a committee investigating poverty and administration of relief in Massachusetts; the report of the committee is in *Massachusetts General Court, Committee on Pauper Laws, Report of the Committee, 1821* (n.p.). Similar investigations occurred a few years later in New York and Philadelphia. See: David Rothman, *The Discovery of the Asylum: Social Order and Disorder in the New Republic* (Boston: Little Brown, 1971), pp. 156-57; John Cummings, *Poor-Laws of Massachusetts and New York* (New York: Macmillan Co., 1895). For a general discussion of Brahmin philanthropy see Howe, *Unitarian*, pp. 236-39. For some examples of Brahmin leaders in charity or-

ganizations see: Winsor, *Memorial*, III, pp. 241n, 271-72; Amos Lawrence, *Extracts from the Diary and Correspondence of Amos Lawrence*, William R. Lawrence (ed.) (Boston: Gould and Lincoln, 1855), pp. 221-33; Bowditch, *Massachusetts General*, pp. 412-31; Freeman Hunt, *Lives of American Merchants*, 2 vols. (New York: Hunt's Merchants' Magazine, 1858), I, p. 159; William Lawrence, *Life of Amos Lawrence*, (Boston: Houghton Mifflin, 1899), p. 53; Robert C. Winthrop, Jr., *Memoir of Robert C. Winthrop* (Boston: Little Brown, 1897), p. 169; Henry James, *Charles W. Eliot*, 2 vols. (Boston: Houghton Mifflin, 1930),I, p. 28.

13. N.a., "The Public and Private Charities of Boston," *The North American Review*, LXI (July, 1845), pp. 141-42 (Quincy's statistics), pp. 143-47 (1845 totals). For examples of individual upper class donors see: David Sears, *Record of Deeds and Gifts of David Sears of Boston* (Cambridge: John Wilson & Son, 1886); *Will of Abbott Lawrence* (Boston: John Wilson & Son, 1857), pp. 21-26; Lawrence, *Extracts*, p. 312; Bowditch, *Massachusetts General*, pp. 442-45.

14. Winthrop, *Memoir of Robert C. Winthrop*, pp. 169, 318; N.a., *Influence*, p. 115; Mitchell, *Handbook*, p. 97; James, *Charles W. Eliot*, I, p. 28; Hunt, *Lives*, II, pp. 288-89; Lawrence, *Life of Amos Lawrence*, pp. 56, 58; *Will of Abbott Lawrence*, pp. 11-21, 25; Walter Muir Whitehill, *The Boston Library: A Centennial History* (Cambridge: Harvard University Press, 1956), pp. 264-65.

15. Albert Bushnell Hart (ed.), *Commonwealth History of Massachusetts*, 6 vols. (New York: The States History Co., 1927-30), III, pp. 581-82, 621-22; N.a., *A Catalogue of the Members of the City Councils of Boston, Roxbury & Charlestown, 1822-1908. A Catalogue of the Selectmen of Boston, 1634-1822. Also of Various Other Towns and Municipal Officers* (Boston: City of Boston Printing Department, 1909); Winsor, *Memorial*, III, pp. 194n, 213, 297; Josiah Quincy, *A Memorial History of the Town and City of Boston from September 17, 1630 to September 17, 1830* (Boston: Little Brown, 1852), pp. 432-42; Charles Warren, *Jacobin and Junto* (Cambridge: Harvard University Press, 1931), p. 164; Morison, *Maritime*, p. 167; Josiah Quincy, *Memoir of the Life of Josiah Quincy, Jr.* (Boston: John Wilson and Son, 1874); Henry Cabot Lodge, *The Life and Letters of George Cabot* (Boston: Little Brown, 1877); Thomas Wentworth Higginson, *The Life and Times of Stephen Higginson* (Boston: Houghton Mifflin, 1907); Morison, *Life and Letters of Harrison Gray Otis*; H.W.L. Dana, *The Dana Saga: Three Centuries of the Family in Cambridge* (Cambridge: The Cambridge Historical Society, 1941), pp. 21-30; Greenslet, *Lowells*, pp. 48-83; William Bruce Wheeler, "Urban Politics in Nature's Republic: The Development of Political Parties in the Seaport Cities" (Ph.D. Dissertation: The University of Virginia, 1957), pp. 338-39; Paul Goodman, *The Democratic-Republicans of Massachusetts: Politics in a Young Re-*

public (Cambridge: Harvard University Press, 1964), pp. 73-75, 108-15; Gray, *William Gray*, pp. 10-11, 38-44.

16. Morison, *Maritime*, p. 165. For a discussion of these policies see Morison, pp. 164-68. For the role of Brahmin Federalists in representing Massachusetts maritime interests see: Lodge, *Life and Letters of George Cabot*, pp. 36-144; T. W. Higginson, *Life and Times of Stephen Higginson*, pp. 69-74; "Letters of Stephen Higginson," *Annual Report of the American Historical Association*, I (1896), pp. 716-840; Edmund Quincy, *The Life of Josiah Quincy* (Boston: Ticknor and Fields, 1868), pp. 40-101; Morison, *Life and Letters of Harrison Gray Otis*; Josiah Quincy, *Speeches Delivered in the Congress of the United States, 1805-1813* (Boston: Little Brown, 1874); John Lowell, *The New England Patriot: A Candid Comparison of the Principles and Conduct of the Washington and Jeffersonian Administrations* (Boston: Russell and Cutler, 1810); Lowell, *An Enquiry Into the Question of the Chesapeake and the Necessity of Expediency of War* (Boston: Greenough and Stebbins, 1807), pp. 1-43; Lowell, *Interesting Political Discussion: The Diplomatic Policy of Mr. Madison Unveiled* (Boston: Russell and Culter, 1812), pp. 1-53.

17. *Journal of the Convention for Framing a Constitution of Government for the State of Massachusetts Bay, 1779-80* (Boston: Dutton and Wentworth, 1832); East, *Business*, p. 202; Morison, *Maritime*, p. 28.

18. Winsor, *Memorial*, III, pp. 193-94; East, *Business*, p. 264; Morison, *Maritime*, pp. 36-37.

19. Winsor, *Memorial*, III, pp. 195-96; Morison, *Maritime*, pp. 39-40; Anson Ely Morse, *The Federalist Party in Massachusetts to the Year 1800* (Princeton: Princeton University Press, 1909), pp. 40-53. For an example of the Boston upper class support of the Federal Constitution see Stephen Higginson to John Adams, August 8, 1788; to Nathan Dane, May 22, 1788, "Letters of Stephen Higginson," pp. 719-26, 761.

20. J. Quincy, *Memorial*, pp. 30-31.

21. Bowditch, "Gleaner," pp. 94, 202-03; Shurtleff, *Topographical*, pp. 330, 338-39, 357, 419-22; Whitehill, *Topographical History*, pp. 48-49, 76-78; Firey, *Land*, pp. 218-33; Morison, *Harrison Gray Otis*, pp. 74-79; 219-26.

22. Chester Phillips Huse, *Financial History of Boston* (Cambridge: Harvard University Press, 1916), pp. 37-39.

23. Oscar and Mary F. Handlin, *Commonwealth: A Study of the Role of Government in the American Economy: Massachusetts 1774-1861* (Cambridge: Harvard University Press, 1969), pp. 99-100, 102-03.

24. Gray, *William Gray*, pp. 38-39; Josiah Quincy, *Memoir of the Life of John Quincy Adams* (Boston: Phillips & Sampson, 1858), pp. 34-37; Goodman, *Democratic-Republicans*, pp. 192-94.

25. Porter, *Jacksons and Lees*, I, p. 121, II, pp. 969-70.

26. Henry Lee to Patrick Tracy Jackson, January 30, 1813, *Ibid.*, II, 1076. T.H. Perkins to W.F. Paine, ?,?, 1815 or 16, Perkins Papers, MHS.

27. For Brahmin activities in the textile industry see: Nathan Appleton, *Introduction of the Power Loom and the Origin of Lowell* (Boston: B.H. Penhallow, 1858); John Amory Lowell, "Memoir of Patrick Tracy Jackson," *Hunt's Merchants' Magazine* (New York: Hunt's Merchants' Magazine,1848), pp. 4-6; Hannah Josephson, *The Golden Threads* (New York: Duell, Sloan and Pearce, 1949); Caroline Ware, *The Early New England Cotton Manufacture* (Boston: Houghton Mifflin, 1931); George Sweet Gibb, *The Saco-Lowell Shops, Textile Machinery Building in New England* (Cambridge: Harvard University Press, 1950); Ovra L. Stone, *History of Massachusetts Industries*, 2 vols. (Boston: The S.J. Clarke Publishing Co., 1930), I; Malcolm Keir, *Industries of American Manufacturing* (New York: The Ronald Press, 1928, pp. 295-300; J. Herbert Burgy, *The New England Cotton Textile Industry* (Baltimore: Waverly Press, 1932); Melvin T. Copeland, *The Cotton Manufacturing Industry of the United States* (Cambridge: Harvard University Press, 1912); H.E. Michl, *The Textile Industries, An Economic Analysis* (Washington, D.C.: The Textile Foundation, 1938); W. Paul Strassman, *Risk and Technological Innovation* (Ithaca: Cornell University Press, 1959), pp. 76-117; Paul F. McGouldrick, *New England Textiles in the Nineteenth Century: Profits and Investment* (Cambridge: Harvard University Press, 1968); Robert F. Dalzell, Jr., "The Rise of the Waltham-Lowell System and Some Thought on the Political Economy of Modernization in Antebellum Massachusetts," *Perspectives in American History*, IX (1975), pp. 229-70. For the history of Brahmin enterprise in New England railroads see: Edwards Chase Kirkland, *Men, Cities and Transportation: A Study in New England History, 1820-1900*, 2 vols. (Cambridge: Harvard University Press, 1948); Alvin F. Harlow, *Steelways of New England* (New York: Creative Age Press, 1948); Thelma M. Kistler, *The Rise of Railroads in the Connecticut River Valley* (Northampton: Smith College Press, 1938); George Pierce Baker, *The Formation of the New England Railroad Systems* (Cambridge: Harvard University Press, 1937); Arthur M. Johnson and Barry Supple, *Boston Capitalists and Western Railroads* (Cambridge: Harvard University Press, 1967), pp. 38-91; Francis B.C. Bradlee, *The Boston and Lowell Railroad, The Nashua and Lowell Railroad and the Salem and Lowell Railroad* (Salem: Essex Institute, 1917); George Bliss, *Historical Memoir of the Western Railroad* (Springfield: Samuel Bowles & Co., 1863); Charles B. Fisher, *The Story of the Old Colony Railroad* (n.p.: no publisher, 1919). The percentages on spindleage, railroad mileage, insurance capital and banking resources are in Copeland, *Cotton*, p. 6.

28. T.H. Perkins to LeRoy, Bayard & Co., May 27, 1820; to James L. Lloyd, May 26, 1820; to Cary & Co., May 10, 1820; September 2, 1820, Perkins Papers, MHS; Henry Lee quoted in Porter, *Jacksons and Lees*, I, p.

44; Cleveland Amory, *The Proper Bostonians* (New York: E.P. Dutton & Co., 1947), pp. 54-55.

29. T.H. Perkins to Samuel Cabot and Thomas G. Cary, January ?, 1835; to Elizabeth Perkins, May 1, 1852, Perkins Papers, MHS; Robert K. Lamb, "Entrepreneur and Community, "William Miller (ed.), *Men in Business* (Cambridge: Harvard University Press, 1952), pp. 110-11; Morison, *Life and Letters of Harrison Gray Otis*, I, pp. 448-50, 454; Porter, *Jacksons and Lees*, I, p. 123; William Appleton, *Selections from the Diaries of William Appleton, 1786-1852*, Susan Loring (ed.) (Boston: privately published, 1922), October 28, 1848, pp. 132-33; Keir, *Industries*, p. 229.

30. Morison, *Life and Letters of Harrison Gray Otis*, II, pp. 94, 243, 248; Warren, *Jacobin*, pp. 164-219.

31. Higginson to Timothy Pickering, January 2, 1800; February 15, 1804, "Letters to Stephen Higginson," pp. 798, 833, 839.

32. John Quincy Adams to Josiah Quincy, December 4, 1804, E. Quincy, *Memoir of Josiah Quincy*, pp. 54-64.

33. H. Lee to P. Remsen and Co., July 8, 1817, Porter, *Jacksons and Lees*, II, 1257. See also: Shaw Livermore, Jr., *The Twilight of Federalism, The Disintegration of the Federalist Party, 1815-1830* (Princeton: Princeton University Press, 1962), pp. 49-54, 59; Morison, *Harrison Gray Otis*, pp. 84-86. For an excellent discussion of the generational split in Federalism see David Hackett Fischer, *The Revolution of American Conservatism* (New York: Harper & Row, 1965).

34. H.G. Otis to S.F. Otis, February 15, 1801, Morison, *Life and Letters of Harrison Gray Otis*, I, p. 208.

35. H. G. Otis, *An Address to the Members of the City Council on the Removal of the Municipal Government to the Old State House* (Boston: John H. Eastburn, 1830), pp. 14-15.

36. J. Quincy, "Farewell Address to Josiah Quincy as Mayor of Boston, 1829," *Old South Leaflets*, VIII (Boston: Old South Meeting House, n.d.), p. 101.

37. Fischer, *Revolution*, pp. 227-412.

38. *Journal of Debates and Proceedings in the Convention of Delegates Chosen to Revise the Constitution of Massachusetts, 1820-21* (Boston: Daily Advertiser, 1821), pp. 5, 133-36, 175-77, 180, 183, 200-07, 215-16, 250-51.

39. Edward Pessen, *Riches, Class and Power Before the Civil War* (Lexington: D.C. Heath and Co., 1973), pp. 284-87; *Catalogue, passim*.

40. *List of Persons, Copartnerships and Corporations, Who Were Taxed Twenty Five Dollars and Upwards, in the City of Boston, in the Year 1835* (Boston: John H. Eastburn, 1836). *List of Persons, Copartnerships and Corporations who were Taxed on Ten Thousand Dollars and Upwards, in the City of Boston, in the Year 1860* (Boston: George C. Rand & Avery, 1861).

41. Pessen, *Riches,* pp. 45-51.

42. See footnote 40 for references to the assessment lists. The Brahmins were identified through the following biographical sources: *New England Historical and Genealogial Register*; Mary Caroline Crawford, *Famous Families of Massachusetts*, 2 vols. (Boston: Houghton Mifflin, 1930); Winsor, *Memorial*; Albert P. Langtry, *Metropolitan Boston. A Modern History*, 5 vols. (New York: Lewis Publishing Co., 1929), IV-V; James Spear Loring, *The Hundred Boston Orators Appointed by the Municipal Authorities and Other Public Bodies from 1770 to 1852; Comprising Historical Gleanings Illustrating the Principles and Progress of our Republican Institutions* (Boston: John P. Jewett & Co., 1852); Hunt, *Lives of the Merchants*; N.a., *Biographical Sketches of Representative Citizens of the Commonwealth of Massachusetts* (Boston: Graves & Steinbarger, 1901); Charles Edwin Hurd, *Representative Citizens of the Commonwealth of Massachusetts* (Boston: New England Publishing Co., 1902); N.a., *Biographical Encyclopedia of Massachusetts of the Nineteenth Century* (New York: Metropolitan Publishing and Engraving Co., 1879); N.a., *Men of Massachusetts* (Boston: Boston Press Club, 1903); Daniel L. Marsh and William H. Clark, *The Story of Massachusetts*, 4 vols. (New York: The American Historical Society, 1938), IV; Samuel Atkins Eliot, *Biographical History of Massachusetts*, 10 vols. (Boston: Massachusetts Biographical Society, 1911-18); Samuel Adams Drake, *Old Landmarks and Historic Personages of Boston*, 5 vols. (Boston: Little Brown, 1895); John C. Rand (ed.), *One of a Thousand: A Series of Biographical Sketches of 1,000 Representative Men Resident in the Commonwealth of Massachusetts. A.D. 1888-1889* (Boston: First National Publishing Co., 1890); William R. Cutter (ed.), *Memorial Encyclopedia of the State of Massachusetts*, 3 vols. (Boston, New York, Chicago: The American Historical Society, 1917); Cutter, et al. (eds.), *Encyclopedia of Biography, Massachusetts*; Cutter (ed.), *Genealogical and Personal Memoirs Relating to the Families of Boston and Eastern Massachusetts*, 4 vols. (New York: Lewis Publishing Co., 1908); Thomas L. Wilson, *The Aristocracy of Boston: Who They Are, and What They Were: Being a History of the Business and Business Men of Boston for the Last Forty Years* (Boston: published by the author, 1848); N.a., *"Our First Men." A Calendar of Wealth, Fashion and Gentility; Containing a List of Those Persons Taxed in the City of Boston, Credibly Reported to be Worth 100,000 Dollars, With Biographical Notices of the Principal Persons* (Boston: n.p., 1846); N.a., *Boston Past and Present. Being an Outline of the History of the City as Exhibited in the Lives of its Prominent Citizens* (Boston and New York: John F. Trow, 1874); Joshua L. Chamberlain, *Universities and Their Sons* (Boston: R. Herndon Co., 1898); Dumas Malone and Robert L. Schuyler (eds.), *Dictionary of American Biography*, 22 vols. (New York: Charles Scribner's Sons, 1928-58). In addition to these collective biographical sources I consulted memoirs, autobiographies and biographies of

eminent Bostonians, obituaries in the New York *Times* and histories of various phases of upper class Boston life.

43. Pessen, "The Egalitarian Myth and the American Social Reality: Wealth, Mobility and Equality in the 'Era of the Common Man,'" *The American Historical Review*, LXXVI (1971), pp. 1020-31; Pessen, *Riches*, pp. 39-40.

44. The political offices held by the rich Bostonians of 1835 and 1860 were derived from *Catalogue of the Members of the City Councils* and the biographical references in footnote 42.

45. Hart, *Commonwealth*, IV, pp. 621-23; *Catalogue, passim.*

46. Thomas H. O'Connor, *Lords of the Loom* (New York: Charles Scribner's Sons, 1968), pp. 35, 66; Kirkland, *Men*, I, pp. 129-33; Baker, *Formation*, p. 101n; Gibb, *Saco-Lowell*, pp. 61-62.

47. Kinley J. Brauer, *Cotton Versus Conscience, Massachusetts Whig Politics and Southwestern Expansion, 1843-48* (Lexington: University of Kentucky Press, 1966), p. 19.

48. Robert Rich, " 'Wilderness of Whigs'. The Wealthy Men of Boston," *The Journal of Social History*, IV (Spring, 1971), pp. 263-67.

49. John Quincy Adams, *Memoirs of John Quincy Adams*, Charles Francis Adams (ed.), 12 vols. (Philadelphia: J.B. Lippincott, 1874), November 16, 1838, X, p. 43; Charles Francis Adams quoted in Brauer, *Cotton*, p. 133; David Donald, *Charles Sumner and the Coming of the Civil War* (New York: Alfred A. Knopf, 1960), p. 137; cf. O'Connor, *Lords*, p. 66.

50. Baker, *Formation*, p. 101n; Kistler, *Rise*, pp. 152-55; Kirkland, *Men*, I, pp. 127-33.

51. For the struggle between Cotton Whigs and their opponents see: Brauer, *Cotton*; O'Connor, *Lords*; Donald, *Charles Sumner*; Arthur B. Darling, *Political Changes in Massachusetts. 1824-1828* (New Haven: Yale University Press, 1925), p. 150ff; Frank Otto Gattell, *John Gorham Palfrey and the New England Conscience* (Cambridge: Harvard University Press, 1963).

52. Firey, *Land*, pp. 65-70; Whitehill, *Boston*, pp. 84-86; Alexander S. Porter, "Changes of Values in Real Estate in Boston in the Past One Hundred Years," *Collections of the Bostonian Society*, I, (1888), pp. 60-62.

53. Huse, *Financial*, pp. 19-106; Winsor, *Memorial*, III, pp. 225-37, 243-44, 251-56; Quincy, *Municipal*, pp. 58-279; Robert A. McCaughey, *Josiah Quincy, 1772-1864: The Last Federalist* (Cambridge: Harvard University Press, 1974), pp. 98-120.

54. Winsor, *Memorial*, III, pp. 255-56. Huse, *Financial*, pp. 58, 86.

55. Constance McLaughlin Green, *American Cities in the Growth of the Nation* (New York: Colophon Books, 1965), pp. 31, 33.

4

Yankee Leadership in a Divided City: Boston, 1860-1910

GEOFFREY BLODGETT

I

The passage of political power from Yankee Bostonians to Irish-American Bostonians during the half-century after the Civil War produced a powerful folk memory with an enduring life of its own as a causal force shaping 20th-century cleavages in the political culture of the city. As the past receded, this folk memory often appeared more passionate, more unmanageable, more real and raw than the historical facts themselves. Paddy versus Brahmin, George Apley and Frank Skeffington, North End, West End, all around the town, it lingered as a lively presence among successors of the original protagonists long after the power transfer was completed and the resentments attending it might have been expected to wane.

The memory also remained useful to scholars searching for the origins of Boston's current ethnic strife. The Harvard psychiatrist Robert Coles, interviewed for a November 1979 article in the *New York Times* about the city's racial troubles, invoked the memory by arguing that Boston blacks today are latter-day victims of the long grudge war fought across class lines between Irishmen and their Yankee oppressors a century before. "What people have to understand," Coles explained, "is that before blacks even came to the city in any numbers, there were a hundred years of racism of another kind. Blacks are taking it on the chin because

Reprinted from Geoffrey Blodgett, "Yankee Leadership in a Divided City: Boston, 1860-1910," *Journal of Urban History*, Vol. 8, No. 4 (August 1982), pp. 371-396, © 1982 Sage Publications, Inc., with permission.

of a rage that was here before they were. And it stems from an arrogant upper class."[1]

The image of upper-class arrogance—"No Irish Need Apply," "Cabots speak only to God"—is central to the Boston folk memory of social conflict. However it does not loom nearly as large or crucial in the actual record of the city's politics in the half-century before 1910. Certainly the arrogance was there, along with an abundance of self-doubt, self-pity, and growing pessimism about the future, all carefully preserved in the diaries and letters and memoirs of the Brahmin literati. But these glum attitudes, however pervasive and influential, did not create a single-minded class stance.[2] Nor did they control the upper-class political response to its displacement during the critical years from 1885 to 1900. In fact the argument can be made that during those years important elements of the Yankee upper class served as mediators of the city's ethno-cultural political strife, helping with like-minded Irish leaders to moderate the passions of power transfer.

The argument may be summarized as follows: Boston was a divided city in the Gilded Age, but its salient divisions did not pit lower class against upper class. Yankee patricians retained a strong working involvement in the city's political structure until the turn of the century, in contrast to their counterparts in New York and Philadelphia, where upper-class political activity had been reduced to angry, episodic, and relatively ineffective reform protests against "machine" politics.[3] The most significant product of patrician involvement in Boston politics was an incongruous, fragile alliance inside the Democratic party between an elite Yankee leadership minority and the leaders of a growing Irish working-class majority. Despite the inherent frictions and instability of this alliance, its arbiters managed to define a fund of shared interests which held the alliance together as the dominant force in the city's politics over the last quarter of the 19th century. The result was a substantial interlude of political detente within the city's Democratic party, detente informed by earnest commitments to ethnic comity, a grudging Irish deference to Yankee patrician leadership, and Yankee acknowledgment of the legitimacy of Irish power in the city. These terms of cooperation spanned precisely those years when the balance of political power was passing into Irish hands.

The main disruptions of comity before 1896 came not from the Yankee elite, nor from Irish political leaders, but rather from middle-class native Protestants and working-class Canadian Protestant immigrants, whose values and interests clashed directly with the mores of the city's Irish Catholic population. When these frictions reached a flash point in the late 1880s, the Yankee elite contributed importantly to the muting of social strife and the protection of Irish interests. One result was the confirmation for a time of Irish deference to Yankee leadership. Within another decade, however, in the wake of the depression of the 1890s and the political upheaval it provoked nationally and locally, the fragile Yankee-Irish Democratic alliance came unstuck. Despite strenuous efforts by Yankee Democratic mayors to preside over the city's restless Irish population, by 1900 the terms of alliance no longer worked.

Thereafter Boston's Irish leaders battled for control of their own power among themselves on their own terms. Meanwhile the city's non-Irish patricians, in retreat toward the periphery of urban political influence, resorted to the sorts of non-partisan, good-government stratagems tried earlier in New York and Philadelphia—tactics aimed at containing what they perceived to be the worst consequences of majority rule, Irish style. By 1910 or thereabout, the old alliance which had moderated the tensions of power transfer was a discarded memory, replaced by the legend of monolithic upper-class political arrogance.[4]

That, in bald outline, is the main pattern which emerges from the complex fabric of Boston's post-Civil War political history. One is tempted to call it the reality behind the myth of relentless polar conflict between Irishmen and Yankees. But there are other patterns in Boston's complexity, and these need examining to see how far they qualify the main pattern.

II

Those who have stressed the theme of polar conflict argue that it was if anything intensified by Boston's slow growth rate as compared with New York, Philadelphia, and Chicago. They note that the big pre-Civil War wave of Irish immigration receded in the 1860s, and in the absence of large arrivals from the European continent until the late 1880s, the city remained ethnically divided in two between Irish stock and native-born. The postwar migration of rural New Englanders and Canadian Protestants into the city served only to sharpen this division. Relatively low rates of mobility at both extremes of the city's social hierarchy—upward mobility among working-class Irishmen and geographical mo-

bility among upper-class Brahmins—enforced a mood of stasis, conges-
tion, and grinding group resentment in the city.[5]

Conflict between native-born and foreign-born also flared in the relations between the people who ran the city and those who ran the state.
Boston was the only big city in America where the distance between
City Hall and the State House could be crossed in a ten-minute walk.
That space was filled with cultural mistrust. The state hovered closely
over the city, an anxious watchdog of municipal behavior. Bulfinch's
18th-century State House remained the seat of Yankee Republicanism,
its majority prompted by the cues of village virtue, fearful of the city's
compact alien mass. From the early 1860s on, even before the Irish
had gained much strength in Boston's city council or police force,
sentiment rose in the General Court for imposing state-sponsored law
and order on the city. Inadequate police protection for abolitionist meetings in downtown Boston, the North End draft riot of 1863, and the
long-term tangled issues of liquor licensing, prostitution, and saloon
control all provoked demands for state intervention. Demands focused
on stripping the city's politicians of their authority over police and liquor
licensing and placing this authority under state-directed metropolitan
oversight. A legislative committee reported in 1863: "It is necessary
to adopt the metropolitan principle in order to prevent the elements
which are destructive of property and laws from keeping practical control
of the city, and . . . undermining the prosperity and peace of the commonwealth." The report went on to call large cities "the common
sewers of the state."[6] Boston was not the only urban menace confronting
the General Court, but it was the biggest, nearest, and most threatening.
The ethnic dimensions of the menace were closely monitored. As the
number of Irish policemen, councilmen, and aldermen rose across the
1870s, the call for state intervention intensified. Following the election
in 1884 of the city's first Irish Democratic mayor, Hugh O'Brien, the
General Court finally made its move, and transferred control of Boston's
police to a metropolitan commission appointed by the governor.[7]

Boston's Irish Democrats bitterly resented this effort by the Yankee
state majority to improve urban behavior by curbing Irish power. Their
party leader, Patrick Maguire, put it this way in his newspaper, *The
Republic*: "The venerable hayseed legislators from Podunk and other
rural sections, aided by Boston hypocrites and frauds, lay and clerical,
[have] deprived Boston of the control of her police for the purpose of
making her a moral city."[8]

In the late 1880s schools joined police and saloons on the list of moral issues dividing the city from the state, and—within Boston—Catholics from Protestants. A coalition of Evangelical ministers, women suffragists, temperance leaders, and anti-Catholic Canadian immigrants (a coalition similar in composition to that caricatured by Maguire) launched a drive to curb the growth of Catholic parochial schools by means of state-sponsored inspection. In 1888 this surveillance impulse merged with an effort to purge the Boston School Committee of Catholic influence. The twin-pronged campaign posed a broader threat to Irish interests than the police issue. It ignited more volatile religious and ethnic passions than any cultural controversy since the Civil War. The quarrel soon spread beyond the boundaries of debate over educational policy to kindle animosities smouldering for years around the liquor issue, the role of women in politics, the aspirations of the Catholic Church hierarchy, and—inevitably—the grip of Irish Democratic politicians on their following. Protestants mobilized by the school crisis vented their zeal in Boston mayoral politics as well. The result was the defeat of Hugh O'Brien's re-election try in 1888 and a momentary Republican restoration at City Hall. Once again the legitimacy of Irish Democratic influence in the governance of Boston had been rebuked.[9]

Police control and school control were two issues, then, which illuminated fierce resistance to the growing Irish presence. A less explosive long-term issue, metropolitan integration, revealed comparable hostility. This issue turned on efforts to extend the city's political dimensions and tax base to match its demographic growth. Boston expanded its territory incrementally in the early post-Civil War years through annexation. The city's population doubled between 1860 and 1880. Half this growth came from the legal absorption, one by one, of Roxbury, Dorchester, Brighton, Charlestown, and West Roxbury between 1867 and 1874. After that, annexation ground to a halt. (Hyde Park was annexed in 1911.) The tactic had worked as long as prosperous Yankee merchants, lawyers, and others living in the annexed areas thought they could control the political life of the center city where they did business. But as Irish Democratic influence in the city swelled, and city tax rates rose, Yankee voters on the perimeter recoiled. Anxiety about the encroachment of the corrupt city on the life of its surrounding towns replaced fading hopes for controlling the center from the rim.

The peculiar values of New England's village past helped to justify this reassessment of suburban self-interest. Unlike many modern American suburbs, most of Boston's 19th-century satellite communities were deep-rooted historic enclaves with habits of self-government dating back a century and more. All the virtues associated with the town meeting tradition—slow cellular growth, neighborhood homogeneity, deference to old families and established local leaders—reinforced a desire to shun the new alien ways of the big city. The survival of the older Yankee virtues seemed to depend on separatism and local autonomy. Therefore, despite growing economic dependence on the center city, the satellite towns stubbornly resisted metropolitan political integration. By the end of the century, modern electric transit and communication systems greatly tightened metropolitan connections. Meanwhile the state had moved to spur the metropolitan integration of water, sewer, and park systems. Nevertheless all proposals for merging the cells of the periphery with the politics of the core ran up against implacable Yankee opposition. By 1910, one-and-a-half million people lived in the metropolitan area hopefully described as Greater Boston; 670,000 of them lived in the city proper, while the rest remained politically scattered among some 39 independent towns and cities surrounding it. Ethnic animosity had gone far to blight the political dimension of the metropolitan idea.[10]

III

Boston was taut, then, with the cross-pull of many overlapping social tensions, stemming from conflict over police control, liquor control, school control, and control of metropolitan growth. In each of these conflicts, bitter ethnic animosity compounded the trouble. Set against this pattern of strife, the working alliance between Irish Democrats and elite Yankee Democrats noted at the outset seems all the more remarkable, and worth closer scrutiny. The alliance enabled the Democratic party to control the Boston mayoralty during twenty of the last thirty years of the century. Although the alliance was built on a growing foundation of Irish votes, the mayors it elected were, with the exception of Hugh O'Brien, native-born Yankee patricians. The three who served the longest—Frederick O. Prince, Nathan Matthews, and Josiah Quincy—were Harvard graduates of impeccable family lineage. They were examples of a political breed that became almost extinct after the turn of the century—upper-class, college-educated, Yankee gentlemen who were also Democrats. Their function was to mediate the emergence of the Irish to power, in the party and in the city, by expedient transactions in coalition politics. Together with their Irish allies—Patrick Collins, Patrick Maguire, Hugh O'Brien, Thomas Gargan, and Joseph O'Neil—they helped manage the most critical ethnic transition in the city's history.

The alliance originated in the party upheavals of the 1850s, when Irish and Yankee opponents of anti-slavery agitation in Boston found themselves thrown together in the Democratic party. The Yankee faction of the party consisted mostly of former Whigs, socially conservative lawyers, merchants, and overseas traders, who were put off by the rampant moral reformism of the antebellum years. Whig-Democrats shared with Irish Democrats a mutual aversion to the moral agenda of the new Republican party for purifying the social order, whether the object of purification was the Southern slave owner or the urban saloon. This mistrust of all measures to promote social purity by public coercion would remain central to Democratic party thought and rhetoric for the rest of the century. It created a crucial bridge of agreement spanning ethnic, religious, and class differences among party leaders.

Four former Whigs served as Democratic mayors of Boston at one time or another between 1860 and 1880. Of these, the courtly blue-blood lawyer F. O. Prince took the most significant steps toward accommodation of Irish interests during his mayoralty in the late 1870s. Prince was a candid Democratic partisan who understood the importance of linkages in the federated structure of the party. Having joined the Democrats in 1860, he served for the next 28 years as secretary of the Democratic National Committee. As mayor, he dropped the pious notion that city governance had nothing to do with national party labels, party regularity, or party patronage. A Democrat with national credentials, but dependent as mayor on local Irish support, Prince acted as both a patron and a client in his dealings with the Irish. He owed his mayoralty to the Democratic city committee, the body that determined mayoral nominations with a close eye on issues of party discipline and rewards. The man who swung Prince's nomination in the city committee was Patrick Maguire, an Ireland-born printer and realtor who was rapidly emerging to replace his mentor Michael Doherty as Boston's most powerful backroom political manager. Thereafter Prince saw to it that Maguire was in regular attendance at the party's national conventions, as Doherty had been since 1860.

By bringing potent local leaders like Doherty and Maguire into the councils of the party at this high echelon, Prince helped to nail down local Irish leadership support for such presidential candidates as Samuel Tilden and Grover Cleveland. Meanwhile as mayor, he courted Irish favor with his patronage, including seats on the municipal boards charged with management of police and liquor licensing. When he named Thomas Gargan to the city's board of police, this was the highest municipal office yet held by an Irishman. In later years, Irish Democrats would look back on Prince's patronage as meager and condescending. Congressman Joseph O'Neil recalled in 1892 that Prince "believed that there were half a dozen men with Irish blood who had brains, but that the balance was fit only to fill places with less than a thousand a year." Nevertheless Prince was a realistic practitioner in the art of patron-client politics, and his response to Irish demands for recognition set useful precedents for both factions in the alliance as they strove to adjust their ways to changing ethnic equilibrium.[11]

Local demographic facts guaranteed a steady growth of Irish power in this balance. The presidential election of 1884, on the other hand, brought fresh recruits and new vitality to the Yankee faction. The dimensions of the Mugwump bolt from Blaine to Cleveland that year were not nearly as large as the bolters claimed. The bolt failed to dislodge the electoral votes of Massachusetts from the Republican column, and it did not significantly affect the ethnic composition of Boston's Democratic vote.[12] But at the level of party leadership the Mugwumps, owing to their social status, their wealth and their connections to wealth, wielded influence disproportionate to their numbers. Their somewhat ostentatious presence in the Democratic coalition after 1884 would have consequences as important to the politics of the city as to the state and nation.

These local consequences of the bolt were not wholly anticipated by the bolters, or easily welcomed by the Irish. Few Mugwumps had any great desire for sustained involvement in the grimy work of city government. Their political priorities were cosmopolitan and national in scope, and only their concern for Grover Cleveland's success as president prompted them to try for cooperation with the local Irish leadership of Cleveland's party. They entered the party holding their noses. Their opinion of the Irish was laced with mistrust, as their frequent private references to "micks" and "bummers" and "saloon Democrats" and "the Irish or dynamite wing" of the party suggest.[13] The vision of a proper politics which they carried in their mind's eye, a vision which celebrated the personal autonomy of the free individual citizen, collided with the behavioral ethic of bloc discipline and party regularity practiced by the Irish. Mugwump devices to crack the wall of party discipline, such as civil service reform and the secret ballot, were purposely aimed at disrupting settled habits and arrangements among the Irish. For all these reasons, as well as fundamental differences of religious, educational, and cultural background which divided Mugwumps and Irishmen into opposing negative reference groups, there did not seem to be much ground for local cooperation between them.

Yet cooperation at the leadership level did occur, even though respective constituencies had little to do with each other. Cooperation began with expedient efforts to maximize Cleveland's local vote in 1884. It continued in negotiations thereafter to regulate the flow of presidential patronage into the city in ways that satisfied both the hunger of party regulars and the lofty standards of the Mugwumps. In their eagerness for closer relations with the Irish, Mugwumps varied widely, depending mostly on the intensity of their political ambition. Among the bolters of 1884, Josiah Quincy and John F. Andrew were most prominent in efforts at cooperation. They were soon joined by other Yankees of similar background—young Harvard-educated lawyers like William E. Russell, Nathan Matthews, Sherman Hoar, and Charles Hamlin. Most of these men came from families in which political involvement was an established family tradition. Their desire to pursue careers in elective politics dictated a willingness to work with local Irish leaders. Acceptance of the tactics of coalition compromise was built into their decision to seek public office as Democrats. By the end of Cleveland's first term, whatever their original party persuasion, they regarded themselves as Democratic regulars, and strove to translate into state and municipal politics the aims they believed Cleveland had vindicated at the national level. More than the Whig Democrats of the 1860s and 1870s, these young Yankee leaders pursued their reformist goals with a lively sense of group identity and positive purpose.

Harvard College had done much to shape their group values, and the Harvard ethos went far to ready them for political accommodation to the Irish. While Harvard remained an elite institution catering mainly to the educational and social needs of Boston's upper classes, under President Eliot it acquired a broad new secular outlook and a vitalizing sense of public mission.[14] Harvard moved toward meritocracy in these years, and began inculcating among its elite graduates what Christopher Jencks and David Riesman have called a "national upper-middle class style: cosmopolitan, moderate, universalistic, somewhat legalistic, concerned with equity and fair play, aspiring to neutrality between regions, religions, and ethnic groups.''[15] While Jencks and Riesman locate this style in a 20th-century setting, it nicely fits the mood of the young Harvard graduates who plunged into Boston politics in the 1880s. To validate the Harvard claim to leadership in a divided city, they were prepared not only to play down cultural differences in their own dealings with the Irish, but to assert their stewardship by defending the Irish from local detractors in the name of community harmony. There was more than civic altruism and noblesse oblige in their motives. Only in a public environment that maintained some degree of cultural comity could their upper-class claim to leadership prevail. From their precarious social perch they sensed that deference to their family pedigrees and educational credentials would not survive very long in an atmosphere of contagious social rancor.

Josiah Quincy captured their mood in his 1880 Harvard commencement speech when he said:

The world has entered upon a period of change.... Upon the horizon may be seen indications of political and social convulsions that must be faced within the lives of many of us who are graduating today. The problem is to make the results of study and cultivated thought acceptable to the mass of the people; for it is into their hands that the government of all civilized states is now rapidly passing.[16]

Quincy and his young colleagues thereafter tried to suppress those bleak misgivings about the future of mass democracy which dogged the minds of so many of their elders, including the Adams brothers of that generation and Harvard professors Charles Eliot Norton and Barrett Wendell. The younger men shunned catastrophic speculation. They tried instead to translate into the accommodations of coalition politics the more sanguine and adaptable outlook of President Eliot, William James, and the old Transcendentalist warrior Thomas Wentworth Higginson. A host of specific local issues gave Yankee leaders a chance to demonstrate their talent for cooperation with the Irish—the parochial school controversy of the late 1880s, the perennial issue of Home Rule for Boston, prohibition, and woman suffrage. In the school controversy, Harvard's Eliot threw the weight of his influence decisively against anti-Catholic efforts to curb parochial schooling by state inspection. Higginson and James took a similar position, while Nathan Matthews mustered opposition to the inspection bill in the General Court. Their motives were complex. They had no special love for the hierarchy of the Catholic Church. Their stance was prompted by political calculation, concern for the general integrity of private schooling systems of which they and their children were beneficiaries, and a strong distaste for Evangelical efforts to impose Protestant cultural uniformity on Boston's varied educational arrangements. In both their public and private statements on the issue, they were firmly committed to latitudinarian diversity, what was later called cultural pluralism.[17]

On the question of Home Rule for Boston, Yankee Democratic sympathy for Irish opposition to state interference in the city's governance was also mixed. As suburban gentlemen, most of them, Yankee Democrats were no happier than their Republican neighbors about center-city law and order or aldermanic spending habits. They made no serious effort after 1885 to return control of Boston police to City Hall or to lift state-imposed ceilings on municipal taxation and indebtedness. But the Democratic party tradition of Jeffersonian laissez-faire localism provided them with the rhetoric with which to pay periodic lip service to the idea of Home Rule for Boston. William E. Russell, who served as Democratic mayor of Cambridge in the mid-80s and won the governorship with Irish support in the early 90s, was particularly skillful at invoking party doctrine to promote tolerance for Irish behavior in the city. "I believe it far better," Russell claimed, "to leave to the public spirit of a community to work out its salvation, if need be, after a period of suffering, rather than to interfere with its self-government by forcing upon it the power of the state."[18] The requirements of intra-party detente persuaded other Yankee Democrats to echo this view from time to time, though with decidedly controlled enthusiasm.

Dislike of public interference with personal drinking habits provided still another bridge of working agreement among coalition leaders. The contrast of ambience between the saloon life of the Irish and the Back Bay card parties and club dinners favored by Yankee lawyers and their friends should not obscure a shared opposition to the dry ethic. Beneath tribal variations in drinking habits, the available evidence suggests that Bostonians at both ends of the social spectrum were caught up to a degree in the ways of an "alcoholic republic."[19] Of course the inclination to drink was no respecter of party, but partisan division on the politics of temperance had long been visible. The division was clarified when in the late 1880s Bay State Republicans began bidding openly for Prohibitionist support. This brought Yankee and Irish Democrats together in defensive opposition to further moral intervention by the state against their "personal liberty" to drink.[20]

The issue of woman suffrage yielded less partisan clarity. Still, the configuration of support and opposition was roughly similar to those precipitated by quarrels over schooling and liquor control. The main thrust of pro-suffrage activity came from middle class Protestants of Republican background. Republican party leadership was divided over the tactical wisdom of backing this thrust. Meanwhile several prominent Yankee Democrats, including Josiah Quincy, Thomas Wentworth Higginson, and *Boston Globe* editor Charles H. Taylor, came out for woman suffrage. But Boston's Irish spokesmen—political, clerical, and journalistic—were almost unanimous in their opposition. And by the mid-1890s Yankee Democratic support for this stance reached substantial proportions. Two more decades would pass before Democratic opposition to woman suffrage began to crack.[21]

What emerged from all these attitudinal alignments were the grounds for a cross-class defensive alliance inside the Democratic party, as upper-class Yankee Democrats collaborated with leaders of the Catholic working class to contain the eclectic moral impulse of Boston's Protestant middle. A Republican Congressman from Worcester, mixing analytical insight with partisan spite, called it an alliance between "Harvard College and the slums."[22]

In the early 1890s the alliance paid off in an impressive resurgence of Democratic strength in gubernatorial and congressional elections, in spreading support for Grover Cleveland's low-tariff initiatives, and in increasingly hard-headed negotiating assumptions about the ethnic division of federal patronage. Nowhere was the latter mood expressed with more candor than in a message from Boston to Washington in 1894, sent by Yankee Democrat Sherman Hoar to Yankee Democrat Richard Olney: "I think with five Yankees now in office here and two Irishmen, another Irishman would be good politics."[23] Hoar's estimate was symptomatic of Yankee calculations across a broad range of issues as they strove to control party equilibrium. He and his colleagues were prepared to go some distance toward conceding Irish power in Boston in order to maintain their own standing in the party at the state and national level.

Meanwhile Irish leaders, nursing the wounds of recent sectarian combat in the city, were ready to reciprocate. Dismayed by the ouster of Hugh O'Brien from the mayoralty in 1888 and the defeat of another Irish candidate a year later, Patrick Maguire persuaded the Democratic city committee to revert to the strategy of the 1870s and run an upperclass Yankee gentleman for mayor, along the lines of his old patron-client F.O. Prince. Only by reviving the politics of deference, Maguire decided, could the Irish regain access to the fruits of City Hall.

Maguire's choice was Nathan Matthews, who since 1884 had emerged as the main architect of the Democratic party's statewide renovation. Matthews, like his father before him, was a wealthy Boston real estate manager with deep roots in the Democratic party. His knack for raising money and organizing campaigns won him respect on all sides as an honest, aggressive party entrepreneur. His mayoralty from 1891 to 1894 proved to be a stringent test of Maguire's strategy. He was the first mayor to exploit fully the new executive power vested in that office by the charter reforms of 1885, which were aimed at curbing the spending habits of the city council. The tight business efficiency which Matthews tried to impose on city management made him a hard man for Boston Democrats to live with. But he got things done. His realtor's familiarity with the needs of urban development enabled him to apply the rudiments of city planning to Boston's growth patterns. New park facilities, a better water supply, drastic reductions in gas rates, and the groundwork for a center-city subway system were his proudest feats. Although he worked hard to cut padding from the city payroll, he understood as well as anyone the political benefits of public spending. Urban growth meant municipal contracts for digging, laying, building and paving. And contracts spelled jobs—especially big contracts to utilities entrepreneurs like Henry M. Whitney, a major Democratic party patron. Maguire's city organization fed grudgingly on this low-wage patronage, and turned out annual majorities to float Matthews' re-elections.[24]

The national economic collapse of 1893 disrupted these growth-oriented arrangements. Hard times brought out the fiscal conservative in Matthews. It triggered his alarm about what he called "the insidious encroachment of socialism," and turned him into a cold ideologue of self-help.[25] As the politics of retrenchment replaced the politics of growth, he wound up resisting all proposals for expanded municipal expenditures to halt the spread of working class unemployment. Matthews left office in January 1895 unloved and unlamented in the Irish wards of Boston, and Patrick Maguire soon thereafter retreated into suburban semi-retirement.

Depression unstrung the city-wide Irish organization Maguire had led for almost twenty years. In the absence of centralized public relief efforts by either the city or the state, hard times had the effect of localizing patterns of dependence among the urban poor, and thus accentuated the role of the ward boss in cushioning their lives against privation. The depression of the '90s radically expanded the power of the men who ran the wards. These were a new generation of Irish leaders—American-born clubhouse professionals, grounded in their inner-city tenement districts, skillfully absorbing Jewish and Italian newcomers into their organizations, proud and secure in the dense mesh of local influence. Martin Lomasney in the West End, John F. Fitzgerald in the North End, James Donovan in the South End, Patrick Kennedy in East Boston were in no mood for deference. Further Yankee stewardship in Boston politics would have to meet their autonomy head on. In fact the acceleration in their rise to power across the depression years would ulti-mately snap the old terms of ethnic collaboration in the running of the city.[26]

IV

The depression, the collapse of national Democratic party fortunes after 1894, and the harsh strife among party regulars during the Bryan campaign of 1896 all combined to ruin the local initiatives launched back in 1884, and left the Boston political environment fundamentally transformed. Basic to the change was the disappearance of that crucial mood of readiness for cross-class cooperation between Irishman and Yankee, the mood which had buoyed Democratic morale over the years that landed Cleveland in the White House, Billy Russell in the gover-nor's chair, and O'Brien and Matthews in the Boston mayoralty. The structure of mutual dependence built by the linkages between national, state, and municipal success lost its logic after 1894, fell apart, and gave way to headstrong local factionalism and mutual mistrust.[27]

Henry Adams caught the social consequences of the new atmosphere when he wrote about the Boston of the turn of the century:

New England standards were various, scarcely reconcilable with each other, and constantly multiplying in number, until balance between them threatened to become impossible.... State Street and the banks exacted one stamp; the old Congregational clergy another; Harvard College, poor in votes but rich in social influence, a third; the foreign element, especially the Irish, held aloof, and seldom consented to approve anyone.... New power was disintegrating society, and setting independent centres of force to work.... No one could represent it faithfully as a whole.[28]

Adams' impressions are verified by the experience of Josiah Quincy, Boston's mayor from 1896 through 1899. His years in office showed a divided city the distance one lonely Yankee Democrat was prepared to travel in order to restore to it some semblance of community. In retrospect his effort may have been doomed from the start. But while it was happening it looked to many like the most far-reaching municipal experiment in America.

The Irish decision to run Quincy for mayor confirmed his reputation among fellow Yankees as a Mugwump who had long since lost his virtue. Each important phase of his career after 1884 propelled him beyond the boundaries of proper Mugwump behavior, while simultaneously improving his credentials among party regulars. After helping to write a new city charter for his native Quincy, he was elected to the General Court in 1886 with support from the Knights of Labor. At the State House he quickly assumed leadership of the Democratic minority and nursed through an impressive modernization of Massachusetts labor law, based on English precedent. Meanwhile he honed his talents as a party manager. He spent most of 1893 in Washington helping President Cleveland swap patronage for votes during the fight to repeal the Sherman Silver Purchase Act. A solitary bachelor, he had bucked the suburban migration and moved in from Quincy to Boston, where he lived in an old house on Charles Street. He shunned the polite society of Back Bay, preferring the company of those closer to the pulse of the city—professional politicians, labor leaders, settlement house workers, and downtown businessmen. He was a keen student of English Fabian thought and continental urban governance. By every criterion except ethnicity he was better prepared to try managing the city than any man in town.[29]

His four years in City Hall struck many contemporaries, and some later historians, as a naive, premature adventure in municipal socialism.

If the urban crisis of the 1890s had turned his friend Nathan Matthews into a grim reactionary, it persuaded Quincy to urge Boston toward a more collectivist future, oddly reminiscent in some ways of Edward Bellamy's urban utopia. A little dazzled perhaps by the possibilities of a new century around the corner, he hoped to bring Bostonians together, despite their differences, in a spirit of advancing civic pluralism gathered in a common cause. "The people of a city constitute a community," he wrote for Boston's radical reform journal, *Arena*, "in all which that significant term implies; their interests are inextricably bound up together, and everything which promotes the well-being of a large part of the population benefits all."[30]

To implement this spacious dream, Quincy practiced administrative sprawl. He radically expanded the reach of the city's public agencies out over the collective life of the city, in what might be called a surge of participatory bureaucracy. Through a rash of new commissions, departments, and ad hoc committees, he tried to enlist from diverse groups not simply cooperation but involvement in the tasks of making Boston work. These groups included suburban Republican merchants doing business in the city, whom he organized into a Merchants Municipal Committee to advise him on taxation and transit; social workers interested in his schemes for public baths, playgrounds, and gymnasia; and patrons of cultural uplift responding to his plans for public lecture series, city-sponsored art shows, and musical events ranging from brass bands on Boston Common to a touring municipal string quartet. To Boston's trade unionists he offered job-oriented incentives to involvement—an expanded public works operation; more direct hiring of union labor by the city in place of reliance on private non-union contractors; and, with an eye on Boston's powerful typographers, the creation of a municipal printing plant. Quincy tried to turn this plant into a showcase of enlightened labor relations, complete with an 8-hour day, paid holidays, and the promise of eventual retirement pensions. Though overshadowed by his celebrated public baths, the printing operation was his main pilot plant experiment in urban reform through public ownership.[31]

Quincy's fellow politicians did not know quite what to make of all this, but most of them were not impressed. Noting the money and jobs involved, some interpreted his innovations as merely an ingenious new version of the spoils system. Even his election to a second two-year term in 1897 did not squelch the skepticism. "The curious thing about it all," one shrewd observer commented, "is that I haven't yet found one single Democrat of first-class standing who has been willing to tell me personally that he believes in Josiah Quincy.''[32] Quincy had in effect moved beyond his party's fund of 19th-century shared beliefs.

The Democrats he worried most about were the Irish ward leaders. Some of his reforms threatened traditional patronage arrangements among them, as in the case of his crackdown on non-union private contracting of city work, a long-standing device for channeling low-wage jobs through aldermanic clubhouses. Other reforms seemed to result only in filling City Hall with Yankee do-gooders inclined to meddle beyond their turf. The mayor's most troublesome enemy among Irish leaders was the West End's unpredictable Martin Lomasney, who scorned what he later called Quincy's ''visionary ideas on government'' and maneuvered endlessly to thwart them.[33]

Quincy tried to sooth the ward leaders' misgivings by bringing them together as a group. He managed to pull every important Irish leader in the city, except Lomasney, into a body called the Board of Strategy, in effect a small successor group to Maguire's old Democratic city committee. This forum for negotiating differences worked until midway through his second term. Then it disintegrated in an angry feud over executive control of city spending, which Quincy recognized had gotten out of hand. His effort to remove budgetary decisions from the influence of ward-based pressures and lift them to the level of ''scientific'' management cast him in a role he had till then avoided—a Yankee elitist who proposed to govern above the crowd. His stance left him vulnerable to attacks by Lomasney, a rebellious city council, and Republican leaders in the state legislature. The fight brought Quincy down, and closed the books on what a journalist for *Harpers Weekly* called his ''insolvent utopia.''[34] The collapse was more than fiscal. It finished the last phase of the Irish-Yankee leadership alliance which had worked to mute the city's power transfer since the days of F.O. Prince. Eighteen years would go by before Boston would again entrust the mayor's office to a Harvard man.

V

The collapse of Quincy's dream for Boston released a kaleidoscopic pattern of new forces in the city's politics. From 1900 to 1910, Democrats were a party in name only. Succeeding elections served mainly to record voter reaction to momentary coalitions emerging from the latest vendettas and bargains. Party leaders, emancipated from concern with national party fortunes or deference to the Harvard connection, were free to swing their strength to immediate local advantage. Patron-client politics did not disappear, but they were no longer contained by party boundaries or ethnic loyalty. Lomasney made that clear at the outset of the new era when he insured Democrat Patrick Collins' defeat for the mayoralty and then proceeded to expand his own power through patronage from the Republican victor.[35] For most of the next decade, Lomasney's baffling insurgency made a counterpoint to the ebb and flow of John F. Fitzgerald's mayoral ambitions. The free-wheeling maneuvers of the Irish leaders did not always cancel each other out, but they enforced a factionalism among their followers that sometimes verged on ethnic fratricide.

Meanwhile Yankee Democrats for the most part backed off from direct involvement in the city's elective politics. Quincy continued to play a backstage role, purged now of his quasi-socialist illusions, trying to restore a semblance of cohesion to the party's state minority. And powerful Democratic businessmen like Henry M. Whitney and William Gaston pursued their interest in urban gas and transit franchises, relying on political collaboration from Fitzgerald. What was left of the "reform" wing of the party, which had been radicalized by the Bryan campaign of 1896, practiced its own brand of unglued insurgency. It rallied sporadically around such men as George Fred Williams, the volatile Mugwump-turned-Bryanite who combined deep mistrust for both the leaders of the Boston Irish and the corporate arrogance of Whitney and Gaston, and John B. Moran, a lapsed Catholic with a strange political past and a talent for blue-nose sensationalism who as Boston's District Attorney in 1906 alarmed the city by reviving strict enforcement of its liquor laws.[36] Both Moran and Williams—who was the son of a German sailor—were men whose background and associations had set them apart from fellow Democrats as political oddities back in the 1890s. In the factionalized setting of the new century they glorified in the arts of splinter leadership.

The most effective reform influence of these years was the "loose army" of civic spokesmen who worked outside the party system to bring the structure of city government and the behavior of elected officials into line with current Progressive ideals. The main leader of this army was another political outsider, Louis Brandeis, the Kentucky-born son of Jewish immigrants who had played only a minor part in Mugwump politics in earlier years. Inspired by his public-interest lobbying as well as their own perceptions of waste, corruption and demagoguery in Boston ward politics, the city's independent reformers merged into the Good Government Association in 1903. Their predominantly upper-class Yankee business and professional backgrounds and their amateur, part-time political activism combined with the name of their organization to earn them the label, Goo-Goo, and the inevitable stigma of righteous propriety which the label carried. They were legitimate successors to the Mugwumps, and open targets for charges fired at them by Irish journalists like James J. Roche, who despised what he called their "smooth, sneaking, pigeon-livered bigotry."[37]

But unlike the Mugwump organizations of the 1880s, the G.G.A. closed in with earnest force on the problems of Boston governance. Its membership was mobilized by Fitzgerald's election as mayor in 1905 and his rollicking abuse of reformist values in the years that followed. For the balance of the decade, Boston's political life was marked by warfare between Fitzgerald and the G.G.A.—between liberated center-city Irish impudence and Yankee disapproval pressing in from the periphery. In this familiar urban contest between the center and the rim, sharpened now by open ethnic hostility, the good government forces had few effective political options. They lacked both plausible candidates and an organized voter following with which to shape electoral outcomes. Their tactic of non-endorsement for candidates who failed to measure up to their standards worked only erratically. And even their own ablest leaders could disappoint them by shunning nominations—as when Brandeis turned down a G.G.A. request to run for mayor against Fitzgerald in 1907.[38]

In the end it was the de-personalized strategy of structural reform, imposed on the city after sustained investigation and publicity, that produced the most substantial G.G.A. success. After a two-year ribbon inquiry into city mismanagement, chaired by former mayor Matthews, Boston voters in 1909 approved a new city charter that decisively altered the city's governance structure. While the changes moved far beyond the charter modifications of 1885 and the aborted changes sought by Quincy in 1898, they aimed in the same direction—toward concentrating and elevating political authority in executive hands and reducing legislative influence. The charter reformers hoped to sanitize City Hall by lifting its business above the reach of the wards. The huge old 75-man city council of ward representatives disappeared, replaced by a tidier body of nine seats to be filled on rotation in non-partisan, at-large elections. The mayor's term of office was extended; his veto power over council action was expanded; and his power of appointment was freed from council approval. Between elections the main check on his behavior now came not from below but from above, in the form of two state-appointed watchdog commissions, one for finance, one for appointments.[39]

The charter of 1909 institutionalized goals that pervaded reform thought in the Progressive era—administrative efficiency through compact executive authority, and a filtration of the popular impulse through staggered city-wide legislative elections.[40] But if charter reform reflected a national mood, still it would have local results that depended on the mood of the city's population. Perhaps in the minds of some Boston civic reformers loomed the dream of using the new machinery to restore a remembered past, when Yankee executive intelligence presided over a chastened and contained majority. It wasn't to be. In the first mayoral election under the new charter, in January 1910, the blueblood Harvard-trained Yankee banker James J. Storrow, the pride of his breed, met Fitzgerald head on. Fitzgerald beat him after waging a campaign unparalleled up to that time in the bitterness of its class and ethnic appeals.[41]

Ironically, by way of compensation for Storrow's defeat by Honey Fitz, in the tiny new city council, elected at large, the candidates of the G.G.A. discovered they had won a legislative majority. Willy-nilly, the roles of reformers and politicos had been reversed. The Boston mayoralty now became the main vehicle of Irish power in the city, while the non-Irish factions of the population were left to press their political influence through legislative tactics of pressure, protest, and containment.

Thereafter Yankee upper-class leadership in Boston largely evacuated the city's electoral arena and resorted to more subtle economic and social ways of registering its influence. Its local political reputation meanwhile began to gather mythic proportions, as the folk memory of upper-class arrogance settled in.

Notes

1. *New York Times Magazine*, Nov. 25, 1979.

2. Arthur Mann, *Yankee Reformers in an Urban Age* (Cambridge: Harvard University Press, 1954), Ch. 2; Frederic C. Jaher, "The Boston Brahmins in

the Age of Industrial Capitalism," in Jaher, ed., *The Age of Industrialism in America* (New York: The Free Press, 1968), 197.

3. Frederic C. Jaher, "Nineteenth-Century Elites in Boston and New York," *Journal of Social History*, 6 (Fall 1972): 60-68; Philip S. Benjamin, "Gentlemen Reformers in the Quaker City, 1870-1912," *Political Science Quarterly*, 85 (March 1970): 61-79.

4. The argument develops themes first broached in Geoffrey Blodgett, *The Gentle Reformers: Massachusetts Democrats in the Cleveland Era* (Cambridge: Harvard University Press, 1966). See also Peter K. Eisinger, "Ethnic Political Transition in Boston, 1884-1933: Some Lessons for Contemporary Cities," *Political Science Quarterly*, 93 (Summer 1978): 217-239.

5. Oscar Handlin, *Boston's Immigrants: A Study in Acculturation*, revised edition (Cambridge: Harvard University Press, 1959), 212-222; William V. Shannon, *The American Irish* (New York: Macmillan, 1963), 182-187; Martin Green, *The Problem of Boston* (New York: W.W. Norton and Co., Inc., 1966), 103; Stephan Thernstrom, *The Other Bostonians* (Cambridge: Harvard University Press, 1973), 39,135, 167. See also Henry Cabot Lodge, *Boston* (New York: Longmans, Green and Co., 1892), 198-204.

6. Quotation from Robert H. Whitten, *Public Administration in Massachusetts: The Relation of Central to Local Authority* (New York: Columbia University Press, 1898), 81. See James M. Bugbee, "Boston Under the Mayors, 1822-1880," in Justin Winsor, ed., *Memorial History of Boston* (Boston: Ticknor, 1881), III, 266-271.

7. Roger Lane, *Policing the City: Boston, 1822-1885* (Cambridge: Harvard University Press, 1967), 141, 176, 210, 216-219.

8. *The Republic* (Boston), June 9, 1894.

9. Robert H. Lord, et al., *History of the Archdiocese of Boston in the Various Stages of its Development, 1604 to 1943* (Boston: Boston Pilot Publishing Co., 1944), III, 100-125; Barbara M. Solomon, *Ancestors and Immigrants: a Changing New England Tradition* (Cambridge: Harvard University Press, 1956), 48-53; Lois B. Merk, "Boston's Historic Public School Crisis," *New England Quarterly*, 31 (June 1958): 172-199; Paul Kleppner, *The Third Electoral System, 1853-1892* (Chapel Hill: University of North Carolina Press, 1979), 349-352.

10. Bugbee, in Winsor, ed., *Memorial History of Boston*, III, 275-276; Lane, *Policing the City*, 161; Jaher, ed., *The Age of Industrialism in America*, 206-208; James A. Merino, "Cooperative Schemes for Greater Boston, 1890-1920," *New England Quarterly*, 45 (June 1972): 196-226; Michael Conzen and George K. Lewis, "Boston: A Geographical Portrait," in John S. Adams, ed., *Contemporary Metropolitan America: Cities of the Nation's Metropolitan Core* (Cambridge: Ballinger Publishing Co., 1976), I, 84-89, 113-116. See also Sam Bass Warner, *Streetcar Suburbs: The Process of Growth in Boston, 1870-1920* (Cambridge: Harvard University Press, 1962), passim.

11. *Boston Herald*, Oct. 26, 1896; "Frederick Octavius Prince," *National Cyclopedia of American Biography* (New York: James T. White and Company, 1900), X, 222; Lane, *Policing the City*, 166, 209, 212-213; Blodgett, *Gentle Reformers*, 59; Kleppner, *Third Electoral System*, 333; Joseph O'Neil to William E. Russell, Feb. 2, 1892, Russell Papers, Massachusetts Historical Society.

12. Dale Baum, " 'Noisy but not Numerous': The Revolt of the Massachusetts Mugwumps," *Historian*, 41 (Feb. 1979): 241-256. The Mugwump bolt should not obscure the fact that most Massachusetts Yankees remained Republicans in national, state, and local politics.

13. Blodgett, *Gentle Reformers*, 35, 52, 93. A Boston critic of Mugwump behavior mocked the awkwardness of their sudden alliance with the Irish in 1884: "The 'innocents at home' here have paid the taxes of ten thousand Irishmen—that they might vote for Cleveland. In three weeks these men will all vote for a Ring administration of Boston. The next week the men who paid their taxes will ask me to a Civil Service Reform meeting. You will come and speak and tell me I must not even laugh at them." E.E. Hale to R.R. Bowker, Nov. 13, 1884, Bowker Papers, Manuscripts Division, Library of Congress.

14. Jaher, *Age of Industrialism*, 215-218; Ronald Story, "Harvard and the Boston Brahmins: A Study in Institutional and Class Development, 1800-1865," *Journal of Social History*, 9 (Spring 1975): 94-121; Hugh Hawkins, *Between Harvard and America: The Educational Leadership of Charles W. Eliot* (New York: Oxford University Press, 1972), Ch. 4, 5, and 6.

15. Christopher Jencks and David Reisman, *The Academic Revolution* (Garden City, N.Y.: Doubleday, 1968), 12.

16. Josiah Quincy, "The Orator in a Modern Democracy," Harvard University Archives.

17. K.E. Conway and M.W. Cameron, *Charles Francis Donnelly: A Memoir* (New York: James T. White and Company, 1909), 31-51 and passim; Hawkins, *Between Harvard and America*, 123, 184; Tilden Edelstein, *Strange Enthusiasm: A Life of Thomas Wentworth Higginson* (New Haven: Yale University Press, 1968), 369-371; Robert A. Silverman, "Nathan Matthews: Politics of Reform in Boston, 1890-1910," *New England Quarterly*, 50 (Dec. 1977): 628; Henry James, ed., *Letters of William James* (Boston: Atlantic Monthly Press, 1920), I, 296-297; Solomon, *Ancestors and Immigrants*, 45-50. For the Boston origins of the concept of cultural pluralism, see Allon Gal, *Brandeis of Boston* (Cambridge: Harvard University Press, 1980), 147-151. Not all Harvard Mugwumps were ready for the concept. Henry Lee wrote to President Eliot in 1886, "Instinct and reading of history prompt me to distrust and repel Catholics. Their usurpation of office, aided by the schools and savings banks benevolently supported by us . . . , the Unitarian merchants and lawyers, & c & c, depresses me seriously." Henry Lee to Charles W. Eliot, Aug. 31, 1886, Eliot Papers, Harvard University Archives.

18. Typewritten speech draft, for delivery Aug. 22, 1895, Russell Papers, Massachusetts Historical Society.

19. The quoted phrase is from the title of W.J. Rorabaugh, *Alcoholic Republic: An American Tradition* (New York: Oxford University Press, 1979). Mugwump Charles Francis Adams, Jr., made this thoughtful entry in his diary in 1875: "A fine boil appeared on my neck today, forcibly suggesting to me that I was drinking too much claret—Knocked off and began on whisky." Charles Francis Adams, Jr., Diary, 1875, Adams Papers, Massachusetts Historical Society. See Robert Grant, *Fourscore: An Autobiography* (Boston: Houghton Mifflin Company, 1934), 129, 132.

20. Richard Harmond, "Troubles of Massachusetts Republicans During the 1880s," *Mid-America*, 56 (April 1974): 91-93; Kleppner, *Third Electoral System*, 343, 349.

21. Blodgett, *Gentle Reformers*, 155-157; James Kenneally, "Woman Suffrage and the Massachusetts 'Referendum' of 1895," *The Historian*, 30 (Aug. 1968): 617-633; John D. Buenker, "The Urban Political Machine and Woman Suffrage: A Study in Political Adaptability," *The Historian*, 33 (Feb. 1971): 264-279.

22. Congressman Joseph H. Walker, quoted in *Boston Herald*, Nov. 6, 1890.

23. Sherman Hoar to Richard Olney, July 17, 1894, Olney Papers, Manuscripts Division, Library of Congress.

24. Blodgett, *Gentle Reformers*, 158-161; Silverman, "Matthews," 626-639.

25. Nathan Matthews, *The City Government of Boston* (Boston: Rockwell and Churchill, city printers, 1895), 104-107, 175, 182.

26. Blodgett, *Gentle Reformers*, 166-171; Shannon, *The American Irish*, 199.

27. George Fred Williams, Diary Notes, 1895, Massachusetts Historical Society, are vivid testimony to the changed atmosphere.

28. Henry Adams, *The Education of Henry Adams* (Boston: Houghton Mifflin Company, 1918), 419.

29. Geoffrey Blodgett, "Josiah Quincy, Brahmin Democrat," *New England Quarterly*, 38 (Dec. 1965): 435-440.

30. Josiah Quincy, "The Development of American Cities," *Arena*, 17 (March 1897): 536.

31. Blodgett, "Quincy," 441-445.

32. George H. Lyman to Henry Cabot Lodge, Dec. 23, 1897, Lodge Papers, Massachusetts Historical Society.

33. *Boston Herald*, Dec. 11 and Dec. 13, 1925; Silverman, "Matthews," 638.

34. G.A. Copeland, "An Insolvent Utopia," *Harper's Weekly*, 44 (June 16, 1900): 549.

35. Richard M. Abrams, *Conservatism in a Progressive Era: Massachusetts Politics, 1900-1912* (Cambridge: Harvard University Press, 1964), 45.

36. Abrams, *Conservatism in a Progressive Era*, 68, 94, 145, 169; Blodgett, *Gentle Reformers*, 276-278.

37. The phrase, "loose army," is from Abrams, *Conservatism in a Progressive Era*, 131. For Brandeis' role, see Gal, *Brandeis of Boston*, 89-92, 118, 119. Roche is quoted in Roger Lane, "James Jeffrey Roche and the Boston *Pilot*," *New England Quarterly*, 33 (Sept. 1960): 363.

38. Abrams, *Conservatism in a Progressive Era*, 131, 136, 144; Melvin Urofsky and David Levy, eds., *Letters of Louis D. Brandeis* (Albany: State University of New York Press, 1971-75), II, 31; Richard Henry Dana, Journal, II, Feb. 1, 1906, Dana Papers, Massachusetts Historical Society.

39. Abrams, *Conservatism in a Progressive Era*, 145-150; Albert Bushnell Hart, ed., *Commonwealth History of Massachusetts* (New York: The Statesman History Co., 1930),V, 80-82.

40. Samuel P. Hays, "The Politics of Reform in Municipal Government in the Progressive Era," *Pacific Northwest Quarterly*, 55 (Oct. 1964): 157-169.

41. John Henry Cutler, '*Honey Fitz': Three Steps to the White House* (Indianapolis: Bobbs-Merrill, 1962), is a colorful account.

5

From Party to Factions: The Dissolution of Boston's Majority Party, 1876-1908

PAUL KLEPPNER

In politics you don't have friends. You have allies.

John Fitzgerald Kennedy

The evolution of party politics in Boston seemingly involves no great analytic puzzles. By the late 1870's, the Hub had become the most predominantly Irish of the nation's major cities and one of its most reliably Democratic bailiwicks. Politicization of the well chronicled clash between Yankee and Irish cultures combined with an underlying change in the ethno-religious composition of the city's electorate to connect these two developments. Cultural antagonism was transferred into partisan politics, as Yankee Protestant Republicans battled Irish Catholic Democrats. In the long run, victory went to the group with the higher birthrate. As the Irish grew in numbers, they came eventually to dominate the city's electorate, to elevate their own to municipal offices, and to wrest political control of the city from the hands of their Yankee enemies.

This is at once a tidy and partially credible explanation of Boston's political history. It correctly draws attention to Protestant-Catholic antagonism as a major and durable cleavage line of the city's partisan politics and to the important roles that differences in migration and birthrates played in eventually producing its Democratic majority. Despite these merits, however, this mode of explanation does not tell us all that we need to know about the evolution of Boston's political

This analysis derives from larger projects designed to explore the contours of mass electoral behavior in all states outside the South. That work has been supported by grants from the National Endowment for the Humanities and the National Science Foundation and administered by the latter as Grant Nos. SES-7714155 and SES-7714155A-01. The author is grateful for the support provided by both agencies.

struggles. By emphasizing the static element, it diverts attention from other factors that may have worked to produce political change. Its preoccupation with Yankee-Irish conflict may exaggerate each group's behavioral cohesiveness (as Geoffrey Blodgett has shown in the case of the small but significant group of Yankees who were Democratic leaders) and overdraw the congruence between cultural and party combat. Its exclusive focus on conflict between the major parties overlooks another source of political tension: the factional struggles that raged within the parties, especially those that ultimately rent the unity of the Democratic majority.

Whether or not such factors need to be taken into account cannot be resolved deductively. In fact, final conclusions must be suspended until we have available studies of designated time periods that have been comparably designed to explore the relationships between social groups and parties, and which are sensitive both to the distinguishable domains of party activity and to the often indiscernible psychological glue that cemented them together. As an interim and preliminary step in that direction, we can explore the behavior of Boston's voters for insights into the character of the city's partisan politics and party development.

What will be reported here is a limited and preliminary reconnaissance. It uses ward-level voting and demographic data to probe two specific aspects of the behavior of Boston's Democratic electorate: its partisan consistency and its degrees of native-stock vs. Irish polarization.[1] The time period examined is also a limited one, 1876 through 1908. That sequence has not been chosen arbitrarily, however; it provides an opportunity to examine both the period during which the Democrats emerged as the city's normal majority party (the late 1870s and early 1880s) and the decade of the 1890s, which elsewhere was a period of shrinking Democratic support and reorganization of electoral coalitions.[2] While so limited an exploration cannot provide a comprehensive portrait of electoral behavior, it can offer some insights that may be useful in constructing a more complete explanation of the city's politics.

We can begin by inquiring into the matter of partisan consistency among the city's Democratic voters. Strong partisans are likely to support all of their party's candidates at each election and to repeat that behavior at subsequent elections. Indices of split-ticket voting and of consistent partisan choices from one election to the next provide good indicators of the extent to which party norms guided individual behavior. However, since Massachusetts introduced a new ballot form in 1889 that facilitated split-ticket voting, the data presented here deal only with party-vote consistency from one election to the next.[3]

Table 1 presents estimates of the mean level of Democratic vote consistency for several offices within designated time periods. To obtain these figures, I began by developing the estimate for each pair of elections. For example, for any pair of presidential elections (say 1876 and 1880, or 1880 and 1884), I used regression procedures to estimate the proportion of Democratic voters at the first contest who repeated that party choice at the second.[4] Then the means were calculated to summarize these results within selected time periods.

Presidential elections occurred at four-year intervals, so for technical as well as substantive reasons we might expect more slippage in these estimates than in the others. Through 1895, when Boston changed from annual to biennial mayoralty elections, the president-to-mayor and governor-to-mayor estimates involve only the interval between the national and state elections in November and the contest for mayor in the second week of December. From 1897 through 1907, the most recent presidential contest was used as the first election in that paired comparison; but, since Massachusetts retained annual gubernatorial elections through the entire period, the governor-to-mayor estimates continued to involve only about a one-month time lapse.

The first three sequences presented in Table 1 follow what by now has become a fairly conventional means of periodizing U.S. electoral history. The 1876-1892 sequence covers the stable phase of the third electoral era; the 1892-1899 sequence covers the period of electoral upheaval in the 1890s; and the 1900-1908 sequence includes the early elections of the stable phase of the fourth electoral era. If the results are summarized in this way, regardless of which category of paired elections one examines, there doesn't appear to be a great deal of difference from one sequence to the other. If a Boston voter cast a Democratic ballot at one election, he was highly likely to repeat that performance at the next opportunity, whether that was a chance to vote for president or for mayor. Obviously, and as we would have expected, Boston's Democratic voters behaved as strong and regular partisans.[5]

The use of this periodization scheme may mask important distinctions. To explore that possibility, sequences 4 through 7 in Table 1 contrast the periods during which the Democrats ran Irish Catholic candidates for mayor with those during which they nominated Yankee Protestants. When the governor-to-mayor and mayor-to-mayor estimates are sum-

Table 1
Estimates of Democratic Voting Consistency between Elections, Boston, 1876-1908[1]

		President to President	President to Mayor	Governor to Mayor	Mayor to Mayor
1)	1876-1892	93.5	93.4	89.7	91.2
2)	1893-1899	85.2	97.2	91.6	91.8
3)	1900-1908	97.2	91.6	87.3	84.3
4)	1876-1882	NC	NC	98.4	97.8
5)	1883-1889[2]	NC	NC	83.4	87.4
6)	1890-1897	NC	NC	95.0	90.5
7)	1899-1908[2]	NC	NC	82.4	88.2

[1] Entries are the mean proportions of Democratic voters at the first election who cast Democratic ballots at the second election for each pair in the sequence

[2] Irish Democratic candidates for Mayor

Table 2
Irish and Native-stock Voting Support for Democratic Candidates, 1876-1908[1]

	1876–1882	1883–1889[2]	1890–1897	1899–1980[2]
BOSTON[3]				
President				
Irish	97.5	100.0	90.1	98.3
Native	15.5	9.8	8.4	3.6
Governor				
Irish	97.6	96.2	95.1	92.8
Native	18.2	9.3	10.4	3.2
Mayor				
Irish	94.4	86.1	97.1	84.9
Native	23.5	1.5	16.8	6.2
OUTSTATE MASSACHUSETTS[4]				
Governor				
Irish	70.8	80.5	88.5	83.1
Native	27.9	26.3	18.9	13.8

[1] Entries are the mean proportions of the voting components of each group that cast Democratic ballots at each election in the sequence.

[2] Irish Democratic candidates for Mayor.

[3] The number of wards for the full time period was 25.

[4] Exludes Boston, and the number of towns and cities varied from 337 to 353.

marized in this way, we can begin to detect a faint but revealing pattern of difference.[6] There was greater consistency in voting selections when Yankees headed the city ticket than when Irish nominees did. The high rates of interelection consistency were especially remarkable during the 1890s, when the depression hit the city and the fortunes of the Democratic party dipped with the employment rate. Thereafter, when the Democrats again nominated Irish candidates for mayor, the levels of partisan consistency plunged downward. These data suggest a clear tendency for party norms to erode whenever the city's Irish Democrats nominated one of their own for mayor.

Since Yankee-Irish conflict was the vital fault line of party politics in Boston, that result should not be too surprising. We would expect Democratic voters who were not Irish Catholics to experience especially strong cross-pressures when their party bestowed its mayoralty nomination on one of their cultural foes. Under that condition, we would expect native-stock voting support for the Democratic candidate for mayor to drop, and we would also expect Irish support to remain stable or even to increase. The regression estimates of Irish and native-stock voting support presented in Table 2 confirm the first part of that expectation, but they disabuse us of the notion that Irish candidates elicited greater than usual electoral support among Irish voters.[7]

We should begin by noticing that there was a difference between the partisan behavior of Boston's Irish and native-stock voters and that of their counterparts in the other cities and towns of the state. Boston's Irish were consistently more Democratic, and its native-stock voters less so, than the same groups in outstate Massachusetts. The Boston context made a difference: it worked to increase the size of the partisan gap between the Irish and native-stock groups.

The comparisons across offices within Boston are even more revealing, however. Notice that during the 1876-1882 and 1890-1897 periods, when Democratic city tickets were headed by Yankee candidates for mayor, native-stock voters gave the Democrats greater support in local elections than in gubernatorial or presidential contests. And the nomination of Yankees did not appreciably reduce Irish voting support for the Democratic party during these sequences. But when Boston's Democrats nominated Irish mayoralty candidates between 1883 and 1889, then local native-stock support virtually evaporated. Moreover, that development seemed to have had some carryover to native-stock voting preferences in presidential and gubernatorial elections. In presidential elections between 1883 and 1889, the proportion of native-stock voters who cast Democratic ballots fell to 63.2 percent of the size it had been during the 1876-1882 period, and the gubernatorial proportion dropped to 51.0 percent of its earlier size. No similar shrinkage occurred in the proportionate share of native-stock votes that the Democrats received in outstate Massachusetts. During the depression decade of the 1890s, the voting support of Boston's native-stock citizens for Democratic mayoralty candidates rebounded to about the same level as native voters elsewhere in the state, but there was no appreciable change in their proportionate preference for Democratic presidential and gubernatorial candidates. Finally, after the depression, when Boston's Democrats again nominated Irish candidates for mayor, native-stock voters once again withdrew from the Democratic coalition.[8]

The behavior of Boston's Irish voters was even more arresting than the expected reaction of its native-stock citizens. The nomination of Irish Catholics for mayor had the apparently anomalous effect of reducing the levels of Irish voting support for the Democrats. While the outstate Irish became more Democratic after 1882, their Boston co-religionists reduced their levels of party voting in mayoralty elections. Significantly, however, there was virtually no change in the levels of Irish support for Democratic presidential and gubernatorial candidates. The reaction of Boston's Irish voters, in other words, was clearly confined to the election in which the Democratic ticket was headed by a fellow Irishman.[9] That reaction abated when the local Democrats nominated Yankees for the mayoralty during the 1890s, but reappeared in the turn-of-the-century elections when Irish nominees headed the Democratic city ticket.

A static conception of congruence between Yankee-Irish cultural conflict and Republican-Democratic party battles does not readily accommodate such findings. It ignores the fact that nearly a fifth of the native-stock voters continued to cast Democratic ballots in local elections—as long as the mayoralty candidate wasn't Irish—well after Boston had become an Irish city. In other words, in assuming that Yankee-Irish grassroots party polarization was a virtually constant feature of Boston's politics, we gloss over the process through which it eventually emerged as well as the conditions that shaped it.

However, the larger flaw relates to the behavior of the Irish. Because the conception assumes that Irish voters exhibited a nearly unvarying degree of partisan cohesiveness, it does not stimulate a search for the conditions that eroded the group's behavioral solidarity. Yet there were clear and consistent differences over time and across offices in the group's response to political stimuli. The data in Table 2 make those distinctions apparent, and we can add some point to that description by summarizing the voting behavior of homogeneous Irish precincts for the three types of elections. In all three, of course, the Irish were strong Democrats; but in presidential and gubernatorial contests there was relatively little variation from one area of the city to another in the Irish percentage cast for the Democratic candidate. The typical range from the lowest to the highest precinct was eight to ten percentage points. The variation across the Irish precincts was usually greater in city elections, and it was especially wide when Irish candidates headed the ticket. Reasonably illustrative was the range that occurred in 1887: Hugh O'Brien polled 91.3 percent of the vote among South Boston's Irish, but only 56.1 percent among Charlestown's Irish. Spreads of twenty-five to forty percentage points were common when either O'Brien or Patrick A. Collins ran for mayor (except for Collins's 1903 race); much smaller spreads occurred when Yankees headed the Democratic city ticket.

This response by Irish voters to Irish mayoralty candidates may seem counterintuitive and contrary to the expected reaction from a self-conscious ethno-religious group.[10] And it does not fit very well into an explanation treating exclusively with Yankee-Irish conflict. But this response is critically important to understanding the dynamic evolution of Boston's politics. Its occurrence underscores the existence of distinctions within the Irish group and points to the conditions under which those were likely to become politically salient. Conflict among the Irish did not affect the group's partisan consistency or cohesiveness as long as the Democrats nominated Yankee candidates for mayor. In the 1880s, when Irish candidates first headed the city ticket, some signs of that conflict appeared. Those were comparatively mild indicators of a factionalism that was then being organized at the grassroots level, and which was still partially constrained by the tactics of the party's leaders and by the symbolic importance that the group must have attached to elevating one of its own to the mayoralty. Conditions were different by the late 1890s; factional struggle was more thoroughly organized and the party organization was less able to constrain it. The transitional candidacy of Patrick Collins (1899-1903) served that purpose reasonably well, but with the nomination of John F. Fitzgerald—himself one of the factional leaders—conflict among contending groups of Irish Democrats burst into the open. As that occurred, the majority party relapsed into a condition of chaotic factionalism and nearly hopeless disarray.

Party factionalism did not materialize suddenly and mysteriously after 1900. Its roots ran deep into the structure of Boston's city government and into the practices of its late-nineteenth-century Democratic party.

Decision-making power in Boston was highly decentralized, as it was generally in nineteenth-century American cities. The city charter of 1854 formally entrusted the administration of the city to the Mayor, a twelve-member Board of Aldermen, and a Common Council, which was composed of an equal number of representatives from each ward.[11] But the charter vested the executive power of the municipal corporation in the Board of Aldermen, so that they had control over the fire department, the health department, the markets, the streets, the county buildings, and the granting of licenses. In practice, and except for their exclusive power to advise and consent to appointments recommended by the Mayor, the Aldermen came to share much of this executive authority with the Common Council, since the concurrence of both bodies was required to enact enabling ordinances. Subsequent actions by the legislature further fragmented decision-making authority; for example, in 1870 the legislature provided for the election of an independent board of street commissioners. But the amendments to the city charter in 1885 ostensibly moved the city in the direction of more centralized authority in the hands of the Mayor. The intent of those changes was to strip the Aldermen and the Common Council of their executive functions and to give the Mayor broad powers of appointment and removal in the city departments and an item veto over appropriations measures. Practice lagged well behind intent, however, and the Common Council especially continued to involve itself in matters that related to the employment of labor, the purchase of city supplies and the award of contracts for public works.[12]

The organization of the city's political parties paralleled its governmental structure. Each party appeared to be somewhat centralized, since it was governed by a city committee, which called annual conventions to nominate candidates for city-wide office. However, that appearance was illusory. The wards were the prime units of the organizational structure. The representatives on each party's city committee were selected at the ward level, as were the delegates to its conventions. Moreover, each ward elected candidates to the Common Council; and, as that body became increasingly involved in the decisions that allocated the city's tangible resources, the ward caucuses acquired even greater political importance. In practice, what evolved was a bottom-heavy structure, in which candidate selection and voter mobilization depended on action at the ward level. The persisting problem faced by party managers was how to forge and sustain alliances among the separate ward leaders to prevent fragmentation of the party. Their problem became greater as the city increased in size and the number of wards grew from twelve, to sixteen, to twenty-two, and finally to twenty-five by December 1875.[13]

By the mid-1870s, Boston's Democratic party—under the chairmanship of Patrick A. Collins—acted to impose order on what was becoming an increasingly unmanageable and unpredictable set of political conditions. Through a series of changes in the by-laws, the party's leadership remodeled their organizational apparatus. Two of these changes were especially important. The first eliminated the city convention and authorized the Democratic City Committee to convene itself as a nominating convention. The second altered the basis for representation on the City Committee. Election to the committee remained at the ward level, but the new by-laws required that an equal number of representatives were to be elected from each precinct and that only one representative could be chosen from the ward at large.[14]

These new by-laws meant that in the future the party organization would be able to designate the party's candidates for mayor. In practice, the Executive Committee of the organization searched for and selected the candidate and presented his name to the full City Committee for ratification. The purpose, however, of the precinct representation requirement for selection of city committeemen is somewhat more elusive. In its assessment of the change, the *Boston Post* offered a revealing clue. Precinct representation was necessary, the *Post* argued, to eliminate "certain associations which by sufferance threatened to become local elements of the organization, and to prohibit certain practices and negligences which were equally at war with the spirit and life of Democratic professions."[15] While the *Post*, like other contemporary party sources, never concretely identified these "certain associations," it seems likely that it had in mind the social clubs that had begun to participate in party affairs by endorsing and working for selected candidates at the ward caucuses. If so, then the provision must have been intended to prevent such organizations from dominating the ward caucuses and selecting only their own members as representatives to the City Committee.

While the second of these new by-laws, and its likely implications, seems to have eluded the attention of analysts, the new power that the City Committee exercised over the mayoralty nomination certainly has not. The dominant view is that Boston's Democratic City Committee of the 1880s functioned as a centralized and powerful institution that was capable of extinguishing dissent and controlling the candidate selection process. The prominent role of Patrick Maguire, its chairman in the mid-1880s and an important force until his death in 1896, fortified that image among both some contemporaries and most later historians. Maguire does seem to have controlled the Executive Committee and to have selected the party's nominees for Mayor. From this angle of view, the Democratic organization seems to have functioned as a classic example of a political machine, with Maguire as its recognized "boss."

However, the application of the machine metaphor distorts reality in this case. It derives from an exclusive emphasis on the mayoralty nomination, combined with an unarticulated assumption that that office was then as powerful and tangibly important as it later became. Maguire could dictate the party's choice for the mayoralty nomination, but the City Committee had no institutionalized means to control the selection process for the increasingly important seats on the Common Council. Since each ward nominated and elected its own council representatives, the ward leaders had direct control over some municipal jobs, and private employers whose business depended on city contracts provided them with access to even larger numbers of employment opportunities for their constituents.[16] Because the City Committee could not either punish recalcitrants or control the distribution of rewards, it was unable to exert discipline over the party's activist cadre, even if its leaders had had the will to try to do so. The legal structure of Boston's city government had encouraged the development of a set of party practices—ward-level nominations and elections—that effectively precluded the City Committee of the 1880s and 1890s from functioning as "a 'structure of control' . . . able to 'concert the action' of those linked to it and thereby to 'centralize influence' within its jurisdiction."[17]

The generation of Irishmen who directed the affairs of the party organization in the 1870s and 1880s—principally Maguire, Collins, Michael M. Cunniff, John F. Fitzgerald, and Thomas J. Gargan—were

not exclusively preoccupied with ward politics. They had wider in-
volvements and broader views, and they used their control over the
organization to work for an appropriately larger objective. They sought
recognition of their own and their group's respectability by the city's
Yankee elite. Their control over the City Committee and the mayoralty
nomination served that end in two ways. First, they used their leverage
to construct a public image of a disciplined and efficiently functioning
city organization. By conducting party activities in an orderly and businesslike way, they sought to show that they were capable of managing
the affairs of the city. Second, they used their control over the nominating process to select mayoralty candidates who would run the city,
not as partisans, but according to those ''highest interests'' and ''best
business principles'' that the Yankee elite valued. It was for that purpose
that they selected either Yankee Democrats or Irish candidates—like
O'Brien and Collins—who were financially successful and uninvolved
in the raging ward battles.[18]

Maguire and his associates were able to pursue these tactics because
the relative weakness of the office worked to minimize factional contention over the mayoralty nomination. The office had considerable
symbolic significance, of course, but it had little tangible value to the
Democratic ward chieftains. Nominating Yankee Democrats proved the
safest route for the party managers, since it immediately served larger
purposes and produced a bonus—higher-than-usual levels of voting
support among the city's native-stock population. Selecting even prestigious Irishmen was a more problematic course, since the reactions of
grassroots voters differed from those of the party's activists. An Irish
candidate at the top of the ticket repelled native-stock voters, while
politicizing the lingering hostility that existed among subgroups of the
Irish. The faint, but still perceptible, signs of Irish-vs.-Irish conflict that
appeared in the 1880s and 1890s were only forerunners of the rampant
factionalism that would reduce Boston's Democratic party to a condition
of total disarray after the turn of the century.

While the party's then dominant Irish leadership worked during the
1870s and 1880s to assuage Yankee anxieties, the future course of
Boston's politics was being shaped in its wardrooms and through the
development of new types of political institutions.

Private clubs and formal associations had long played important roles
in promoting the careers of Irish politicians in Boston. But the ''certain
associations'' that the *Post* had noticed in 1874 were primarily social

organizations—like the Red Berry Club, a fraternity of older residents of the North End, and the Neptune Associates, one of the many boat clubs in the waterfront wards.[19] These organizations mobilized their ranks to support those members who sought public offices; otherwise their involvement in politics was sporadic and peripheral to their original and major purposes. During the 1880s, the political importance of these older types of social-political associations faded, as new grassroots institutions began to emerge. These were clubs organized expressly to engage in political activities, in general, and to promote the political careers of their founders, in particular. The emergence of these personally controlled political clubs altered the institutional infrastructure of Boston's ward politics.

One of the earliest, and certainly the most notorious, of the new political clubs was the Hendricks Club, organized by Martin Lomasney in 1885; through it he dominated Democratic politics in the West End for over a generation. For all practical purposes, Lomasney's club was the Democratic organization of the eighth ward. Candidates who claimed to be running under the Democratic label, but who lacked the club's (and, hence, the organization's) endorsement, had only tenuous claims on the party's symbols and on the habituated loyalties of its electorate.[20]

There was nothing mysterious or even sinister in the way in which Lomasney built the Hendricks Club, identified it with the Democratic organization of his ward, and thereby enlisted the loyalties of the ward's voters. The club was more than an electioneering mechanism; it was a social service and employment agency. As a political institution that implicated itself in the social life of its members, Lomasney's organization operated somewhat like a European party of integration.

Other ward chieftains soon followed Lomasney's example. In 1888 Thomas W. Flood organized the Somerset Associates in South Boston (Ward 14), and in the early 1890s John F. Fitzgerald founded the Jefferson Club in the North End (Ward 6). Other ward leaders reorganized and reoriented older social clubs, especially Joseph J. Corbett in Charlestown, James Donovan in the South End, and Patrick J. Kennedy in East Boston. And in 1901 what was to become the most famous of the city's political clubs came to life: the Tammany Club of Roxbury (Ward 17), which was founded to promote the political career of James Michael Curley.[21]

It may appear that the development of these personal ward organizations simply extended and perpetuated past practices. The internal workings of Boston's newly emerging majority party long had projected something of a feudal appearance, with the City Committee lacking the power to compel either the obeisance or obedience of the ward barons. Even in the 1870s, alliances were fluid, and the leaders of the party had to negotiate annually with the ward chairmen to patch together a consensus. While the seeming weakness of the City Committee was quite real, the security of the ward leaders of the 1870s and 1880s was more fragile than it may appear in retrospect. The ward caucuses provided annual opportunities to challenge incumbent leaders, and those opportunities were frequently seized, especially in the early 1880s. Sometimes the challenges were repulsed; on other occasions they were successful; and nearly as often one year's victors became the next year's vanquished. Even leaders who managed to retain control for an extended period faced the likelihood of repeated conflict and the possibility of eventual defeat. Lomasney himself, for example, had used an "Independent Democrat" movement to challenge the incumbent leader in several annual caucuses before finally winning control in the West End. For the most part, the ward barons of the 1870s and 1880s were no more able than the City Committee to "concert the action" of their nominal subalterns within the party and to "centralize influence" within their jurisdictions.[22]

Lomasney's Hendricks Club was the prototype of a new institutional infrastructure that changed the rules of the game. Through personally controlled political clubs that became virtually indistinguishable from the party organizations, ward barons became "ward bosses." They solidified their control over their wards by pre-empting the support of the clientele necessary to organize and sustain challenges. In the process, Democratic party factionalism acquired a durable institutional base.

The emergence of personal and integrative ward organizations was a phased development. Moreover, as long as other political conditions remained unaltered, there was no necessary reason why that development had to produce chaotic factionalism. Since the powers of the city government were decentralized, and the ward leaders retained control over the distribution of city jobs and the award of public contracts through their representatives on the Common Council, they had no reason to battle each other over the mayoralty nomination. As these conditions changed during the 1890s, however, ward leaders began a struggle for control over the party organization (and the city government), the party's mechanisms for managing and constraining conflict eroded in effectiveness, and the majority party fell into a condition of factional disarray.

As long as the office of Mayor was relatively weak, as it was through the 1880s, the City Committee operated rather efficiently to dispense the party's nomination. The efforts to strengthen the office, by Nathan Matthews, Jr. in the early 1890s and Josiah Quincy in the mid-1890s, unbalanced the equation, and the increasingly powerful and secure ward leaders responded in kind.

Matthews was nominated by the Democrats and elected Mayor in 1890, and subsequently re-elected for three additional one-year terms. Unlike his immediate predecessors, Matthews saw the implications of the 1885 charter amendments and acted to enlarge the Mayor's role in the city government. He used his power over appointments to exert control over the executive departments, a move which reduced their responsiveness to the Common Council. Even this limited effort to centralize control aroused the ward leaders and led them to challenge the City Committee's control over the candidate selection process.[23]

At the expiration of Matthews's fourth term, Maguire and the City Committee were unable routinely to dictate their choice of Francis Peabody for Mayor. Grassroots opposition to Peabody seems to have been unusually strong, and to prevent open conflict the Chairman of the City Committee, James Donovan, made an unprecedented move. Prior to presenting Peabody's name to the City Committee for ratification, he called a conference of the twenty-five ward chairmen. This attempt to quiet the opposition was largely successful, principally because it produced public endorsements of Peabody by three of the key ward leaders—Fitzgerald, Kennedy, and Lomasney. When the City Committee convened as a nominating convention two days later, Peabody received 70.0 percent of the votes, with most of the opposition concentrated in the Charlestown and South Boston delegations.[24] However, the city's electorate was generally less receptive to Peabody's candidacy: he polled 47.2 percent of the popular vote, and the mayoralty fell into Republican hands. Compared with Matthews's percentages in 1893, Peabody's support remained about the same in only three wards and declined in the remaining twenty-two, with especially large drops in the Beacon Hill, Back Bay, and Roxbury wards.

Peabody's defeat was significant, of course; but even more so was the fact that the City Committee, for the first time in twenty years, had been unable to designate the nominee without first consulting with the ward chairmen. For all practical purposes, the City Committee had lost effective control. With the defeat of Peabody, the ward leaders moved quickly to strip away even the remaining appearance of control by the City Committee. In 1895 they successfully pressured the City Committee to alter its by-laws and to restore the older practice of nominating mayoralty candidates through an elected delegate convention. Henceforth, the mayoralty nomination would be thrashed out in the rough and tumble of the ward caucuses.[25]

In 1895, with a two-year mayoralty term at stake, Josiah Quincy endured the caucus test and easily secured the Democratic nomination. Quincy's actions as Mayor raised the stakes of the game and ignited open conflict between opposing sets of ward "bosses."

When he became Mayor in January 1896, Quincy embarked on a greatly expanded program of street improvements and public works, including a system of playgrounds, gymnasia, and public baths. In part his actions represented a response to requests from the city's unions, which from the onset of the depression had been urging larger expenditures for public works and street improvements to create jobs for the unemployed. It also reflected his own conception of the role of municipal government, which included a conviction that the interests of social harmony were best served by providing poorer citizens with some of the conveniences and comforts enjoyed by those who were better off.[26] In any case, Quincy's version of municipal socialism meant more city jobs and contracts and potentially more tangible benefits to be distributed by the ward leaders.

How was this larger benefits pie to be sliced? During his first two years as Mayor, Quincy worked with a select group of ward leaders to prevent Martin Lomasney from gaining a disproportionate share. Dubbed the Board of Strategy by contemporaries, this informal and shifting combination included as its prime actors Joseph Corbett, James Donovan, Patrick Kennedy, and John F. Fitzgerald, who had earlier been a Lomasney ally, with secondary roles being played from time to time by John A. Keliher and John H. Lee. After the death of Patrick Maguire in November 1896, the combination assumed greater importance, as it worked to prevent Lomasney from securing control over the city organization. In turn, Lomasney constructed his own working alliances with James E. Hayes, Corbett's Charlestown rival, and William S. McNary of South Boston. By 1897 the battle lines were drawn, and the rival combinations struggled for control over the party's aldermanic nominations. However, Quincy's general popularity discouraged the Lomasney group from challenging his renomination for Mayor.[27]

After his reelection, Quincy moved to implement another of his conceptions of proper municipal government—the centralization of executive authority. He requested the state legislature to create a Board of Apportionment to operate independently of Aldermen and Common Council in developing and allocating the city budget. The plan threatened the operation of the ward organizations and antagonized even his former allies among the ward leaders. The effect of Quincy's proposal was to increase both his vulnerability to Lomasney's attacks and the intensity of factional strife among the city's Democrats.[28]

In an attempt to restore order (if not harmony), Corbett and the other Board of Strategy participants turned to Patrick Collins as their choice for the mayoralty nomination in 1899. They recruited Collins from political retirement because he had not been closely allied with the factional combatants. Collins was hardly a consensus choice for the nomination, although he finally secured 64.2 percent of the votes at the nominating convention. The Lomasney combination supported John R. Murphy of Charlestown for the nomination, and Murphy subsequently refused to endorse Collins and contested for the mayoralty on an independent ticket. In the general election, Lomasney's ward gave Collins 61.7 percent of its vote, only slightly below its usual level of Democratic support; but Collins lost the election because of lagging support in the Charlestown and South Boston precincts.[29]

Over the next two years, Collins labored tirelessly to placate his opponents within the party, and by 1901 even the warring Charleston factions were reported to be "vying with each other in the desire to be first in line for General Collins."[30] When he was nominated and elected in 1901, Collins became Boston's second Irish Catholic Mayor. While his nomination for a second term encountered some opposition within the party, especially from the delegates representing the Dorchester, West Roxbury, and Brighton wards, Collins was renominated and reelected in 1903.

In one sense, the re-election of Collins in 1903 was the culmination of the older Democratic strategy that aimed at securing Yankee acceptance of Irish municipal leadership. At the mass level, the dimension of Collins's victory was without recent precedent: he polled 63.0 percent of the vote and carried every ward in the city.[31] At the elite level, the indicator was no less dramatic: five days before the election, Collins was the guest of honor at a reception at the Somerset Club, the exclusive sanctuary of the Brahmin elite.[32]

On the surface, Collins's sweeping victory in 1903 seemed to secure Democratic—and Irish—political hegemony in Boston. Even the 1901 election, and more certainly the 1903 results, signalled the extinction of viable party opposition on the part of the Republicans. Their dispirited and perfunctory effort in 1903 was a tacit admission that the nomination of a Democrat who surmounted that party's factional battles was tantamount to election. But factional antagonism festered barely beneath the surface of these election results, and within two years it burst into the open and fragmented the Democratic party.

Once in office, Collins worked to develop a disciplined and efficiently functioning Democratic organization. As Chairman of the City Committee in 1874, he had engineered the removal of the mayoralty nomination from the ward caucuses. The ward leaders had since reversed that change, but Collins now attempted to restore order and discipline in another way—by encouraging the conversion of the Board of Strategy into the functional equivalent of a city-wide machine. To accomplish that Collins used his power over appointments to name those designated by the Board of Strategy to head the executive departments. Once in control of the executive departments, the members of the Board of Strategy could use the flow of city contracts and jobs to undermine the opposing ward leaders and to build a city-wide organization strong enough to exert discipline and control.

Matthews and Quincy had challenged the ward leaders by attempting to centralize power in the office of the Mayor. Collins challenged them on their own ground by attempting to centralize power in a city-wide organization. If that was itself an ominous development to Lomasney and other outsiders, then Collins's appointment of James Donovan as Superintendent of Streets was even more so. The Department of Streets controlled more patronage than any other city department, and Donovan could use the position to attain personal control over a strengthened city organization. What Collins had perhaps not anticipated was that Donovan's colleagues on the Board of Strategy were equally apprehensive. Centralizing power in his hands threatened their own organizations and ambitions.[33]

There was no doubt that the ward leaders would respond to this new effort to centralize power just as they had to earlier attempts. However, their response, which led to a complete collapse of party discipline, was hastened by the state law that required mayoralty candidates to be nominated at a primary election. That change reduced the influence of the ward organizations and placed a premium on name recognition and campaign style. In 1905 John F. Fitzgerald, one of the original members of the Board of Strategy, took advantage of the primary requirement to challenge James Donovan's designated candidate for the mayoralty nomination.[34] Under these conditions, even the apparent cohesiveness of the Board of Strategy broke down. Joseph Corbett, John Lee, and former Mayor Quincy endorsed Fitzgerald. In one of those strange twists that characterize a politics of factions and shifting alliances, James Donovan's candidate drew support from Martin Lomasney, against whom the Board of Strategy had plotted for over a decade. Lomasney's old allies William S. McNary and John R. Murphy also opposed Fitzgerald, as did his old foes John A. Keliher and Patrick Kennedy.[35]

The primary was "bitterly contested" and marked by "an unprecedented amount of rancor," and the wounds that were opened did not heal quickly.[36] Fitzgerald polled 53.5 percent of the primary vote, but he lost Kennedy's East Boston ward (with 49.3 percent), Lomasney's West End (with 15.9 percent), and Keliher's bailiwick (with 36.8 percent). In the mayoralty election, Lomasney's ward went Republican: it delivered 58.0 percent of its vote to Fitzgerald's opponent. Keliher's ward gave Fitzgerald 55.5 percent of its vote, but that was its lowest Democratic proportion since 1895. Overall, Fitzgerald received about 79.0 percent of the ballots cast by Irish voters in 1905, and that dropped further to 70.5 percent in his unsuccessful re-election bid in 1907.[37]

In his 1905 race, Fitzgerald promised the city's voters a "Bigger, Better, Busier Boston."[38] What he delivered was a Boston whose majority party was hopelessly factionalized and incapable of performing the functions of a party in government. With Fitzgerald's success through the direct primary in 1905 and again in 1907, the Democratic organization's attempts to manage factional conflict and constrain its effects within the party effectively ended. Thereafter strife among personally oriented factions of Democrats became the dominant mode of municipal politics.[39]

Notes

1. The ward vote returns are reported in *The [Boston] Municipal Register* (Boston: City of Boston Printing Department, date varies) for the appropriate

years, and more detailed ward and precinct data are in the "Annual Report of the Election Department," in *Documents of the City of Boston* (Boston: City of Boston Printing Department, date varies). Data describing the ethnic composition of Boston's wards and Massachusetts towns and cities have been taken from: Massachusetts Bureau of Statistics of Labor, *The Census of Massachusetts: 1875*, 3 vols. (Boston: A. J. Wright, 1876-77); idem, *The Census of Massachusetts: 1880* (Boston: Wright and Potter, 1883); idem, *The Census of Massachusetts: 1885*, 3 vols. (Boston, 1887-88); idem, *Census of the Commonwealth of Massachusetts: 1895*, 7 vols. (Boston, 1896-1900); idem, *Census of the Commonwealth of Massachusetts, 1905*, 4 vols. (Boston, 1908-10). Linear interpolations were used to cover election years that fell between censuses. Changes in ward and precinct boundaries were followed in the *Municipal Register*, and the data were reaggregated accordingly.

2. In twenty-three contests for president, governor, and mayor, between 1876 and 1885, inclusive, the Democrats failed to poll a majority of Boston's vote only twice. They lacked a majority in five of the eleven contests between 1893 and 1898.

3. Massachusetts was the first state to introduce the Australian ballot, which listed all of the candidates for an office on a single ballot. Until then each party distributed ballots that listed only its own nominees, a practice which made split-ticket voting cumbersome. On the introduction of the Australian ballot, see Jerrold G. Rusk, "The Effects of the Australian Ballot Reform on Split-Ticket Voting: 1876-1908," *American Political Science Review* 64 (December 1970): 1220-38; and also see Walter Dean Burnham, "Theory and Voting Research: Some Reflections on Converse's 'Change in the American Electorate,' " *American Political Science Review* 68 (September 1974): 1002-23.

4. For the use of regression procedures to develop estimates of individual-level behavior from aggregate-level data, see Leo A. Goodman, "Ecological Regression and the Behavior of Individuals," *American Sociological Review* 18 (December 1953): 663-64; Goodman, "Some Alternatives to Ecological Correlation," *American Journal of Sociology* 64 (May 1959): 610-25; Laura Irwin Langbein and Allan J. Lichtman, *Ecological Inference* (Beverly Hills, Calif.: Sage Publications, 1978); and Ray M. Shortridge, "Voting for Minor Parties in the Antebellum Midwest," *Indiana Magazine of History* 74 (June 1978): 117-34.

5. The "low" point in the presidential series is the 85.2 percent consistency rate during the 1890s. That mean was pulled down by the 1892 to 1896 estimate of 70.5 percent which was 11.5 percentage points lower than any other estimate in the series. The Bryan candidacy induced a split in Boston's Democratic party, and that development underlay this abnormally low level of party consistency. The same sort of result appears in the 1896 gubernatorial results; but, since those elections were held annually, its impact on the mean is muted.

6. The means for the president-to-president and president-to-mayor estimates have not been calculated for these sequences, since no more than one pair of presidential elections fell within any of the periods, except the one from 1899 to 1908.

7. The Irish variable includes adult males who were born in Ireland as well as those who were native born of Irish-born parents. The native-stock measure includes adult males who were native born of native-born parents. Given the social and geographic context and the period being dicussed, it is a good surrogate for a more precise measurement of the Yankee component of the population.

8. The 6.2 percent estimate for native-stock voting for Mayor over the 1899-1907 elections exaggerates the case. Virtually all of that can be attributed to the 1903 estimate of 23.5 percent, and in that year the incumbent Democrat was virtually a consensus candidate for re-election.

9. In each city election between 1883 and 1888, Hugh O'Brien was the Democratic candidate for Mayor; in 1889 the Democrats nominated another Irish candidate, Owen A. Galvin.

10. For discussion and evidence relating to the political effects of the cohesive psychology of ethnicity, see Edgar Litt, *Ethnic Politics in America* (Glenview, Ill.: Scott, Foresman and Company, 1970), pp. 127-41; John 0. Stitely, *Rhode Island Voting Patterns, 1940-1964* (Kingston, R.I.: Bureau of Government Research, 1966); and David B. Walker, *Politics and Ethnocentrism: The Case of the Franco-Americans* (Brunswick, Maine: Bowdoin College Bureau for Research in Municipal Government, 1961). For a penetrating analysis of attitudinal differences within the Irish group, see Victor A. Walsh, " 'A Fanatic Heart': The Cause of Irish-American Nationalism in Pittsburgh During the Gilded Age," *Journal of Social History* 15 (Winter 1981): 187-204.

11. The 1854 charter provided for four representatives to the Common Council from each ward, but that was changed to three from each ward in 1875. In 1854 there were twelve wards; by 1875 there were twenty-four wards, and that number increased to twenty-five in 1876 with the division of Ward 22 into two separate wards. From that point and until the charter of 1909 became effective, the Common Council had seventy-five members.

12. The text of each charter then in force is conveniently reprinted in the annual *Municipal Register*. Also see *The Memorial History of Boston, Including Suffolk County, Massachusetts, 1630-1880*, ed. Justin Winsor, 4 vols. (Boston: James P. Osgood and Company, 1880-81), 3:260-61, 278; *Commonwealth History of Massachusetts*, ed. Albert Bushnell Hart, 5 vols. (New York: The States History Company, 1930), 5:69-70, 74. And for the limited effects of the 1885 charter amendments, see *Metropolitan Boston: A Modern History*, ed. Albert P. Langtry, 4 vols. (New York: Lewis Historical Publishing Company, Inc., 1929), 2:736. In 1885 the legislature also authorized the governor to appoint an independent police board for the city.

13. Between 1868 and 1874 Boston annexed Roxbury, Dorchester, Brighton, West Roxbury, and Charlestown. These additions required new wards, and increased population also led to subdivisions of other wards.

14. For information on these changes, see *Boston Post*, 4 and 9 Apr., 13 June 1874, 28 Nov. 1876, 26 June 1878, and 24 Apr. 1879. The reorganization actually spanned the years from 1874 through 1879, but the core changes were made in 1874. The precise number of members on the City Committee was altered at several points during the five-year period, but the precinct requirement was not changed. It was only in 1879 that the committee dropped the name "Ward and City Committee" and designated itself as the Democratic City Committee of Boston.

15. *Boston Post*, 10 Apr. 1874. And for the Republican reaction to this Democratic reorganization, see *Boston Daily Advertiser*, 3 Nov. 1876.

16. John H. Cutler, *"Honey Fitz": Three Steps to the White House* (Indianapolis: Bobbs-Merrill, 1962), p. 53.

17. Martin Shefter, "The Electoral Foundations of the Political Machine: New York City, 1884-1897," in *The History of American Electoral Behavior*, eds. Joel H. Silbey, Allan G. Bogue, and William H. Flanigan (Princeton, N.J: Princeton University Press, 1978), p. 292. Also see Edward C. Banfield, *Political Influence: A New Theory of Urban Politics* (New York, 1961), pp. 307-23.

18. This was an important component of the public image constructed for O'Brien; see the issues of the *Boston Post*, 3, 15, and 30 November 1883, 26 November and 8 December 1884, and 28 November and 14 December 1885. On the backgrounds and perspectives of O'Brien and Collins, see Geoffrey Blodgett, *The Gentle Reformers: Massachusetts Democrats in the Cleveland Era* (Cambridge, Mass: Harvard University Press, 1966), pp. 53-55, 61-63, and 144-46. And for the values and perspectives of Boston's upper class, see E. Digby Baltzell, *Puritan Boston and Quaker Philadelphia: Two Protestant Ethics and the Spirit of Class Authority and Leadership* (New York: Free Press, 1979).

19. Cutler, *"Honey Fitz,"* pp. 51-52.

20. See Shefter, "Electoral Foundations of the Political Machine," pp. 293-96, for the role of this type of organization in general and its particular significance in New York City. For descriptions of Lomasney's organization and its activities, see Joseph F. Dinneen, *Ward Eight* (New York: Harper, 1936); and Leslie G. Ainsley, *Boston Mahatma: Martin Lomasney* (Boston: Bruce Humphreys, 1949); and for his own view, see "Martin Lomasney: The Story of His Life as Related by Him to Thomas Carens," *Boston Herald*, 2 through 27 Dec. 1925. The best sources of information are the newspaper reports of the ward caucuses and political meetings, especially the detailed accounts that regularly appeared in the *Boston Post*.

21. For descriptions of Curley's Tammany Club, see James Michael Curley,

I'd Do It Again: A Record of All My Uproarious Years (Englewood Cliffs, N.J.: Prentice Hall, 1957), pp. 52-53 and 63-66; and *Boston Post*, 6 December 1903. Other Tammany Clubs also existed in the city; e.g., George H. Murphy and Richard W. Garrity established the "Tammany Club of Ward 20 [part of Roxbury]" in 1893; *Post* 30 October 1893. For an example of reorientation of one of the older social-political clubs, see the discussion of the Fort Hill Fishing Club, in *Post*, 29 September 1896. The Somerset Associates became better known under the leadership of Flood's successor in Ward 14, Joseph J. Norton.

22. With a minor exception or so, there is not even a remote hint that the leaders of the City Committee, and especially Maguire, were implicated in the organizations of these types of challenges. Indeed, they were just as likely to be composed of their allies as of their foes. The details can most conveniently be followed in the *Boston Post*, especially in the issues of October through early December of each year, which was the period immediately preceding the city election.

23. On Matthews, see Blodgett, *Gentle Reformers*, pp. 84, 159-65; *Commonwealth History of Massachusetts*, ed. Hart, 5:75-76; and *Metropolitan Boston*, ed. Langtry, 2:725-26. For his own views, see Nathan Matthews, *The City Government of Boston* (Boston: Rockwell and Churchill, 1895).

24. *Boston Post*, 15 and 17 Nov. 1894. The Charlestown delegation was itself split, with Joseph J. Corbett's faction supporting Peabody and the James E. Hayes group opposing him. I do not discount the high unemployment in the laboring areas and the city's limited response to that problem as sources of the opposition to the nomination of a member of the Yankee elite for mayor.

25. *Boston Post*, 12 and 13 Dec. 1894, 8 and 9 Nov. 1895. For Lomasney's earlier tactical switches on the question of restoring the elected delegate convention, see *Post* 27 May and 27 June 1890. There was also an "Independent Democrat" movement organized in 1894, but that had little significance and was unrelated to the demands by the ward chieftains for a direct role in selecting the nominee; see *Post* 15 and 26 Nov., and 7 and 8 Dec. 1894.

26. *Commonwealth History of Massachusetts*, ed. Hart, 5:76-77; *Metropolitan Boston*, ed. Langtry, 2:726-27; Blodgett, *Gentle Reformers*, pp. 246-55. On the early impact of the depression, see *Boston Post*, 26 and 27 Nov., and 12 and 13 Dec., 1893.

27. *Boston Post*, 4, 19, 27, 29 Nov., 1897, and 1, 2 Dec. 1897. The opposition within the party to Quincy's re-election came from the Bryanite wing; see Blodgett, *Gentle Reformers*, pp. 256-57. For the conflict in 1896 between the Bryanites and the ward leaders for control over the Democratic party organization in Boston, see *Boston Post*, 12, 24, 26, 27 Sept. 1896, and 4, 18, 19, 22, 29, and 30 Nov. 1896.

28. Blodgett, *Gentle Reformers*, pp. 258-59.

29. Apart from Lomasney, the opposition to Collins's nomination in 1899

centered in South Boston and in the rivalry between the Charlestown factions; see *Boston Post*, 3, 10, 14, 16, and 21 Nov., and 4, 6, and 13 Dec. 1899.

30. *Post*, 1 Nov. 1901.

31. Collins had polled 60.0 percent in 1901, but he lost eight wards, including both the Back Bay and Beacon Hill areas that he carried in 1903.

32. *Boston Post*, 11 Dec. 1903. The Somerset Club was organized in 1851 and its "clubhouse" moved to No. 42 Beacon Street in April 1872; for a list of its 550 members, see *Constitution of the Somerset Club with a List of Its Officers and Members June 1903* (Boston: Somerset Clubs, 1903).

33. On Donovan's appointment, see Cutler, *"Honey Fitz,"* p. 78. Earlier Donovan had been Superintendent of Lamps; see Blodgett, *Gentle Reformers*, p. 248. On the changed patterns of awarding city contracts and the effects on the ward organizations, see the discussion in the *Boston Post*, 14 Nov. 1903.

34. The candidate's name was Edward J. Donovan, who was then the City Clerk and not related to James Donovan. To avoid confusion, the references in the paragraph are to James Donovan.

35. For the alignments, see *Boston Post*, 1, 3, 8, 17, 18, and 23 Nov., and 1, 9 Dec. 1905.

36. *Metropolitan Boston*, ed. Langtry, 2:278; and *Boston Post*, 13 Nov. 1905.

37. The primary election results are in "Annual Report of the Election Department for the Year 1905," in *Documents of the City of Boston* (Document No. 14; Boston: City of Boston Printing Department, 1906), p. 107. Fitzgerald made peace with Kennedy after the primary and carried his East Boston ward against the Republican and Citzens nominee, Lewis A. Frothingham, with 72.0 percent of the vote, which was only 5.2 and 6.4 percentage points below Collins's percentages in 1901 and 1903, respectively. On the Fitzgerald-Kennedy detente, see Cutler, *"Honey Fitz,"* pp. 91-92. But Cutler incorrectly identifies Keliher as a Fitzgerald supporter; see *Boston Post*, 17 Nov. 1905.

38. *Post*, 9 Dec. 1905.

39. By abolishing party designations in city elections, the 1909 charter institutionalized the mode of factional politics that had emerged earlier. By 1907 the factional alliances had shifted slightly from 1905: Lomasney and McNary supported Fitzgerald for re-election, while Daniel J. Kiley, a former Lomasney stalwart, led the opposition. On these developments, see *Boston Post*, 28 Nov. and 9 Dec. 1907. In Roxbury's Ward 17, there was a rupture between James Michael Curley and Thomas F. Curley (no relation), and it is significant that what was at immediate stake in their struggle was the presidency of the Tammany Club. When Thomas F. Curley lost that battle, he countered by organizing the Jefferson Club of Ward 17. On these matters, see Curley, *I'd Do It Again*, pp. 80-81; and *Boston Post*, 8 Nov. 1907.

6

The Irony of Progressive Reform:
Boston 1898-1910

CONSTANCE K. BURNS

Boston's mayoral election of January 10, 1910 was politics at its theatrical best. The candidates seemed to have been typecast to represent the extremes of the city's two principal groups: millionaire Yankee banker and philanthropist James Jackson Storrow opposed the self-made Irish leader and North End ward boss John Francis Fitzgerald. The intense campaign featured bitter charges of personal unfitness and of linkages to corporate and personal corruption. The heat of the rhetoric contrasted sharply with the frigid weather of the Boston winter during which the candidates toured all sections of the city in a frenetic search for votes. The voters were caught up in the drama, turning out in record numbers when over 90 percent of those eligible voted. The suspense was carried on through the final count, for the result was virtually a dead heat, with the final tally showing Fitzgerald with 47,177; Storrow, 45,775; and a third candidate, George Hibbard, 1,814. It was a fitting climax to a decade marked by political volatility and by the excitement of reform campaigns.[1]

It was also one of the most significant of the city's elections, for underlying it was the critical issue of the relationship that Boston's Yankees and Irish would have toward one another in the changing conditions of the twentieth century. The nineteenth century had been marked by a large and unwelcomed immigration of Irish into Boston, a strong and lasting nativist reaction among many Yankees, and animosity and distrust between native Yankees and immigrant Irish. As the shock of immigration receded, there had also developed an alternative, more fragile, tradition of accommodation and civility between the groups as they became accustomed to sharing the citizenship of a great city. The issue had not been resolved as the twentieth century opened. Although the decade's politics had reflected both traditions, as evident in the two preceding chapters, it had also blurred them by focusing much attention on the issue of political corruption. This was an issue that derived from a national movement for urban reform, but it was an issue of lesser importance in Boston.

It is not surprising that there should have been such a reform movement in American cities in those years of the Progressive Era (1890-1915); the two requisites for such a movement, conditions in need of change and people with a sense of mission to effect that change, were both present. The unprecedented urban growth of the late nineteenth century, marked by increases in the scale of urban environments, in the size and heterogeneity of urban populations, in the opportunities for wealth, in the conditions of poverty and disorder, cried out for action by city governments, but these governments were unable to meet such obligations. The results of the spectacular growth and disorder, including political and corporate corruption, organized crime and vice, disease, poverty, official incompetence—all apparently beyond the reach of city governments to control—made these governments "the one conspicuous failure" among American governments, and created the image of "the shame of the cities."[2]

However, urban growth also offered conditions of considerable opportunity, and these same cities produced vital new citizen coalitions, "strategic elites" composed of the "new middle class" of younger businessmen and professionals allied to segments of the older urban philanthropic elites. Inspired by an activist philosophy, these coalitions of Progressive Era reformers were eager to lead movements for a new civic order with a strong emphasis on a reformed politics. They indicted the political bosses (and sometimes their business allies) by documenting and publicizing "corruption" in graphic detail, then offered their own leadership in reform movements which challenged the bosses in a series of hard-fought, dramatic elections. These "great reform wars" usually reached their climaxes in mayoral elections that were fought in cities across the nation, from New York to Los Angeles, in the years from 1890 to 1917. Highly publicized, especially by the muckraking press, these reform politicians and their causes became symbols of national morality while their opponents, the bosses, were symbols of urban evil.[3]

Boston, however, was not the most logical place for such a reform movement for it was, as municipal expert Delos Wilcox noted, "one of the best governed cities in the nation." Such good conditions were usual in the city and not the products of reform. Paul Kellogg, pioneer social scientist and Pittsburgh reformer, remarked that Boston enjoyed urban conditions without benefit of reform that most cities would be pleased to have after a protracted reform effort. In an era when city governments were unable to order either themselves or their citizens, Boston's government was responsible, its politics credible. This remarkable accomplishment reflected a Yankee civic ethos built on a tradition of historic pride and communal responsibility. The city's standards were set in a cooperative effort by a patrician elite with strong civic concerns together with the non-elite majority. The city's growth had been steady rather than abrupt and its wealth consistent. The government had accepted its responsibility to tax property-owners heavily— more heavily than in any other city in the nation—and to set minimum standards for business. It was a remarkable civic achievement.[4]

If Boston lacked the bad government that was the first requisite for reform movements in other American cities, it did have the second requisite, an activist coalition with a desire for civic leadership and civic power. Boston's Progressive coalition was small but included some of the city's most distinguished and important men and women: it included Brahmins like James Jackson Storrow, John F. Moors, Robert Treat Paine; businessmen Edward A. Filene, Bernard Rothwell, Laurence Minot, John Mason Little; social activist-professionals like Louis Brandeis, Mary Morton Kehew, Dr. Richard Cabot; social workers Robert Woods and Edmund Billings, journalists Edward Clement of the *Transcript* and Edward Grozier of the *Post*. Although drawn from all groups in the city, this leadership was overwhelmingly Yankee, and uniformly inspired by the activities of their counterparts in cities across the nation.[5]

Although incompetence and corruption were not pressing in Boston, the city did have its own particular concerns. The first was the extraordinarily high cost of responsible government. Nathan Matthews, a vigorous mayor and astute student of municipal affairs, remarked in 1895 that "the problem here is not Corruption but Expenditure." The city was the most heavily taxed in the nation, possibly in "the entire world." Matthews proceeded to give sobering statistics from the 1890 census.[6] In the first decade of the new century the city maintained its pace of outspending and outtaxing all other cities (though New York continued to come close). It also increased its pace of spending in comparison with its own past rate. In the decade 1885-1895, spending rose only slightly in excess of the rise in population (30 percent to 27 percent), but in the decade 1895-1905, it rose twice as fast (55 percent to 22 percent). There seemed no easy way to stop the acceleration.[7]

The other problem related to relations between Yankees and Irish in the city. The hostile response to Irish Catholic immigrants had become marked in the 1840s and persisted, waxing and waning, in the succeeding decades; it had become matched by Irish hostility toward Yankees.[8] There had developed as well an alternative tradition that stressed accommodation and civility. Politics had encouraged the development of both traditions. By 1870 Boston politics was structured in a two-party system: the bulk of Yankee Bostonians and immigrants from British Canada were represented by the Republican Party while the Irish found a place in the Democratic Party under the tutelage of the Yankee gentlemen who were its leaders. The Irish had ward organizations led by familiar "bosses" but deferred to or cooperated with Yankee leadership on citywide matters. Both parties preserved the tradition of responsible government while providing representation for all groups in the public life of the city. Sometimes the growing power of the Irish in city politics brought on a nativist backlash, as in 1888 when Hugh O'Brien, the mayor, and most other major Irish officeholders were driven from office by nativist protest. The political process also worked for accommodation, however, and was doing so as the twentieth century opened. The decisive election and re-election of Patrick Collins as mayor in 1901 and 1903 resulted from Yankee-Irish political cooperation. Collins was a cosmopolitan gentleman of noted rectitude and an appropriate successor to such Yankee Democratic mayors as Nathan Matthews and Josiah Quincy.[9]

By the turn of the century, however, the political structure—with its two party system and Yankee-Irish collaboration in the Democratic Party—was becoming a thing of the past. Demographic shifts in the city were making the Republican Party (and its Yankee constituents) into a permanent minority for the first time since the 1850s, even as they were lessening Yankee influence in the Democratic Party and making the Irish Democrats the dominant force in political affairs.

These changes were accompanied by uncertainty. Among the Irish, for example, leadership patterns were changing: Collins died suddenly in 1905, and it became clear that his successor would not be a cosmopolitan gentleman like himself but one of the ward bosses, a professional, local politician. This, in a city where professional politicians usually deferred to non-political leaders, was alarming to many, especially to Yankees. Further clouding the political scene was the factionalism that tore at the Irish ward leadership as they struggled bitterly among themselves to produce the leader who would both represent their group and gain legitimacy for their new dominance. The uncertainty of the Yankee response to losing their traditional political dominance (or at least shared dominance) in politics was made more acute by the apparent decline in the economic climate of the city and the possible loss of Boston's place in the national economic order. All these uncertainties and changes were reinforcing one another at a time when the national urban reform movement was enjoying public attention and electoral success.[10]

"Reform will come to Boston," the *Herald* predicted as early as 1898,[11] but how it would come and what its effects would be were very uncertain. The decay of the political structure provided a unique opportunity for activists seeking a place in the political world of the city: the opening for their leadership would be there. However, there were unique problems facing reform in Boston. In other cities reformers had gained their legitimacy by championing the public's interest in opposing political corruption and corporate greed. In Boston the task would be more subtle, for civic needs were different. Maintaining a civic ethos and lessening ethnic tensions were not prominent parts of the national agenda for reform nor were they easily included in reform crusades. But Boston reformers would have to be judged on how they responded to Boston's needs. As the volatile electoral results of the decade indicated, the Boston voters were willing to consider new departures and new leadership.

Reform did come to Boston, and it climaxed in the election of January, 1910. That reform and that climax are little remembered, but they left an enduring and an ironic legacy to Boston.

The Coming of Progressive Reform: The Public School Association

"Reform" came to Boston first in school affairs—and its course in the years between 1898 and 1905 highlighted the pitfalls and the opportunities it offered to the city. In Boston reform always must be understood against a national backdrop. In many American cities the state of public education illustrated "the conspicuous failure" of urban

governments to resist political exploitation and to provide adequate
services to their citizens. By the 1890s public education was under great
pressure to provide facilities and courses of studies to the new millions
of urban children, many of them immigrants. Yet urban schools were
failing in these critical tasks: city systems had thousands of children
without accommodation, teachers tyrannized by political leaders, meager school budgets plundered for political purposes, instruction too often
routine, insensitive, and unrelated to the evolving urban world.[12]

In city after city, the newly developing coalitions of urban activists
led a growing wave of protest against such conditions, bitterly attacking
politicians for having caused them. Appealing to voting publics and
state legislatures, the reformers waged a series of astute, hard-fought
campaigns to oust the old system and to install themselves as leaders
of the public's interest in good education. The most notable of the
"Great School Wars" was fought in New York City where the Progressives' Public Education Association fought Tammany Hall and succeeded in establishing their leadership and program by 1895. In cities
elsewhere, including Philadelphia, Baltimore, St. Louis, and Chicago,
successful efforts at school reform on the New York model took place.[13]

In Boston, however, the school system did not seem to offer fertile
ground for reformers who sought to improve deplorable conditions.
Commitment to education had been traditional in Boston and was an
impressive part of the city's civic ethos. In the 1890s, when political
exploitation and educational shortcomings were notorious in other cities,
Boston's educational system appeared to be functioning well. The city
had traditionally spent more on education than any other city and in the
1890s spent additional millions for buildings to house the rapidly growing school population even as they enlarged the curriculum and upgraded
standards for teachers. Although the political parties nominated the
candidates for School Committee, they traditionally chose non-political,
disinterested people, and the Committee was largely scandal-free.[14]

There were legacies from the past that had the potential to be unsettling in a period of rapid change. Principal among them was the
ubiquitous matter of Protestant-Catholic relations. Education had long
had sensitive religious and cultural significance, and the nativist movement of the 1880s in Boston had been directly triggered by Protestant
fears of growing Catholic influence in school affairs. After the elections
of 1888 and 1889 had driven all Catholics from the School Committee,
accommodationist Protestants had assumed leadership and arranged a

tacit *modus vivendi* between Catholics and militant Protestants. For Catholics the moderate Protestants offered educational practices that would not affront their religious sensibilities as well as a lessening of the virulent anti-Catholic rhetoric of the time. To the Protestants they offered a guarantee of continued Yankee Protestant domination of the School Committee and teaching staff as well as of traditional values in education. This arrangement was monitored by the Independent Women Voters, a nativist group of Protestant women whose principal concern was that Catholics not participate in school affairs. The compromise was inherently unstable, and in a period of shifting populations and politics school affairs could again become the focus of religious acrimony.[15]

Beyond this there was a school administration with a structure coming to appear outdated. In an era that stressed centralization and professionalization, Boston's schools were still directly administered by elected, non-professional School Committee members in a system that was built upon district autonomy. Further, the increasingly large school budgets seemed to make School Committee service more attractive to politicians. However, for all their disruptive potential, school affairs were not roiled by religious tensions or structural anachronisms or political influence when educational reform began in Boston.[16]

Reform began because Boston had an activist coalition eager to assert leadership in educational affairs and denied these aspirations by both political parties. These educational activists typified the new Progressive leadership: they included patrician lawyer-educator A. Lawrence Lowell, banker-philanthropist John F. Moors, lawyer-activist Louis Brandeis, women's rights leader Mary Morton Kehew, social worker Robert Woods. The segment of the coalition most notably absent was the journalists, possibly because conditions in education were not sensational enough to attract them. Rebuffed by the regular parties, the activists proceeded to form the Public School Association in 1898 and to nominate their own candidates for the annual elections. They justified their leadership by the need for improvement, not in the schools, but in the people who directed them. They stridently attacked the incumbent members as politically motivated and unfit, focusing on the few examples of school politicking as if they were typical of the entire committee. Intent on establishing the necessity of their candidates' election, the PSA ignored the accomplishments of the school system. They coupled extravagant attacks on incumbents with claims for the moral superiority and distinguished, disinterested nature of their own candidates. They waged their campaigns with a vigor unusual in school elections where candidates had traditionally "stood" rather than "run" for election. Lawrence Lowell once felt the need to apologize to his listeners for such an unseemly show of political enthusiasm and self-endorsement.

Initially this was a successful ploy, attractive for its novelty as well as for the distinguished people who were nominated. By 1901 the PSA had elected a majority of the 24-member Committee.[17] However, the strategy soon backfired because of their mishandling of the religious issue. Their reform goals became inextricably tangled with religious ones. They had no major educational conditions to improve, but as reformers they wanted to modernize the system by giving its administration to professional educators and they wanted to keep political influence at a minimum; as Bostonians they wanted to maintain the Protestant ascendancy in the schools. Toward this last goal, their nominees were 90 percent Protestant, they cooperated with the Independent Women Voters, and they did not challenge the traditional policy of discrimination against Catholics on the school staff. As these practices became more evident in the course of a few years, they produced a devastating backlash that threatened to discredit all the goals of reform and the reformers themselves.[18]

Some Catholic politicians, affronted as Catholics, threatened as politicians, led a vigorous protest against reform and the PSA. Mrs. Julia Duff, former teacher, School Committee woman from Charlestown, and member of a political family, challenged the Democratic City Committee to disavow the reformers and to nominate a slate of anti-reform, anti-PSA Democrats. Cowed by her vehemence and popular backing, the Democratic leaders bowed to her wishes, and the Democratic slates in 1902 and 1903 were selected by Mrs. Duff for their loyalty to her goals. Using the slogan "Boston Schools for Boston Girls" [i.e., for Boston Irish teachers] she focused on the issue of job discrimination. In a startling setback for the PSA she was able to overturn their majority and to elect a majority of her supporters within two years. She capped her triumph in 1904 when her Committee supporters ousted veteran superintendent Edwin Seaver and elected instead his deputy George Conley. Both were competent men, but Seaver was Protestant and Conley Catholic; Mrs. Duff was using the schools for religious ends, as she perceived the Protestants to have done. And both Mrs. Duff and the PSA were able to ignore the issue of quality of education itself.[19]

Painfully reconsidering their goals and strategies in the light of this new reality, the PSA chose to face the religious issue head on. In an historic statement for Boston they declared

We are all American citizens. It is therefore clear that no attempt should be made to ostracize any class of citizens because of religious difference. As it is contrary to the spirit of American citizenship to organize on a sectarian basis, it is the plain duty of the Public School Association, so long as the attitude of the Independent Women Voters remains unchanged, to insist that our candidates shall not accept a nomination which is refused to good citizens because of their religion.[20]

They followed this renunciation of nativism with the sponsorship of a balanced ticket, for the first time nominating four Irish Bostonians with Democratic affiliations, four Yankee Bostonians with Republican affiliation, all of whom were non-politicians. Ignoring Mrs. Duff's cries of betrayal, the Democratic City Committee joined the PSA in joint sponsorship of the Democrats. Both Republicans and Democrats renounced the Independent Women. Incredulous at this turn of fortune, Mrs. Duff and the Women each nominated slates, and each was defeated. In the election of 1904 all eight Democrats were elected to the School Committee, as were almost all Democratic candidates for any office. School Committee affairs were solidly in the hands of one political party with only an uncertain commitment to the ideal of the non-political School Committee.[21]

After seven years of reform activity, the PSA's record was ambiguous. They had attacked nativism and had helped eliminate two of the extremist groups in School Committee politics. But they had weakened the Boston tradition of an apolitical School Committee and had lost their own position, so recently attained, of power. Worst of all, they had created a cynicism about "reform" among the emerging Irish majority which would not encourage trust or cooperation between the two groups.

The unpredictability of the decade's politics was exhibited again as School Committee matters took another sharp turn, one that restored the PSA to power and demonstrated a viable way to achieve reform goals. The successful strategy emphasized the linkage of reform with civic consensus rather than with adversarial challenge and emphasized the benefits that good education could offer to all Bostonians. To understand this critical shift, it is necessary to return to 1901 when the PSA nominated as one of their candidates the patrician banker James Jackson Storrow.

Storrow was a member of a wealthy old family, senior partner in the prestigious investment banking house of Lee Higginson and a nominal Democrat. Together with his wife Helen Osborne Storrow he had a strong philanthropic commitment to the city and a special interest in children's causes. Together they sponsored settlement houses, helped found a new juvenile court, acted as benefactors to such organizations as Newsboys and Scouts. Hence Storrow was a logical person to stand for School Committee in 1901 as a PSA candidate. He was successful in his first hurrah—1901 was a good PSA year—even though his stiff public manner precluded much active campaigning.[22]

Once on the Committee he achieved a reputation for absolute fairness in the sensitive matter of hiring and promoting Boston teachers and administrators. His stand for equity and merit regardless of religious background came in sharp contrast to the traditional discrimination against Catholics. He pursued his own policy quietly, never raising the issue in any public or divisive manner, never courting an Irish vote, but very quickly he achieved a reputation for fairness in ethnic matters. When he ran for School Committee in the critical election of 1905, he received the clear endorsement of the *Boston Pilot*, the Irish Catholic newspaper of the city:

Mr. Storrow is a Protestant but he has hosts of friends and admirers among the Catholics, clergy and laity alike, for his philanthropy which knows no test of religion nor of color; for his upright life; and for his sincere devotion to the best interests of those citizens who most need the public schools.

He will be found where he has been found heretofore, alert for the largest possible moral, material, and intellectual benefits for the neediest rather than seeking to control appointments for personal or political motives. Give him not merely a majority but an overwhelming majority.[23]

He was concerned, too, to make the schools as useful to as many Bostonians as possible. He sponsored Evening Centres, neighborhood evening schools, hoping to keep schools and neighborhoods as a focus in the lives of local Bostonians. He campaigned for "school houses thrown open out of school hours where every evening in the week can be found a thousand neighbors meeting together for their mutual im-

provement and enjoyment." He also encouraged movements for vocational guidance and skilled trade education as a means of offering
relevant educational experiences to those youth who traditionally left
school early in their lives.[24] He led no crusade for reform, but the city
responded to his quiet sense of purpose. The extent of the trust that he
inspired among Bostonians was soon demonstrated.

When the PSA conciliation measures of 1904 had gained them some
Democratic good will but no political power, Storrow used his personal
prestige to redirect the course of educational reform. In January 1905
he petitioned the State Legislature for a new charter for the School
Committee. He proposed a small School Committee to be elected at
large, that would set policy for the schools while (it was implied) giving
administrative responsibilities to a professional staff. This was the accepted model for modernized educational systems, but in Boston it had
the potential for creating religious bitterness anew. Sponsored by a
Yankee Protestant, it could appear to take from Irish politicians and
their constituents the control of the School Committee and the schools
at just the time when they had acquired such power, without the jus-
tification of a demoralized school system. Storrow's prestige was such
that the reform was accepted in the public interest and passed with little
rancor in April, 1905. It is likely that the Republican Legislature would
have given him the reform charter in any event; his real triumph came
in getting it accepted with so little religious resentment. His nomination
by Irish Democrats in December, 1905, and his endorsement by the
Pilot are clear indications of the esteem in which most Irish Bostonians
held him and of their willingness to accept his leadership.[25]

The next step was the election of a Committee compatible with his
consensus-oriented, modernizing program. Differences between Democrats and the PSA about nominations again injected ethnic bitterness
into the campaign, but Storrow and an ad hoc "Citizens Union" managed to sidestep the issue and the balanced PSA slate of two Protestants
(including Storrow), two Catholics, one Jew was elected.[26] The PSA
had thus been restored to its role as the "non-political" center of School
Committee politics, a position in which it continued for several decades.
In the longer run its influence was a mixed blessing; nevertheless among
its real accomplishments was the sponsorship of non-political Boston
Irishmen who had a bent for public service. Too often the Boston Irish
would be content to be represented by their politicians (and sometimes
by their priests) to the exclusion of their best men. But for a decade

and more the PSA gave some of these men a chance to serve the larger public interest under its auspices.

Storrow, meanwhile, continued with his activities designed to build a civic consensus in Boston. He helped found the City Club as a place where businessmen and professionals of all creeds could come together for sociability and civic concern, breaking down the barriers that had characterized so much of the city's public life. He put his prestige and his money behind the venture and it proved remarkably successful. He was concerned as well with the economic state of the city. Believing, with Progressive optimism, in the efficacy of organization and rationalization, he brought together the various commercial groups of the city into a single, newly invigorated Chamber of Commerce to work for the economic and civic concerns in Boston. Here too he retained his ethnic sensitivity: the Chamber emphasized that it would be "democratic" (i.e., multi-ethnic) and its members elected Storrow as first president together with his close friend, the Irish immigrant turned grain merchant, Bernard Rothwell, as vice president. He organized the City Club in 1906, finished his School Committee term in 1908, and reorganized the Chamber of Commerce in 1909.[27]

In 1982, when School Committee problems have so bitterly divided the city for so many years, Storrow's achievements have real significance. He had established a base other than group antagonisms for political activism—and it is significant that the majority of Bostonians appeared to welcome his initiatives. His style of seeking consensus rather than the original reform style of stressing conflict worked to lessen social tension, while maintaining the tradition of educational accomplishment that was one of the city's proudest achievements. Finally, he made "reform" an endeavor that represented the public interest rather than a mask for group interest.

But School Committee politics was only a sideshow; the major political arena was found in the politics of the city government, and other Boston activists became eager to inject reform there. In 1903, even as the school reformers were attempting to deal with Mrs. Duff's challenge to their power, political reformers founded the Good Government Association for political activism.

Urban Political Reform I: The Good Government Association

Nationally, reformers justified their cause and their leadership of it by documenting and publicizing the inadequate or corrupt conditions in their cities. Vice in New York, extortion in San Francisco, bankruptcy in Houston, corporate arrogance in Milwaukee, provided the base for reform in those cities. Ironically for the Boston reformers, incompetence and corruption in government were not commonplace in their city. In 1895 Nathan Matthews had dismissed corruption as a major concern with his casual statement that "Expenditure" and not "Corruption" was Boston's problem. Some years later, in 1902, his successor Patrick Collins, welcoming the urban reformers of the National Municipal League to Boston, noted that "Up in this corner of the land there is very little corruption . . . and if you should find anything wrong here in any part of it . . . come down to City Hall and let me know." The answering remarks of the national experts seemed to indicate that they shared his assessment of the conditions of public life in Boston.[28]

Yet national awareness of urban corruption was becoming widespread; in 1903 the subject was given its enduring and damning title of "The Shame of the Cities" upon publication of Lincoln Steffens' book with that name. In 1903 Chamber of Commerce president William Lincoln included in his annual address general complaints about the high spending, irresponsible City Council, "as bankrupt in morals as in pocket," men who would promote "their schemes for personal benefit at the expense of the people." The national press, attuned to the trendy topic and fascinated with the possibility of corruption in Boston, took his remarks as a call for a reform movement of the kind that Steffens had reported about in St. Louis, Pittsburgh, Chicago, and other cities. The *New York Times* featured Lincoln's remarks on page one, then mused with evident pleasure on their significance:

One might almost fear from the statement in his annual address by the president of Boston's Chamber of Commerce that we are about to hear from that city tales of municipal misgovernment and corruption as dreadful as those which came not long ago from Minneapolis and still later from St. Louis. That would be hard indeed to bear, for we all have a great affection for Boston and would be only too glad to maintain our ancient belief in her superiority to the rest of the country—and to the rest of the world for that matter. New York's evil preeminence as a badly governed city is now threatened. . . .[29]

And in Boston, a nascent group of Progressive activists from the city's business community began to coalesce. Inspired by Lincoln's remarks as well as by their own convictions that—in Louis Brandeis'

words—"misgovernment in Boston has reached the danger point,"
leaders from the city's commercial and trade associations came together
to form the Good Government Association. New to their task of political
reform, they were encouraged by the heartening examples of businessmen in other cities who had sparked reform movements. Especially they
were heartened by the businessmen-directed Municipal Voters League
in Chicago which had achieved a national reputation in challenging and
defeating the "Grey Wolves" of the notorious Chicago City Council.
That unsavory group had been engaged in large-scale extortion of and
collusion with public utility corporations as well as in the organization
of city-wide vice, among other activities.[30] In order to justify a reform
movement in Boston the activists would need to document such activities
in their city. As Louis Brandeis noted,

No one can grow enthusiastic over virtue in general or become indignant over
evil in general. It is the particular virtuous or vicious act in all its details which
receives our admiration or excites our condemnation. Among hopeful people
such indignation and shame are followed by remedial action.[31]

Thus the GGA set out to prove the particular "vicious acts" of
politicians in Boston and to arouse the people to their leadership in the
cause of reform. Assembling a small professional staff and enlisting
the services of college students and young lawyers the GGA directors
set out to organize the vanguard of political reform. The city awaited
with some anticipation the expected revelations as the winter came on
and the December election came closer.

Alas for the cause of reform, the GGA could unearth nothing that
was either sensational or new; they could only repeat Lincoln's charges
about the irresponsibility of the Council, its expense account padding
and a few questionable land deals. The only individual they could
identify and condemn was James Michael Curley ("ought not to be
reelected") whose illegal act, taking a civil service examination for a
constituent without financial reward, had already been prosecuted. (In
1903 Curley was but one of a score of local ward bosses of uncertain
tenure, all eager to obtain some city-wide identification. Curley welcomed the publicity from the GGA, then and later, but in his early
years, before he became mayor in 1913, it was especially welcome.)
All the charges they brought were of small consequence compared to
the charges of city-wide vice and millions in extortion that had been

leveled against the Chicago City Council by the MVL there; the charges were stale even in responsible Boston. Failing to establish the great need for reform in Boston, the GGA was unable to challenge the majority Democrats, almost all of whose candidates won. Most humiliating of all, their *bete-noir*, Curley, won re-election handily. Their electoral attempt did produce a reputation for arrogant self-righteousness and their nickname of Goo-Goo. Brandeis bluntly described the campaign as a failure.[32] This dubious beginning caused most of the business groups to lose interest in political activism and to drop out of the GGA. Within a short time, as a consequence, the GGA and political reform became the property of a small, specialized group of businessmen, the downtown landowners, their lawyers and bankers, whose principal concern was the tax rate. It was a valid concern, certainly, given the growing size of city expenditures and debt, but it was their only concern. Reform in GGA terms came to mean fiscal restraint at best, penny pinching at worst. It also meant a continuing attack on politicians who were the agents of all the spending. It was not the sort of platform to rally a wide coalition of voters.[33]

Their appeal narrowed too as the GGA became closely identified with the Republican Party, notably in the important mayoral elections. In 1905 they joined the Republicans in endorsing Louis Frothingham of Back Bay, former Republican Speaker of the House of Representatives, for mayor. It was difficult to perceive Frothingham as anything other than a partisan Republican and a Yankee of chilling personality, and the voters chose the Democratic candidate, North End boss John F. Fitzgerald, on partisan lines. Two years later, in 1907, the GGA appeared to have a fine opportunity to establish the image of independent reform. The Republicans nominated the undistinguished party regular, George Hibbard, about whom the GGA was less than enthusiastic. Fitzgerald, running for re-election, was tainted by scandal and opposed by another Irish Democrat. Despite the hopeful opening for a reform candidate, the GGA could not or would not sponsor a candidate of its own and tacitly endorsed the Republican. Fitzgerald, damaged by scandal and opposition, lost, but to a Republican rather than a reformer.[34]

At the end of five years of activity the GGA was unable to establish valid reasons for a reform movement and was linked to a partisan minority in the city. They had been unable to mobilize a broad coalition of voters—indeed there is evidence that they were alienating their own supporters—and they had been unable to produce a popular leader. In

short, they were becoming increasingly irrelevant to the politics of the
city. However, like school reform in 1905, political reform took a new
turn in 1907. Unlike school reformers, the political reformers did not
turn to consensus; instead they chose to emphasize the adversarial nature
of reform and to continue the focus on corruption. A Finance Commission was formed to establish, finally, the existence of corruption
and thus to lay the basis for a reform struggle.

Urban Political Reform II: The Finance Commission

With the failure of the joint Republican/GGA mayoral campaign of
1905, John F. Fitzgerald, ward boss, professional politician, and Irish
Catholic, became mayor. The *Herald* spoke for many Bostonians when
it feared that the city was about to be led by "wanton mercenaries."
Fitzgerald did not want to humiliate Boston; like many Boston Irish
who admired the accomplishments of Brahmin leadership Fitzgerald
was not motivated by the cultural antagonisms that dominated some of
his contemporaries like James M. Curley or Julia Duff. Fitzgerald was
an ambitious man who wanted to build a city-wide machine loyal to
himself, and he perceived the Yankee Republicans more as political
opponents than as cultural oppressors. But his political ambitions were
reason enough for Yankees and Republicans to equate his success with
humiliation and bankruptcy for the city.[35]

He became mayor in January, 1906. With the city's Republicans
politically powerless and the GGA unable to mobilize a reform opposition, Republican businessmen turned to the Republican legislature for
a state-sponsored investigation of the Fitzgerald administration's first
year's record. Such an investigation would be modeled on New York
investigations, notably the Lexow and Mazet commissions which had
produced such evidence of corruption that Tammany was defeated in
1895 and again in 1901. To ward off the legislature Fitzgerald proposed
that the city itself sponsor an independent commission to undertake a
"comprehensive inquiry into the finances of the city." Such an investigation would blunt Republican zeal in dealing with the intractable
topic of city expenditures and finances.[36]

With some skepticism seven "representative" Bostonians accepted
Fitzgerald's invitation to serve, and the Fin Com, as it soon came to
be known, was formed. The dominant figure, in terms of knowledge,
experience, and force of personality was former Democratic Mayor

Nathan Matthews. Matthews had been out of public office since his retirement from the mayoralty in 1895, but he maintained an important place in the public life of the city with his large real estate holdings and his municipal expertise.[37]

Matthews had a long-standing commitment to the well being of the city. A concerned, intelligent conservative, he fully believed an activist government necessary to preserve the traditional order and civic ethos of Boston. Aware of the inequities and tensions in the new great cities, he valued politics, despite all the "inefficiencies" entailed, as a means of assimilating the heterogeneous urban populations into American life. Since the 1880s he had been prominent among those Yankees working to integrate the Irish into the Democratic Party and the public life of the city.

In 1895 he had left office believing that "Expenditure" but not "Corruption" was plaguing the city. By 1907, however, he was convinced that both expenditure and corruption had become threats to the city, and that both were linked to the self-serving and corrupt ways of politicians. Compounding his anger was his conviction that the high cost of government was causing the real estate and commerce of the city to stagnate. A reform movement to unseat the politicians and alter the form of government was needed, and to aid it he joined the Fin Com.[38]

The Commission assembled a staff of lawyers, investigators, accountants, and engineers who began their investigation in July, 1907. Their investigations achieved initial success that summer and fall when they exposed collusion between city officials and coal dealers and linked Fitzgerald—though not in any criminal fashion—to the guilty officials. The investigators conducted well publicized public hearings which created a swell of indignation in the press as real, documented scandal was finally exposed. The shock caused by the revelations was enough to defeat Fitzgerald in December, 1907. It was also enough to obscure the fact that the scandals were small-scale. One could assume that there was more, and worse, to come.[39]

There was more to come, in the 18 months of the Commission's life, but there was not worse: the Fin Com failed to unearth the devastating kind of scandal that rocked New York and St. Louis and San Francisco and had led to the overthrow of political machines in those cities and elsewhere. While there was much that was tawdry and shoddy and even pettily criminal in Boston, there was nothing like the vast linkages to vice and exploitation and larceny or the murderous living conditions that marked the public life of other cities. The payroll padding and inefficiency and patronage, the demoralization and cynicism of city workers were unsettling from a Boston viewpoint, but conditions still were good in comparison with other cities, and the Fin Com was aware that such was the case. Yet they were willing to talk in terms of massive corruption.[40]

Their failure to unearth serious wrongdoing was emphasized by the convictions that came from the investigations. The Suffolk County District Attorney, Arthur Dehon Hill, was a man of rectitude and skill, yet he obtained convictions only against three city councillors for petty embezzlement of several hundred dollars and against the coal dealer and purchasing agent who had been involved in the initial scandalous news. And that was all among the politicians. (There were convictions against several large corporations for conspiring among themselves to defraud the city of tens of thousands of dollars for construction work, but little was made of this matter by the Fin Com.)[41] The Fin Com never developed the balanced perspective that would have allowed Bostonians to understand the city's achievements as well as its failures. They allowed a proud civic ethos to slip into obscurity, and reform left the city without a sense of its former pride.

More immediately they failed to address the problem of high governmental costs. They had little plan to their investigation, other than to link politics to financial corruption. Failing to discover this to any great degree, they had no alternative way of investigating city government. From the first to the last, their 18 months' activity was a hodgepodge of investigations with no common themes or questions, nor any suggestions for overall improvement. They identified the problem of city labor as one of the most critical facing the city, but here too they failed to set any standards for understanding the problem or to propose remedies. Beyond identifying the extraordinary growth of city labor from 8,000 to 13,000 in less than a decade they offered only a random assortment of observations such as the comparison of bricks laid by public and private sector employees or the number of men needed to clean catch basins. Most importantly they did not make an effort to distinguish between valid city labor and patronage.[42]

But their most immediate failure lay in the creating of a backlash as a consequence of the attacks on Irish politicians, notably on Fitzgerald. The Fin Com was "out to catch Fitz," as one member injudiciously admitted, but they did not catch him, in any criminal fashion. Able to defeat him in 1907 through public disgust at the initial disclosures, the Fin Com was unable to link him further to wrongdoing. As their particular animus became clearer, as their tactics became too heavy handed, Fitzgerald began to claim prejudice and to make plans to run for mayor again. He began to cry for "Vindication" to his fellow Irish Bostonians for his mistreatment at the hands of the Yankee reformers. Once again, reform was dividing rather than uniting Bostonians.[43]

The final act of the Finance Commission was to propose a new charter for the city. Like the School Committee reformers, like Progressive activists everywhere, they sought to make their reforms permanent by changing the structure of government. They proposed an innovative new charter for the city and asked the state legislature to enact it. They proposed to centralize the government and to take local influence and partisan politics out of the government of the city. All city politics would be non-partisan. The new politics would be dominated by a powerful mayor, checked only by a weak council and a permanent Finance Commission. The small, at-large council would serve only half as long as the mayor (two-year terms to his four-year term). The mayor would have near-absolute power over the budget and over appointments.[44]

There were points of unreality in this proposal. One was the faith that the reformers put in the mayor to implement all the reforms. Martin Lomasney, legendary boss of ward eight, was incredulous at the reformers' faith: "I've known all the mayors in my time," he said, "and they could all be bought, all of them." But the reformers persisted. Their belief in the possibility of legislating political identities out of existence, of creating a non-partisan city by the change of a charter, was another leap of faith. Their willingness to have a Republican legislature enact this radical change for a hostile Democratic city was yet another touch of unreality.[45]

This last unreality brought James J. Storrow finally into the camp of the political activists. He had never been identified with the GGA or the Fin Com although as a wealthy Yankee he had an identity in common with the leaders of both. Alone among the reformers he had stressed a consensual rather than adversarial approach to change, and had been concerned with public support for measures he proposed. Now, in 1909, he used his prestige to dramatize the possibilities of consensus for the Fin Com charter as he had for his own School Committee charter. Believing that it was folly to impose the charter on the people of the

city by legislative fiat, he supported a move for a binding referendum
on the charter. He made a plea to the legislative committee to place the
charter before the voters of Boston in such a referendum. In most
dramatic fashion he marched at the head of several hundred fellow
Chamber of Commerce members to the State House and there he addressed the committee and an overflow crowd:

We believe that the amended charter should be submitted to the voters of Boston
for their acceptance and ratification.... We believe the fact can be driven home
that in civic affairs the interests of all good citizens from the humblest to the
most exalted are identical.... We do not believe that the question involved is
too complicated to be understood by the average voter. He should be afforded
ample opportunity to express himself upon them.... Your directors [of the
Chamber of Commerce] do not think it wise that a new charter should be
imposed upon the city of Boston by a Legislature differing in political com-
plexion from the city without the approbation and good will of a majority of
the voters of the city of Boston. It will be starting out a new era without the
backing and moral support of those without whose assistance it cannot possibly
be a success.[46]

Perhaps moved by this logic the Legislature adopted a compromise.
Those provisions which pertained to fiscal matters—the mayor's control
over the budget, the new Finance Commission—were to be enacted
without referendum. The voters were to be given a choice on political
issues: they would choose between the reformers' proposal of non-
partisan elections, strong mayor, and small, at-large council or another
which allowed for partisan elections and ward councillors (albeit in a
single chamber) and a less powerful mayor.[47]

The activists campaigned for their charter in the name of "the People!"
and against "the Bosses" while the scattered opposition was led by an
uncoordinated assortment of politicians of both parties. Fitzgerald, however, realized that the power given to the mayor under the "reform"
charter would be useful to any incumbent mayor, "reform" or otherwise, and he chose to endorse it. However embarrassing such an un-
sought endorsement may have been to the Progressives, they ignored
it and continued to inveigh against "the Bosses." The reform charter
was approved by the voters in the November, 1909, election by a narrow
margin, and Fitzgerald's support was probably important in its success.
The Fin Com proposal was now the official charter of the city of Boston.[48]

The legacy of the Fin Com was an ambiguous one. They produced enough material in their investigations to discredit politicians but too little to produce a widespread protest movement. They had produced evidence of municipal mismanagement but few suggestions for improvement. They had reinforced cynicism about politics among many Bostonians and about reform among others. They had produced a new governing structure for the city but did not produce any leader to make it work as its planners hoped.

However uncertain their legacy in most areas, the problem of leadership would have to be faced immediately, for the election for the new mayor under the new charter would take place in just two months, in January, 1910.

The Election of 1910

Political reform had reached the point in 1909 that school reform had reached in 1905: a new charter and a new structure for governance, but with the critical struggle to elect leaders yet to be faced. For the school reformers, Storrow had set the consensual tone for the reform, steered the new charter to acceptance, and led the election fight to implement it. Political reform had produced no kind of consensual tone, nor had it produced any public leaders. In such circumstances it seemed logical that Storrow lend his prestige and his leadership to political reform by running for mayor. He was most willing to do so.

He was, the newspapers unanimously reported, "unquestionably the best man"; there was "no better man in point of public service and dedication." His achievements and his stature seemed to contrast sharply with those of his opponent, John F. Fitzgerald, ward boss and suspect politician. It seemed that the voters would participate in a civic morality play, choosing between the Best Man and the Boss. Morality plays can be dangerous in politics, however: what would be the judgment if the Best Man were to be defeated? Or if he failed to live up to the standards that had been expected of him?[49]

In any event, Progressive activism needed more than a Best Man; it needed a skilled politician who could make its goals believable to a large and diverse voting public. Storrow had displayed such political skill in his School Committee activities as he linked ethnic patronage and managerial competence to an effective political style in the service of the public interest. He had given credibility to reform. But none of the newspaper reports stressed this aspect of his public service; all seemed to stress philanthropy and selflessness rather than politics and achievement.

This apparent lack of understanding of the importance of his political skill was but one of the handicaps facing his candidacy. Among others was the hostility he engendered among politicians of both parties. However non-partisan the new elections were supposed to be, parties were still strong and could not be easily ignored. The Democratic leaders were largely Irish, and their success was based on maintaining the solidarity of their ethnic vote. Yet Storrow's appeal to the Irish had been proved, and he could be expected to divide that vote. Further, however much Fitzgerald's fellow bosses might distrust his ambition, they knew him and shared his core values. By campaign time, only two Irish Democratic figures of any stature supported Storrow.[50]

Also critical was the threat that he posed to Yankee Republicans and they to him. Most obvious was the refusal of incumbent Republican Mayor George Hibbard to bow out of the race. His candidacy was a puzzle for he was seriously ill, short of money, and without any sizeable personal following, but it posed a serious threat to Storrow if he could attract critical Republican votes. Beyond Hibbard moreover there was the austere and powerful figure of Republican Senator Henry Cabot Lodge. Should Storrow be successful in the mayoral contest, it was highly possible that he would seek statewide office—as a Democrat—and would threaten Lodge's statewide domination. Rumors persisted throughout the campaign that Hibbard was being kept in the race by Lodge (and alternatively by Fitzgerald); even when Lodge finally made his neutrality clear, it was grudgingly done.[51]

Storrow's personal prestige and his accomplishments were vital to his success, but here too, in an apparent area of strength, there were problems. He was a modest man who was reluctant to praise himself. He said little about his work for the schools, saying only that

I am interested in whatever I can do for Boston... I did not go in the School Committee for selfish purposes. I thought I might be of some use to the school children of Boston. It is not for me to say whether I was of use, but I tried to be.[52]

Fitzgerald however was willing to talk about Storrow, but in ways that caricatured him as a man of great wealth, greedy for all the power he could buy. Storrow was a banker, a millionaire, a member of more than thirty corporate boards. In an age suspicious of corporate power, these were damaging linkages. Storrow's personal reticence coupled with Fitzgerald's caricature gave his candidacy an odd twist: it was as if, the *New York Post* noted, J. P. Morgan were running for mayor of New York.[53]

Most damaging of all was his abandoning his earlier consensual approach that had minimized attacks on (Irish) politicians and emphasized the public good, the approach that he had used with such effectiveness. He chose instead to adopt the GGA/Fin Com adversarial style directed against politicians. He chose GGA leaders to be his chief strategists, and included the everlasting GGA theme of finances as one of his principal themes. In light of his own prior successes and of their failures, this decision seems incomprehensible. Yet he made such a choice voluntarily: he was among the wealthiest and most powerful of Bostonians and there was no one who could dictate strategy to him. And he made the choice consciously: Nathan Matthews wanted him to campaign on the charter issue itself, and Storrow had demonstrated, in his advocacy of the referendum provision, that he could have done so. Yet he rejected Matthews' counsel and Matthews himself, and chose GGA themes and people. It was a fateful decision. The Best Man was not going to be the best candidate.[54]

Fitzgerald's campaign began quickly, his organization circulating his papers and easily gaining the required 5000 signatures. His strategy was to portray Storrow as the wealthy man, himself as the representative of the ordinary people. "The issue," he said over and over, "is whether a poor man can rise to govern his city or whether the man of wealth can reach out and control the city as he already controls its businesses." These attacks on the wealthy man alternated with attacks on the corporate manipulator. He made scathing attacks on Storrow's business affairs, charging him with everything from gaining illicit millions in underwriting fees to raising the price of bananas through monopoly control of tropical fruit. By contrast he stressed his own common beginnings and his identity with the people of the city, especially with the Irish. Moving back and forth across the city, speaking to small groups in the North End or to "monster rallies" in Faneuil Hall, he constantly emphasized his closeness to the great part of the Boston population, Storrow's aloofness. He may have tried to raise the charge of anti-Catholicism against Storrow, but this was quickly shot down; in any event he had more than enough other material with which to attack his opponent.[55]

Storrow's campaign by contrast was halting. Instead of circulating his own nomination papers, he allowed himself to be nominated by the "Citizens Municipal League," an ad hoc group largely composed of Yankee establishment figures. His linkage to the GGA was emphasized in his opening speech:

The one real question at stake in the campaign is how the annual sum of 20 or more million dollars taken from the people shall be expended by the city officials and what principles should govern the expenditure. First and foremost in importance is that every dollar of the city's money should be expended in pursuance of an orderly and efficient plan.

This was pure GGA.[56]

He alternated these calls for fiscal restraint with bitter attacks on Fitzgerald. Using the old Fin Com accusations as the basis for an attack on "FITZGERALDISM," he discussed Fitzgerald's links with cronyism, the illegal contracts, padded payrolls. These issues had all been debated and discussed for the past two years, yet Storrow raked them up again, in a heavy-handed, lavishly financed advertising blitz. Fitzgerald pointed to the obviously great cost that the rich man could afford and again asked for popular support.[57]

Storrow did have another theme, his old one of what his leadership and his vision of the public interest offered to the people of Boston. This appeared only in fragments, never as part of a coherent program, and he used it only at the end. For example, speaking to workers and explaining why he was concerned to establish a more favorable business climate in Boston, one that would attract modern industry, he explained that

[Such industry would mean] higher wages and therefore the best for our people. This means keeping the children longer in school, this means that the mothers can stay at home and look after their children, this means better hours, more pleasure and less drudgery . . . by hard work and a reasonable amount of good fortune we can create in Boston thousands of high class jobs which are in the interest of every man, whether he be laborer, mechanic, merchant or banker.[58]

He outlined a "constructive program" for the city which included a program to deal with unemployment and to institute pension plans for city workers (as he had already begun to do for teachers). He outlined his hopes for a pluralistic Boston, a new, multi-ethnic city, while speaking to Boston Italians who were honoring him for his generosity to the victims of the recent Messina earthquake.[59] Taken together such fragments suggest a leadership sensitive to the needs of the city. His prior record of executive competence and humane commitment made this leadership credible. But this Storrow appeared only in fragments and only at the end of the campaign.

Fitzgerald's campaign had begun rapidly and well, while Storrow lagged along, talking of the GGA and trying to answer Fitz's barrage of charges. The *Times* despaired by Christmas: "reform was dead" their Boston reporter lamented. But suddenly, in the last weeks, Storrow's campaign caught fire, and the contest took on an air of great intensity, fierce partisanship and brilliant excitement as both men toured the city in the sharp cold of a bitter winter while Hibbard remained at home too ill to speak.[60]

And suddenly it was over. The intensity of the contest was reflected in the size and the closeness of the vote. A record 90 percent of eligible Bostonians voted on January 10, 1910, with results that were heartbreakingly close for Storrow, a vindication for Fitzgerald: Fitzgerald, 47,177; Storrow, 45,775; Hibbard, 1,814.[61]

To most Progressives the results were explicable enough. The Irish majority of the city had gotten what it wanted, and that had been "one of their own," however tarnished he may have been. "The city has the kind of mayor its voters wished", the *New York Times* editorialized; they had responded to a "straight appeal to racial ties" as Storrow himself put it. The Irish might govern the city but they would not be accorded legitimacy in the eyes of an important segment of the population.[62]

Some Bostonians did conjecture that Storrow might have lost because of the failings of his own campaign. This view was particularly plausible in light of the successes of the reform candidates for City Council and School Committee. Writing in the *Nation*, "One of the Framers of the Charter Amendments" [Matthews?] said:

Except for the return to office of Mr. Fitzgerald, the election was a signal success. The chairman of the present excellent School Committee was elected by 13,000 votes over an extreme and almost as well known Irish Democratic candidate as Fitzgerald [Mrs. Duff]. Seven of the reform candidates for the new Council out of a possible nine, were also elected, showing that where the prejudices of the voters were not actively roused, they tended to choose the best, party labels being absent. [Curley finished a lackluster fifth in the Council race.]

It should be added that the School Committee and City Council campaigns were waged without rancor, and without personal charges of wrongdoing by the candidates against their opponents. This permitted independent [i.e., non-ethnic] voting on the part of the Irish to seem less an act of disloyalty than in the case of the hard pressed Fitz.[63]

But this was a view that appears to have been little expressed as the decade of urban reform came to its ironic end.

Certainly the ironies abounded and endured. The fragile but hopeful tradition of ethnic comity in the city, so visible in the successes of most of Storrow's initiatives, vanished in the cynicism of the aftermath of the election. In its place the cleavage line of Yankee-Irish hostility was maintained long after the immigrant period had passed. In politics cynicism and group interest became enshrined. Despite their dismal record, including Storrow's loss, the GGA was a big winner: in the non-partisan electoral system, they assumed the role of opposition party and continued to act like Republicans while continuing their railing at Democratic extravagance and corruption in politics. They proved a splendid adversary for the other long-term winner, James M. Curley. Fitzgerald's successor in 1913, he found his own adversarial, anti-Yankee rhetoric perfectly suited to a politics of Yankee-baiting his GGA opponents. For a generation and more, these successors of the reform decade kept the city tied to the old tradition of ethnic mistrust and the somewhat newer one of political cynicism. In such an environment, it is not surprising that the proud tradition of civic accomplishment came to be irrelevant and largely forgotten.

It would be easy to see this hardening of ethnic tension, this abandonment of the civic ethos, as inevitable in light of the bitter history of the nineteenth century, and indeed that is the way in which Bostonians have perceived it. But this gives a falsely static view to a history that had the potential for incorporating much change. Certainly the career of James Jackson Storrow did show that a majority of the city would accept political leadership that would be sensitive to, but also transcend, ethnic interests. He had embodied the best hope for the new city of the twentieth century—and in the end he came to embody the destruction of those hopes.

Fully sixty years after the election of 1910, two old men reminisced, independently of one another, about its implications. One, who had been a young, second-generation Boston Irishman, a teacher in the city, still felt compelled to justify his vote for Fitzgerald, whom he did not much respect. "You have to remember," he said, pounding his fist on a table, "you have to remember that Storrow was a State Street banker, and those people wanted to control everything in the city." The other, a Yankee, a student at Harvard Law School, said with bitterness in his reminiscing still, "We gave them the best there was, but they wanted 'Sweet Adeline'."[64]

Storrow himself became part of the irony of Progressive reform.

Notes

1. Coverage of the campaign from November, 1909, through January, 1910, was extensive in all Boston newspapers. For election results, Board of Election Commissioners of the City of Boston, *Annual Report, 1909* (Boston, 1910).

2. For information and bibliographic suggestions for detailed information on American cities during this period, begin with one of the general urban histories such as Howard Chudacoff, *Evolution of American Urban Society* (Englewood Cliffs, N.J.: Prentice-Hall, 1972) or Sam Bass Warner, *The Urban Wilderness: A History of the American City* (New York: Harper & Row, 1972).

3. The terms "reformer," "activist," and "Progressive" are used interchangeably and loosely to identify those who worked in the many groups engaged in ordering some form of civic change in the Progressive Era. As such they are applied to a wide variety of people. These "activists" and their motives have evoked a significant historical literature which includes such works as Samuel Hays, "Politics of Reform in Municipal Government in the Progressive Era," *Pacific Northwest Quarterly* 55 (October, 1964): 157-69; Richard Hofstadter, *The Age of Reform* (New York: Random House, 1955); Otis Pease, "Urban Reformers in the Progressive Era: A Reassessment," *Pacific Northwest Quarterly* 62 (April, 1970): 490-538; Robert Wiebe, *The Search for Order* (New York: Hill & Wang 1967); James Weinstein, *The Corporate Ideal in the Liberal State, 1900-1918* (Boston: Atheneum, 1964). For the term "strategic elite," Suzanne Keller, *Beyond the Ruling Class: Strategic Elites in Modern Society* (New York: Random House, 1973).

There were "Great Reform Wars" in virtually every large American city. For a bibliography of urban reform and reformers, Michael H. Ebner and Eugene

M. Tobin, eds., *The Age of Urban Reform* (Port Washington, N.Y.: Kennikat Press, 1977).

4. Delos Wilcox, *Great Cities in America and the Problem of Government* (New York: Macmillan, 1910), p. 361; Frederic C. Howe, *The City, the Hope of Democracy* (New York: Scribners, 1909), p. 58; Charles Zueblin, *A Decade of Civic Improvement* (New York: Macmillan, 1905), pp. 86-102; Paul U. Kellogg, "Boston, 1915", *New Boston* 1 (April, 1910): 1. Lincoln Steffens failed to find the kind of muck in Boston that he had unearthed everywhere else with relative ease: *The Autobiography of Lincoln Steffens* (New York: Scribners, 1931), pp. 598-622.

For a sampling of modern works on facets of the civic ethos in Boston and Massachusetts, Richard Abrams, *Conservatism in a Progressive Era: Massachusetts Politics 1900-1912* (Cambridge: Harvard University Press, 1964); Charles W. Cheape, *Moving the Masses: Urban Public Transit in New York, Boston, Philadelphia, 1880-1912* (Cambridge, Mass.: Harvard University Press, 1980), ch. 4, p. 5; Frederic C. Jaher, *Urban Establishments: Upper Strata in Boston, New York, Chicago, Charleston, and Los Angeles* (Urbana, Ill.: University of Illinois Press, 1982).

5. The activists never formed a single group nor worked in a single cause, but many of them cooperated in overlapping activities. They are best understood through the groups they participated in. In Boston these would include Boston 1915, The Finance Commission, the Good Government Association, the Public Franchise League, the Public School Association, the South End House, the Women's Educational and Industrial Union.

6. Nathan Matthews, *The City Government of Boston: A Valedictory Address* (Boston, 1895), p. 28.

7. U.S. Bureau of the Census, *Statistics of Municipalities of Over 25,000, 1902; 1907; 1913* (Washington, D.C.: Government Printing Office, 1905, 1908, 1914). For the remark that Boston's per capita costs were probably the heaviest in the world, Howe, *The City*, p. 58. The accelerating rate of expenditures and debt were detailed in the Finance Commission of the City of Boston, *Final Report* (4 vols., Boston, 1909) II, 170-73, 228-30.

8. Oscar Handlin, *Boston's Immigrants* (rev. ed., Cambridge: Harvard University Press, 1959); Barbara M. Solomon, *Ancestors and Immigrants, A Changing New England Tradition* (Cambridge, Mass.: Harvard University Press, 1956).

9. Geoffrey Blodgett, *The Gentle Reformers: Massachusetts Democrats in the Cleveland Era* (Cambridge, Mass.: Harvard University Press, 1966); Melvin Holli and Peter d'Arcy Jones, eds., *Biographical Dictionary of American Mayors* (Westport, Ct.: Greenwood, 1981).

Collins' victory in 1903 was by an unprecedented total of 48,745 to his Republican opponent's 22,369: *Election Commission Report, 1903*.

10. Paul Kleppner, "From Party to Faction: The Dissolution of Boston's Majority Party 1876-1900," in Ronald P. Formisano and Constance K. Burns eds., *Boston 1700-1980: The Evolution of Urban Politics* Westport, Ct.: Greenwood Press, 1984).

11. *Boston Herald*, Dec. 10, 1898.

12. David B. Tyack, *One Best System, A History of Urban Education* (Cambridge, Mass.: Harvard University Press, 1978).

13. For the "Great School Wars" in New York City, Sol Cohen, *Progressives and Urban School Reform* (New York: Columbia University Press, 1964) and Diane Ravitch, *The Great School Wars, New York City, 1805-1975* (New York: Basic Books, 1974), pp. 107-230. For other cities, see Andrea R. Andrews, "Baltimore Building Program, 1870-1910: A Study of Urban Reform," *Maryland History* 70 (Fall, 1975): 260-74; William H. Issel, "Modernizers in Philadelphia School Reform, 1882-1905," *Pennsylvania Magazine of History and Biography* 94 (July, 1970): 358-83; Selwyn K. Troen, *The Public and the Schools: Shaping the St. Louis System, 1838-1920* (Columbia, Mo.: University of Missouri Press, 1975).

14. Boston education had a favorable national reputation, although the system was considered to be hampered by excessive formalism. Joseph M. Rice, "Public Schools of Boston," *Forum* 14 (Feb., 1893): 753-67; Wilcox, *Great Cities*, p. 361; Zueblin, *Civic Development*, pp. 100-01.

For information on how the School Committee dealt with the great influx of pupils, over 2000 per year for more than a decade, in terms of buildings, finance, curriculum, staff, see the *Report of the Superintendent of Schools of Boston 1895-1905* (Boston: 1896-1906). For women who served on the Committee prior to 1905, see Polly Kaufman, "Boston Women and School Committee Politics: Women on the School Committee, 1872-1905," unpublished Ed.D. dissertation, Boston University, 1978. Newspaper biographies at the annual election time confirm the non-political character of most candidacies.

15. George W. Anderson, "Politics and the Public Schools," *Atlantic Monthly* 89 (April, 1900): 433-47; Lois W. Merk, "Boston's Historic Public School Crisis," *New England Quarterly* 31 (June, 1958): 172-99; *Women's Voice and Public School Champion*, the journal of the Independent Women Voters, is the best source for their activities.

16. Samuel A. Wetmore, "Boston School Administration," *Educational Review* 21 (September, 1897): 105-17. For concern about the activities of Harrison Atwood, Republican, architect, and School Committee member, see *Herald*, Nov. 22, 1899, Nov. 20, 1900.

17. No records of the PSA exist. These names were taken from newspaper accounts during the annual campaigns which took place during the first two weeks in December. For Lowell's remark, *Herald*, Dec. 4, 1898. Anderson,

"Politics in Schools," for his anger at reformers' exaggerations. GAO Ernst, "Movement for School Reform in Boston," *Educational Review* 28 (Dec., 1905): 433-43.

18. PSA's campaigns were always more moralistic than programmatic. Their goals are best understood through their actions. For the Protestant presence, see Lowell's move to abolish the Boston Normal School, passed and then rescinded, *Herald*, May 4, 1898, Nov. 23, 1898; for separation of School Committee from lucrative building program, *Herald*, May 5, 1901. The stress on nonpoliticians as candidates was constant, but see *Herald* Nov. 30, 1898, Dec. 3, 1899.

19. For a sympathetic portrait of Mrs. Duff, Kaufman, "Boston Women," ch. 10. *Post*, Dec. 10, 1902; *Transcript*, July 3, 1904.

20. *Boston Journal*, July 24, 1904; *Women's Voice*, July, August, September, 1904; *Herald*, Oct. 11, 1904.

21. *Post*, Nov. 27, 1904, Nov. 28, 1904, Dec. 5, 1904.

22. Henry G. Pearson, *Son of New England, James Jackson Storrow* (Boston, n.p., 1930). For a view of Storrow that does not distinguish him from other Progressive activists, Thomas Mason, "Reform Politics in Boston, A Study of Ideology and Culture," unpublished Ph.D. Dissertation, Harvard University, 1963.

23. *Boston Pilot*, Dec. 9, 1905. See also a defense of Storrow against charges by Mrs. Duff by his fellow School Committee member, Irish doctor James McDonald, *Transcript*, Dec. 8, 1905.

24. School Committee of the City of Boston, *Documents, 1903*, #9 (Boston, 1904). For an example of Storrow's public relations campaign in support of the Evening Centres, see letter with attached speech in this interest to William H. Pritchett, April 9, 1903, Pritchett Papers, Library of Congress, Washington, D.C.

25. *Transcript*, March 7, 1905, April 4, 1905, April 29, 1905.

26. *Herald*, Nov. 17, 1905, Dec. 2, 1905, Dec. 13, 1905.

27. *Herald*, Dec. 10, 1906; Pearson, *Son of New England*, pp. 70-81; *Herald*, Jun. 17, 1909.

28. Charles Garrett, *La Guardia Years: Machine and Reform Politics in New York City* (New Brunswick, N.J.: Rutgers University Press, 1961) pp. 1-3; Walton Bean, *Boss Reuf's San Francisco* (Berkely: University of California Press, 1952); David Thelen, *The New Citizenship: Origins of Progressivism in Wisconsin 1885-1900* (Columbia, Mo.: University of Missouri Press, 1972); Harold Platt, "City Building and Progressive Reform . . . Houston 1892-1905," in Michael Elmer and Eugene Tobin, eds., *Age of Urban Reform* (Port Washington, N.Y.: Kennikat Press, 1977), pp. 28-42.

Matthews, "City Government," p. 174. National Municipal League, *Proceedings of the Boston Conference on Good City Government, 1902* (Philadelphia: n.p., 1902), pp. 5-7, passim.

29. *New York Times*, Jan. 21, 22, 1903; *Transcript*, Jan. 21, 1903.

30. *Herald*, April 9, 1903; *City Affairs* 1 (March, 1905): 1-3; unfinished memoir by George Reed Nutter in Good Government Papers, Massachusetts Historical Society, Boston.

Sidney J. Roberts, "Municipal Voters League and Chicago's Boodlers," *Journal of Illinois State Historical Society* 53 (Summer, 1960): 117-48. For Boston activists' use of their model, *Herald*, Dec. 17, 1903.

31. *Herald*, March 12, 1903.

32. *Herald*, Dec. 10, 17, 1903.

33. The GGA never published a list of officers or directors, nor does any such accounting appear in the Papers at the MHS. The few names which were published correlate with those who signed a petition in protest to Storrow's action at the time of the Finance Committee Charter referendum issue.

34. For Fitzgerald and Hibbard, *Dictionary of American Mayors. City Affairs* 2 (Oct. 1907): 1-2; *Herald*, Dec. 5, 1905, Dec. 7, 1907. The third candidate was John Coulthurst, who ran on Hearst's Independence Party ticket.

35. *Herald*, Dec. 12, 1905.

36. *Journal*, June–October, 1906, kept a running commentary on Fitzgerald's patronage and contract practices as well as his use of city perks such as a touring car.

37. Members of the Finance Commission and sponsoring organizations were Matthews, Real Estate Exchange; Randall Morris, Chamber of Commerce; George Crocker, Clearing House; GAO Ernst, United Neighborhood Improvement Association; John A. Sullivan, Board of Trade; John Kennedy, Central Labor Union; John F. Moors, Merchants Association.

38. For Matthews, Robert A. Silverman, "Nathan Matthews and the Politics of Reform in Boston, 1890-1910," *New England Quarterly* 50 (December, 1977): 626-43; *Biographical Dictionary of American Mayors*.

39. All the Boston papers made the investigations front page news, September-December 1907.

40. Finance Commission of the City of Boston, *Final Report* (4 vols., Boston: 1909). *Herald*, July 4, 1909, for comments of Commission member John A. Sullivan.

41. *Herald*, June 4, 1909, July 1,2, 1909, Sept. 21, 1909, Dec. 9, 1909.

42. On the scattershot treatment of the city's labor problem, see the index in the Finance Commission *Report*, I, on that topic. For their cursory summary, see II, 201-16.

43. *Herald*, June 2, 1909. This became a recurring theme in Fitzgerald's campaign. See, for example, *Herald*, Nov. 18, 1909, Dec. 23, 1909, Jan. 9, 1910.

44. Finance Commission, *Report*, II, 2, 243, 277. *Herald*, Jan. 30, 1909.

45. *Herald*, March, 11, 1909.

46. Ibid.

47. *Herald*, June 21, 1909.

48. Final Tally: Plan 2 (reform charter), 39,179; Plan 1, 35,276. Election Commission, *Report, 1909*.

49. *New York Times*, Nov. 9, 1909; *New York Post*, Nov. 9, 1909; *Herald*, Nov. 18, 1909.

50. They were Congressman John A. Keliher (*Herald*, Nov. 27, 1909) and South End leader James M. Donovan (*Herald*, Nov. 23, 1909). Both were long-time Fitzgerald opponents.

51. *Herald*, July 13, 1909, Nov. 23, 1909, Dec. 23, 1909. See also correspondence between Lodge and Henry Lee Higginson in which the latter was threatening and pleading with Lodge to disavow Hibbard: Lodge Papers, Massachusetts Historical Society, Nov. 10, 29, 1909, Jan. 6, 1910. "Tammanyizing Boston," *Colliers* 44 (Jan. 8, 1910): 10. In the aftermath Fitzgerald gave Hibbard a city job which the State Civil Service Commission disallowed. Hibbard died in 1910.

52. *Herald*, Jan. 6, 1910.

53. *Herald*, Nov. 18, 19, 1909, Dec. 19, 1909; *New York Post*, Jan. 12, 1910.

54. *Herald*, Nov. 19, 1909, Dec. 5, 1909; George Reed Nutter Diary, Massachusetts Historical Society, Boston, Dec. 5, 1909.

55. All papers carried the speeches of the candidates and their supporters in lengthy excerpts. For example, *Herald*, Dec. 27, 29, 1909, Jan. 3, 1910, for Fitz's attacks.

56. *Herald*, Nov. 7, 18, 1909, Dec. 14, 1909.

57. The ads and Fitzgerald's objections to the cost were a major feature of the conclusion of the campaign. For example, *Herald*, Dec. 29, 1909, Jan. 4, 1910 ("city hall is not for sale"), Jan. 6, 1910.

58. *Herald*, Jan. 4, 6, 8, 1910.

59. *Herald*, Jan. 6, 1910.

60. *New York Times*, Dec. 20, 1909.

61. Election Commission, *Report, 1909*.

62. *New York Times*, Jan. 11, 1910, Pearson, *Son of New England*, p. 94.

63. *Nation* 70 (Jan. 27, 1910): 83.

64. Fitzgerald often broke into song during his rallies, and "Sweet Adeline" was one of his favorites on such occasions. His supporters liked him for it, but to his detractors such habits symbolized his vacuity.

7

Curley of Boston: The Search for Irish Legitimacy

CHARLES H. TROUT

From the days of John Winthrop into the early nineteenth century, Boston's political leaders by and large were the beneficiaries of religious, patriarchal, or traditional legitimation. Even a man as unpopular as Thomas Hutchinson, the beleaguered governor driven from power on the eve of the Revolution, was spared accusations that his genealogical credentials were somehow out of order. In the nineteenth century, no one doubted the right of the three Josiah Quincys to serve as mayor, even when the third turned out to have socialistic inclinations. One could disagree with a Harrison Gray Otis, a Theodore Lyman or a Samuel Eliot but their right to office was unchallenged: "deference democracy," as Professor Baltzell has called it,[1] was intact. Usually graduates of Harvard, members if not founders of the city's most esteemed clubs, and affiliates of the correct churches, these scions of pre-revolutionary families received the regalia of office almost as if by divine right. Confident of their legitimacy, they saw no need to circumvent a political system that had for so long sustained the authority of their class.

From the Revolution to the early twentieth century, a new political type emerged. As Boston's so-called "natural leaders" retreated from public life,[2] a relatively drab coterie of unremarkable mayors administered the city's business. In the old days, men had *stood* for office; this group, in contrast, *ran* for a place in government. Once in power, they showed themselves loyal to the precepts of the City Charter, and they drew their legitimacy from what Max Weber has called a legal, or constitutional, or bureaucratic source. Masters of a bureaucratic system that had grown up to superintend an even more populous city, these men met Boston's "calculable and recurrent needs by means of a normal routine.''[3] Their ability to inspire moral visions might be questioned. Their relevance to the city in times of "psychic, physical, economic, ethical, religious, political distress" might be called into doubt.[4] Few, however, could question their legitimacy.

When those of Irish descent first turned to politics, it was self-evident that they could not draw their sanction from traditional or patriarchal sources—and this left them two choices. They could, like Hugh O'Brien in the 1880s, or Maurice Tobin some fifty years later, rely upon their bureaucratic capabilities and their constitutional position to justify their authority—or, as we shall see, they could turn to a charismatic mode of leadership. Initially, most selected the bureaucratic. O'Brien, for instance, studiously avoided whatever temptations he might have felt to wander outside the bounds of accepted civilities and make direct appeals to an Irish Catholic electorate. Although O'Brien had sent a shudder through Brahmin Boston by pledging an administration that would "be liberal in all expenditures,"[5] he proved to be an unwavering fiscal conservative. A man who balked at public works projects that would have employed immigrant laborers, he in no way altered the system with which he had been entrusted. Indeed, O'Brien's chief importance, aside from his being the first Irishman to capture the mayoralty and thereby encouraging others to run for office, may well have been to allay fears that the city, if not in Yankee hands, would go to ruin. By the time he had completed his four consecutive one-year terms, O'Brien had blended into a routinized conception of the mayoralty that made him indistinguishable from his Yankee counterparts.

Another choice existed for those Irish who were seeking a source of legitimacy, and it was neither traditional nor bureaucratic. Rather, it rested upon a charismatic foundation. According to this model (and the model, again, is Weber's), the charismatic leader, often summoned in times of crisis, is not required to have expert knowledge, nor does he choose to stay within either traditional or bureaucratic structures. Called to power by those in distress, the charismatic leader has, throughout history, been thought to possess "specific gifts of the body and spirit; and these gifts have been believed to be supernatural, not accessible to everybody." Capable of "heroic frenzy," the charismatic leader is not subject to "an ordered procedure of appointment or dismissal." He is not subject to an "agency of control or appeal," nor is he limited by "exclusive functional jurisdictions." "Charisma," Weber has written, "knows only inner determination and inner restraint." In the matter of economics, Weber reminds us, this restraint is not likely to be great: "Charismatic political heroes seek booty...." They reject "as undignified any pecuniary gain that is methodical and rational." Weber continues:

> The holder of charisma seizes the task that is adequate for him and demands obedience and a following by virtue of his mission. His success determines whether he finds them. His charismatic claim breaks down if his mission is not recognized by those to whom he feels he has been sent. If they recognize him, he is their master—so long as he knows how to maintain recognition through 'proving' himself. But he does not derive his 'right' from their will, in the manner of an election. Rather, the reverse holds: it is the *duty* of those to whom he addresses his mission to recognize him as their charismatically qualified leader.[6]

Cut off from the possibility of traditional legitimation, and—for a variety of reasons that this chapter will explore—disinclined to seek authority by virtue of constitutional office alone, a number of Irish politicians in the first half of this century explored the possibilities of charismatic leadership.

It is important to recognize, nevertheless, that not all Irish Democrats embarked upon this exploration. Indeed, the persistent tendency to see "the Boston Irish" as a political monolith is fatal to an understanding of the city's twentieth-century political history and must be resisted. It might be argued, for instance, that men like Patrick A. Collins and John A. Sullivan tried to develop a foundation not at all unlike that of Boston's so-called "deference democracy." Linking themselves to the rich intellectual heritage bequeathed by John Boyle O'Reilly and John Jeffrey Roche, eager to present themselves as the literate and refined leaders that they were, and capable of building bridges to Yankee notables without renouncing their roots, they struggled mightily to suggest that there existed among the Irish a group of "best people" who had a right to rule by virtue of who they were. In this sense, men of the Collins stripe sought a course parallel to that of the Joseph Lees, the Henry Shattucks, the Henry Parkmans, the Leverett Saltonstalls. In short, they, too, developed a strong feeling that they belonged in Boston, that their influence derived from a rich patrimony, that they had a right to exercise moral as well as political leadership. Others—mayors like Frederick Mansfield, Maurice Tobin, John Hynes, John Collins—followed more in the footsteps of Hugh O'Brien: with varying degrees of competence, they ran the city without demagoguery; without frequent appeals to ethnicity, class, and religion; without straying from the bureaucratic model that formed part of the O'Brien legacy. Still others sought refuge almost exclusively in the charismatic mode—a rogue like Daniel Coakley, perhaps a ward boss like Martin Lomasney, aldermen in the century's opening decade like Frank Linehan and Jerry Watson, city council members of the 1930s like Clement Norton and Francis E. "Frankie" Kelly, maybe contemporaries of ours who shall (discretion being the better part of valor) remain nameless.

But John F. Fitzgerald and James Michael Curley, the two giants of the period with which this chapter is concerned, resist easy categorization, and it is precisely for this reason that both are extraordinarily interesting. In their lifetimes, and surely after their deaths, every effort has been made to enshroud them with folkloric qualities. To this end, they themselves made contributions, especially Curley, but novelists, newspapermen, politicians looking for a laugh, and, alas, historians have all chimed in. Endless anecdotes (a collection that we might entitle *The Large Green Book According to Chairman James*), although admittedly entertaining, have been substituted for history. What makes Fitzgerald and Curley fascinating is not their anecdotal value, however, but their quixotic hunt for sources of authority and acceptance. In Curley's case (and it is with Curley that this chapter is primarily concerned), the search for legitimacy was, I am convinced, absolutely desperate, constantly oscillating, and lifelong. He was never able to achieve it, and in seeking it he covered himself with so many identities that he lost his grip on who he was. By the end of his life, he had retreated into the identity picked up by Edwin O'Connor in *The Last Hurrah*, a portrait that does not do him justice. In fact, the distance between what Curley had been and the O'Connor portrait is a fair measure of what it had cost him to be politically ambitious in the City of Boston. While more often than not casting himself in the charismatic guise (and I am here using Weber's value-neutral model), he time and again tried other modes. In many respects Curley's search for acceptance is tragic: his quest provides a means of calibrating the not-so-dimly hidden injuries of caste and class in Boston, allows us to understand something about the boundaries imposed by his station in life, and sheds light on his struggles to push aside those limits. If, as William Shannon has suggested, he was in the end "a self-crippled giant on a provincial stage,"[7] it is small wonder. To make a cultural and political declaration of freedom requires confidence. For all his bravado, James Michael Curley lacked the requisite assuredness.

There were, of course, reasons why Curley and other products of the nineteenth century who invigorated Boston's twentieth-century politics might have lacked certainty about their legitimacy. From the moment the first ships carrying their human cargo appeared in Boston Harbor, the newcomers from Ireland faced a chilly reception: their sons and grandsons, who would come of political age in the late nineteenth or early twentieth centuries, men like Fitzgerald and Curley, shared in an oral tradition that made clear they belonged to an unwanted group. To a man, they had been told of the mob that had sacked the Ursuline Convent in Charlestown. Those who grew up in Roxbury were constantly reminded that the construction of their church, St. Patrick's, had been made possible because the men of the parish, many of them on horseback and equipped with loaded muskets and bayonets, had guarded the construction site against "the profanation of the bigoted savage." Recruited from those who toiled in Roxbury's iron-rolling mill, its nail factory, and its cordage works, "nearly every man of the parish took his night in turn to perform the work of the literal soldier of the cross."[8]

Culturally unacceptable, the Irish also encountered substantial difficulties in establishing an economic foothold in Boston. From 1845 to 1860, the expenses of the Overseers of the Poor increased nearly eightfold, and Irish immigrants comprised much of the caseload. Instead of expressing sympathy for people styled by Oscar Handlin as "the guano" of America's industrial system,[9] the Overseers believed the soaring costs were unacceptable, that the expenses ought to "startle even the extravagant, and . . . make prudent men inquire with more than usual strictness into the character and necessity of the expenditure." Moreover, immigrants were accused of taking advantage of Yankee generosity. "The idea of one's speculating upon the benevolent disposition of his neighbors," the Overseers complained, "and of making money out of the easy kindness of the City Council, is peculiarly offensive to all who are endowed with the smallest portion of Yankee shrewdness."[10] With nearly 70 percent of those on aid having been born across the Atlantic, or children of Irish born in America but with parents who had recently arrived, the Overseers believed they had a point.[11]

To native elements, there was something appalling about the bulk, the sheer mass of Irish immigration to Boston. As customs officials released the annual count, the magnitude of the numbers themselves obscured the lives those statistics represented. Curley's mother was a Clancy, and from 1848 to 1891, eighteen Bridget Clancys, fifty-two Mary Clancys, and an uncountable number of Ann Clancys, most of them listed as servants, paid their $16 to $20 for steerage to Boston. Curley's father was named Michael, and in this same period, nineteen Michael Curleys shipped into the city. With the exception of a single "color-mixer" from Scotland, all were listed as laborers who had embarked from Irish ports.[12] Twenty years after arriving in Boston, James Michael's father was one of 104 employed, adult Curleys listed in the *City Directory*. Of the 104, fully 85 per cent were, like Michael, mired in blue-collar occupations, a figure that approximated the norm for all the city's Irish in this period.[13] In such a setting, Yankee hosts could not differentiate, could not see individual faces or envision separate aspirations—could not see etched in each face the heroism of one who had survived. There could be no recognition of regional differences, no knowledge that immigrants from County Galway differed from those of County Kerry, no recognition that not all were, as feared, Catholic. To native Bostonians, these immigrants were simply "The Irish"— Bridgets and Paddys; micks and harps; pot-wallopers, biddies, and kitchen canaries; greenhorns and clodhoppers—muckers all.

The sense of what it was to be economically marginal, the sense of precariousness that came in a city where the death rate for Irish children far exceeded the norm for other elements,[14] and the sense of being part of a group that, try as it might, suffered from blocked mobility—the sense of being part of what was wrongly perceived as an undifferentiated mass—placed an indelible mark upon many of those who forged their political careers in the twentieth century. For these political neophytes, the dawn of a new century represented no watershed: men of Fitzgerald's and Curley's generation cannot be understood without observing that they carried into a new era the baggage acquired in their youth. For them, history was continuous, and despite the many attempts to portray the Irish encounter with poverty as picturesque (Curley, indeed, liked to refer to his humble birthplace at 28 Northampton Street as his "log cabin"), it was not. Curley, for one, bore the scars throughout his life.

From the time James Michael Curley's father arrived in Boston, he was part of a limitless pool of day laborers, men who "informed the census takers that they were just laborers—a classification descriptive not of their function, but their lack of function,"[15] and he could not protect his two young sons, John and James, from tragedy. During abnormally high tides, seepage from outhouses in back of places like 28 Northampton Street befouled the neighborhood, and in 1879 a third son, Michael Curley, Jr., languished: in 1881, at the age of two-and-a-half, he died. Three years later, Michael Curley set off one morning for his job with the city's street-paving department. When his wife and two surviving sons next saw him, he was comatose. Seventy-two hours later, he was dead from the exertions of having lifted a curbstone. No obituary marked his death, and not even a death notice appeared in the Boston newspapers. Michael Curley had arrived in Boston unnoticed, worked in Boston unnoticed, died in Boston unnoticed.

In the next twenty-four hours, James Michael Curley's mother, Sarah, had to make the all-too-familiar burial arrangements: for $15, she purchased a plot in Old Calvary, the sprawling immigrant cemetery off Mt. Hope Street in Roslindale where her infant son had been buried earlier. Over the next many months, she paid off the cost of the plot at 25 cents a week, payments taken out of the paltry wages she now was earning as a scrub-woman.[16] However hard she might try, she could not shield her 10-year-old son from the corrosive sadness produced by the losses of a brother and a father, nor could she shield him from economic uncertainties. The youngster's education at the Yeoman Primary School, and then at the Dearborn Grammer School, where Yankee teachers and Irish janitors reminded him of his humble station,[17] was threatened by the need to take a job. For four years, he put in as much as sixty hours a week at Stephen Gale's pharmacy and, at the age of fifteen, he quit school and went to work briefly for the New England Piano Company, probably the most arduous and unpleasant job of his life. Then, for the next eight years he gave himself over to groceries. Hired by C.S. Johnson as "boy of all work,"[18] Curley learned the values of a faithful employee. During young Curley's tenure in these positions, his employers parlayed small capital outlays into solid profits.[19] James Michael, in contrast, did not correspondingly prosper. His early years were singularly unremarkable, and for all his subsequent attempts to romanticize his boyhood, and despite his efforts to assert that his sweatshop job at the piano factory had stirred his social conscience, he showed no signs of having learned the rebel's song. A sort of Horatio Alger manqué, he had carved out a reasonably secure niche, but no more. Whatever, it is palpably clear that neither his father nor his mother had had the power to save their son from the travails of a hard-scrabble life.

Although generalizations about the impact of his early years on his subsequent behavior must be advanced with caution, a few speculations are in order. His subsequent treatment of his father's death is striking. Before James Michael Curley died, he had invested his father with an elaborate mythology: at various points Michael Curley was transmuted into a man who "could fight beyond the powers of the flesh," "a gentle and lovable man," a "warm-hearted family man," a "hard and un-complaining worker," "a grand man," but—and this is crucial—a man who "never made much money."[20] That, I am persuaded, was the bottom line. The flattering remarks Curley reserved for his father were, in a sense, an effort to give meaning to a life that he, James Michael, may well have regarded as meaningless.

Over his career, James Michael Curley made much of another Amer-ican who had lost his father at an early age and whose mother also lacked the capacity to cope. That American was Thomas Jefferson. Jefferson, fatherless at the age of fourteen, was, according to Curley, "a lad of delicate health," and his mother was "a confirmed invalid." "Stunned by the loss of his father and at the thoughts of his mother," Jefferson developed "an impediment in his speech which remained with him through a lifetime. . . ." Nevertheless, Jefferson's mother, although unable to furnish physical protection, provided her son with spiritual and intellectual inspiration. According to Curley, "the presence . . . of the word equality" in that "immortal document," the Declaration of Independence, could "undeniably be traced to his mother, who during his lifetime served both as counsel and inspirer to her gifted son."[21] For Curley, the parallels were obvious. His father was gone. His mother, down on her knees scrubbing floors, was figuratively crippled. Sarah Curley could not provide the economic security of a Monticello, but within the limits of her paralysis she could furnish love and maternal wisdom. For these gifts, Curley would repeatedly pay her fulsome tribute. The rest—economic survival, the steely determination that there be no "impediment" of speech—Curley would have to accomplish on his own.

As his career unfolded, Curley constantly oscillated between a re-jection of his past and a belligerent recognition of his origins. One moment, a political enemy noted in the 1930s, his language was pure

Oxford; the next, it derived from Dogpatch.[22] At the Staley School of Speech, he, like other twentieth-century Boston politicos, devoted eight years to remaking his oratorical style and, in a sense, to refashioning his identity.[23] Throughout his life, he told so many whoppers that it is doubtful that he knew what was true and what was untrue, but the apocryphal has a validity of its own. On the one hand, he depicted his early years as a great deal better than they were: the first time his name appears in the *City Directory*, for instance, he had himself listed as a "piano tuner," an occupation that must have struck him as far more elegant than that of the sweatshop employee that he was.[24] At times, he attributed his impressive acquaintance with literature to omnivorous boyhood reading, when the truth was that his first reading binge occurred at age 29 when he was in jail.[25] On another occasion, he told a reporter of his honeymoon—how he and his bride had taken a thirty-day trip all the way to Banff and Lake Louise, for that is what an ardent groom of social standing might do: the truth was that his honeymoon lasted thirteen days, and he never traveled west of Niagara Falls. On the other hand, he liked to dwell upon the theme of privation, and, as the stories were told and retold, they were transmuted in interesting ways: he and his brother, lacking the money to buy a 25-pound bag of coal, may not literally have gone to the dump to "forage for unburned pieces of anthracite and scraps of wood," as he liked to claim, yet it is evident that the possibility of having to comb through scrap piles was real enough. He liked to tell his audiences that he had frequently gone barefoot. Most youngsters did. Whether he went barefoot because he had no shoes is unknown. That he lived close enough to poverty so that the possibility of shoelessness was an issue in his life, is, on the other hand, wholly plausible.

As Curley's political career evolved, he persistently exhibited wild ideological and programmatic fluctuations. The number of times he befriended and then denounced John F. Fitzgerald, for instance, defies reckoning. In the same aldermanic session, he could inveigh against those he suspected of handing over a valuable franchise to private interests, and the next moment he would give one away. He favored municipal ownership of utilities one minute and opposed it the next. He called for honesty in government, but in Congress he twice voted against a corrupt practices act. Repeatedly, he tried to earn the esteem of men of aristocratic bearing, and then he would attack them: his relationship with Franklin Delano Roosevelt is only one of many such instances. Several of these shifts can, of course, be ascribed to practical politics. At the same time, however, it must be understood that the tragedies and privations of his boyhood along "The Corned-Beef-and-Cabbage Riviera," as he sometimes called his Roxbury neighborhood, played a part as well. Like many of his political contemporaries, James Michael Curley wore what Leon Edel has called "the revealing mask of life," and it is important to search for what Edel has called "the figure under the carpet, the evidence in the reverse of the tapestry, the life-myth of a given mask." Admittedly, this search is speculative, but as Edel reminds us:

We must read certain psychological signs that enable us to understand what people are really saying behind the faces they put on, behind the utterances they allow themselves to make before the world. The aggressive emotion that masquerades as a cutting witticism; the excessive endearment that conceals a certain animus; the pleasant joint remark that is accompanied by a hostile gesture; the sudden slip of the tongue that says the opposite of what has been intended. This is "psychological evidence" a biographer must learn to read....[26]

I would concur, and I would further contend that the history of Curley and his contemporaries—those who gave Boston politics its peculiar flavor from 1900 to 1950—not only wore masks, but that these masks were dictated by circumstances of their birth. In many cases, the donning of masks and the disposition toward a charismatic style of leadership did not represent a conscious, volitional decision. Instead, the choice may well have been inevitable.

Curley's rise to political prominence has been told often and need not long detain us. Suffice it to say that James Michael's first flutterings were closely tied to the infrastructure of his immigrant neighborhood—first to St. Patrick's and then St. Philip's churches, to politicians in his ward, and to Division 9 of the Ancient Order of Hibernians. Savoring recognition as an organizer of countless activities at St. Philip's, he used the local ward leaders and the A.O.H. for lessons in political flummery. Before long, he was running for office—twice in losing struggles for a seat on the old Common Council and then, in 1889, with success. From that point on, it was, he recalled, "like Caesar's legions. One fight was hardly over before another fight was started." Curley enjoyed the struggle. Indeed, his behavior reflected what Sylvan Tomkins has called an unshakeable psychology of commitment: whenever he came under siege, not only did he decline to capitulate but his affect grew even stronger. Each attack deepened his belief in his own powers, his own causes.[27] Each attack drove him to ever bolder designs. Each attack pushed him further toward a charismatic role. This role, in turn, could be seen in the seraglio politics of the Tammany Club he founded. It was on display in the campaigns that from 1900 to 1913 swept him into the Common Council, then the state legislature, the Board of Aldermen, the City Council, the Congress of the United States, and finally into Room One at City Hall. Perhaps most of all, this tendency was revealed in his trip to prison in 1904.

On October 15, 1902, James M. and Thomas F. Curley, Tammany allies but otherwise unrelated, discussed a civil service examination for postal workers that would be given in December. Both men faced elections, and both needed campaign workers. Two ward heelers, Bartholomew Fahey (born in County Galway) and James J. Hughes (born in County Meath), had been acquaintances of the Curleys for over six years but, like many Irish before them, stood little chance of passing the examination. "Why not impersonate them?" the Curleys speculated, and James Michael not only signed a voucher for Hughes but also agreed to impersonate Fahey. On October 31, the applications were filed at the Boston civil service office, and a crime against "the peace and dignity of the United States of America," as the indictment put it, had begun.[28] On December 4, 1902, the two Curleys entered the Federal Building together and began to write. Apparently, they also helped each other with the more difficult questions. Thus the District Attorney in the case could point to "deadly parallels" in the two examinations. "There are," he indicated, "twelve duplicated blunders that cannot be mere coincidence." The two Curleys, for instance, had at first located Fort Scott in Illinois, reconsidered, and then amended their answers to place it correctly in Arkansas.[29] Two heads were apparently better than one, and the impersonators easily passed the test. They did not, however, pass judicial muster, and after protracted court proceedings, they were pronounced guilty and sentenced to sixty days in the Suffolk County jail. "IN THE NAME OF THE PRESIDENT OF THE UNITED STATES," read the quaintly worded but no less sobering "Warrant to Commit," "[we] command you the said Marshal or Deputies . . . forthwith to convey and deliver into the custody of the Keeper of our said Jail, the body of James M. Curley." Legal appeals followed, and it was not until November 7, 1904, almost two years after the original crime had been committed, that Curley was locked up in a Charles Street cell.

When Curley had heard the foreman of the jury pronounce him guilty, "a slight shudder seemed to pass over him,"[30] but this was one of the few times he appeared chastened. Curley knew full well that Boston's mayors, including the third Josiah Quincy, had shoehorned their favorites onto the municipal payroll by inventing special job categories not covered by civil service regulations: the Water Department, for instance, boasted a "ship-caulker," "miners," and "expert swimmer"—stroke unspecified.[31] Because of this ethos, Curley could not believe that he had done anything so dreadfully wrong. Moreover, the fact that a Brahmin judge, Francis Cabot Lowell, had set bail at the extraordinarily punitive level of $2,500 heightened Curley's sense of having been wronged. When the Good Government Association (GGA), heavy with Bostonians who were no strangers to anti-Irish causes, came into being in 1903, in part to block Curley's election to the Board of Aldermen, James Michael was apoplectic. Predictably, he lashed back, and in this regard, he was encouraged by his followers. The men of Tammany raised money for the legal defense, and the women of Ward 17—"The Creole Belles," they called themselves—tendered the two Curleys a complimentary banquet.[32] In this regard, James Michael's followers were performing their "*duty* . . . to recognize him as their charismatically qualified leader," and they delivered him a stunning majority in both the aldermanic election of 1903, when he was not in jail, and that of 1904, when he was.

Emboldened by these developments, Curley attended a Tammany Hall send-off the night before he left for prison—"the most remarkable political meeting ever held in Boston," reported the Boston *Journal* with only a modicum of exaggeration. Curleyites stood shoulder to shoulder at Tammany headquarters, many of them crammed in so tight they could "applaud" only "with husky voices." Meanwhile, a massive crowd outside the hall "ripped the night air with their voices." Speakers denounced the civil service law as "insidious," "iniquitous," "corrupt," and "imperfect." Politicians who had knifed James Michael in the back were variously excoriated for being "the octopus of the ward," a "political pirate," a "cur," a "vulture." Curley also employed religious metaphors: some "Judas Iscariot" had betrayed him, and his enemies would "find resurrection as far beyond them as the sun in the heavens." As Curley reached the end of his tirade, he was shouting. His voice grew hoarse. Then, "with pallid face and eyes flashing," he led the Tammanyites in the singing of "America" and "The Star-Spangled Banner." The window panes rattled with "the series of cheers and tigers" accorded him, and, as he left the hall, scores of followers accompanied him to his home, cheering him as he walked.[33]

And when he was released from jail, these scenes were repeated. Again he chastised his political enemies. More interestingly, he attacked the civil service. The system, he scoffed, "is contrary to human nature, for every man knows that if an influential man has a friend who stands tenth in an examination and an enemy who stands first, the poorest man will get the job." He therefore was only doing what everyone in the city government was doing. (Theodore Roosevelt, he added, was doing it too.) At worst, he had committed a misdemeanor, but it would have been far more unconscionable, he argued, not to have helped his friends. Unrepentant, Curley vowed that in the future, "we will go as far as justice will permit and good sense allow in doing all that we can for you."[34] In essence, Curley had pledged that he would venture beyond the constitutional, the legal, the bureaucratic, and when he walked out of the Tammany Club onto George Street, scores of shouting supporters stood in the snow waiting to let him know they approved.

This single event, followed seven months later by the notorious Dock Trust case in which Curley and other aldermen were investigated by a grand jury for taking bribes in return for their votes, awakened Boston's so-called "best people" into a flurry of activity. Republicans on Beacon Hill unseated James Michael's sidekick, Thomas F. Curley, from the state legislature, and Curley himself was denounced. The Good Government Association kept him on the list of those proscribed all the way to its demise in 1933, and the city's ministers viewed him as morally rotten, as a common criminal. Even a court in Colorado, wrestling with another civil service violation, found the Curley episode a useless precedent, for the case it was considering did not "involve . . . such baseness, vileness and depravity as exists in *Curley v. United States.* . . ."[35] Judge Lowell could not have said it better.

But in election after election, attempts by enemies to exploit Curley's misadventure boomeranged every bit as much as they had in the days when the saga was unfolding. Not all of the city's poor, and not all of its Irish Catholics either,[36] felt alike toward Curley's actions, but a majority clearly believed he had not been venal, nor were his backers necessarily pernicious because they continued to lionize him. Informal, personal government, one that operated outside the constitutional structure, was more to be trusted than the state. That is the way things had worked in the old country, and they worked no differently in Boston, "the Dublin of America." By these lights, Curley's deed had been fully justified.

The cost to Curley, however, was great, for his jailing forever circumscribed his political horizons: only in 1934, an extraordinary year in American politics, would Curley win state-wide election. Any number of progressives and, later, liberal Democrats thought him tainted. Even in his days as the senior member of the Board of Aldermen he could not capture the aldermanic presidency. Until the day he died, Democratic administrations refused him patronage and declined to appoint him to anything of importance. He would forever be the "Jailbird Mayor of Boston," a man unable to extend his following much beyond selected portions of the city. After the civil service imbroglio, Curley was hung on the ethnic and class petards he had hoisted. Contrary to the argument recently advanced by Peter Eisinger, Boston's native-born elite, those pushed aside by Curley and Fitzgerald, were ungenerous toward the Irish in general and toward Curley in particular. The "displaced group," I would argue, did not "make its resources available" for purposes of "economic and urban development, political support, and public service."[37] No matter what Curley did, the city's notables never tendered him the validating gesture of respectability he so desperately desired.

James Michael Curley deserved better. During the Progressive Era, his record in the City Council, as a Congressman, and as Mayor of Boston should have earned him accolades from anyone who cared about the broader contours of social justice. For most of his career, Curley was a social reformer, while the Yankee reformers who opposed him mainly confined themselves to structural concerns—to the creation of the Boston Finance Commission, to the Charter of 1909, to schemes for proportional representation and plans for a City Council elected at large.[38] The structural reformers, in contrast to Curley, wanted a well-policed bureaucratic system, an administrative mode incompatible with Curley's charismatic style.

In office, Curley showed himself to be what Eric Goldman would call a "reform Darwinist."[39] Alcoholism plagued the neighborhoods of the poor not because of moral depravity but because of poverty. Youngsters committed crimes not because they were bad but, again, because they were poor: the city's insistence upon incarcerating young offenders constituted, in his view, a class-biased system for regulating the poor. Tuberculosis victims languished in the Long Island hospital where they were branded as paupers. The hospital, he proclaimed, "bears the same relationship to a cemetery as does an incubator to a hennery."[40] Remove the badge of poverty, give the patients fresh-air treatment, and they would, he believed, stand a reasonable chance for recovery. In short, if the environment were altered, a number of social problems would disappear. If men were paid decent wages, if they were given time off on Saturdays, a milestone would be reached "along the line of progress, along the line of humanity, along the line of right living. . . . "[41] Whenever a department head removed an elderly worker to make room for someone younger, Curley went to the barricades against "the kind of economy that drives [the superannuated] to the poor house . . . and makes of them a public charge. . . . "[42] Repeatedly, he advocated pensions for elderly city workers and the creation of a state-wide old-age assistance plan. Like progressives in the social justice movement, he equated contract labor "to the padrone system," invariably voted for wage increases and shorter hours for government workers, and persistently supported the goals of organized labor—workmen's compensation, factory inspection laws, the abolition of convict labor, wages and hours legislation. Repeatedly and often with sarcasm, he urged his fellow aldermen to display toward blue-collar Bostonians "the same broad, liberal treatment that we accord to horses."[43] Like other urban progressives, he fought to maintain the nickel fare on all street railways, and he also tried to abolish ferry charges for the boat trip to East Boston. At a time when progressives were beginning to recognize the limitations of rigid, highly academic public education, Curley also saw that the traditional schools were not serving the needs of every working-class child. Accordingly, he took initiatives to found a commercial high school, a cause to which John F. Fitzgerald was also devoted. In an era when progressives were beginning to speak of "blighted" neighborhoods and were discovering the slums, Curley opposed construction of elevated lines in every part of Boston: elevateds not only created unwanted noise but the unsightly structures defiled the neighborhoods of the poor. Spearheading efforts to impose tenement-house regulation, he also introduced ordinances against subterranean dwelling places. Curley would use the power of government to achieve beneficent change for the plain people of his city, and authentic progressives could not have asked for more.[44]

In Congress from 1911 to 1914, Curley, the sort of man progressives loved to revile as a corrupt boss, wrote further chapters in what was fast emerging as a significant development in Boston's twentieth-century political history—namely the emergence of what J. Joseph Huthmacher has termed "urban liberalism."[45] Indeed, Curley's votes during his two terms in Washington with few exceptions[46] demonstrate that his political sentiments conformed almost precisely with those of the insurgent Republicans and with progressive elements in his own party. A champion of tariff reform, he favored reciprocity with Canada "because the Lumber Trust and all its allied interests are opposing it and because it typifies the most advanced character of progressive legislation in behalf of the great masses of our people."[47] Moreover, he voted for tariff reductions on woolen and cotton manufactures, he argued that the tariff on agricultural equipment added "to the gigantic wealth of special interests,[48] and he applauded the Underwood-Simmons Tariff of 1913, even though he realized that manufacturers in his district would be hurt.[49]

During his time in office, congressional conservatives attempted to shut off immigration by imposing a literacy test. Curley, a member of the Committee on Immigration and Naturalization, was, like most authentic progressives, convinced that the bill was an "iniquitous measure."[50] Literacy, he believed, did not make a man. Rather, "[t]he need of the hour is an honesty of purpose, a clear conscience, and a sturdy frame."[51] Had the test been applied in the nineteenth century, a host of Irish patriots would have been excluded:

It is the old cry, 'Keep out the alien; keep out the undesirable.' It is the same cry, Mr. Chairman, that prompted the governor of New York in 1860 to dissolve the Irish brigade, commanded by Michael Corcoran, because they were Irish and might be a menace to the Republic, since they refused to turn out in honor of Prince Albert; but when the first blow was struck at Sumter it was the gallant Corcoran who came to the front and volunteered the services of the Irish brigade in the cause of the Union. [Applause.][52]

When President Taft vetoed the immigration bill, Curley received one of the pens, and the tribute was deserved—just as it would have been had he been rewarded for his support of compulsory arbitration in labor disputes, his stand in favor of a bill to limit the use of injunctions against unions, his advocacy of judicial recall, and his lobbying on behalf of a federal child labor act.[53]

As Mayor of Boston from 1914 to 1918, Curley again exhibited a number of signs that should have gladdened progressives. For his corporation counsel, he selected John A. Sullivan, former chairman of the Boston Finance Commission and a man who was widely respected as "the better sort" of Irishman, a man long associated with the O'Reilly-Roche-Collins tradition, a tradition with which James Michael dearly would have liked to have been associated. Although Curley issued dismissal notices to several department heads, he initially went much more slowly with spoilsmanship than had been widely feared. As the *Herald* quipped, Curley had visited the Marine Park aquarium, yet "no fish have died, resigned or been suspended."[54] Even the Good Government Association conceded that the Mayor's restraint entitled him "to the highest praise."[55] Instead of running up the city's expenses, Curley instituted a number of economies. Before long, he had set up a credit union for municipal employees, closed down the worst of the city's homes for juvenile delinquents, called for a municipally-owned pasteurization plant, cracked down on building codes and fire regulations, and used these codes to drive several of the city's sweatshops out of business. In one of his most famous steps, he ordered the municipal scrubwomen off their knees, equipped them with mops, and hiked their pay. Under Curley, both the spirit and the substance of urban liberalism were, for a time, alive and well.

For his achievements during his first twenty years of public life, Curley earned infrequent praise from Boston's "best people." To Brahmin reformers, most of them more concerned with honesty in government than with social justice, Curley represented an "ethnic challenge, which in race-conscious America meant only barely less than a challenge to civilization itself."[56] Deemed an ignorant and venal spoilsman, the practitioner of a loutish, brutal, opportunistic, offensive political style, Curley could not gain acceptance, and with each rebuff he became more churlish, more reckless, more given to demagogic appeals, more inconsistent in his political positions. Accused of being self-serving because he played up to the poor, he at times shifted positions to show that he was not. Nevertheless, he increasingly came to view municipal workers as *his* employees, not as *city* employees, and as his first mayoralty progressed, the line of job seekers outside his door lengthened. His relationship with so-called "pet contractors" became increasingly suspect. More and more, he filled the charismatic role.

Unquestionably, Curley's excesses made plausible the Good Government Association's view that he was not fit for public office, yet it was not so much that James Michael wanted *bad* government, as the GGA implied. Rather, Curley was at many points talking about a wholly *different* government—one that would spend; one that would not be slavishly devoted to balanced budgets, especially during slumps in the economy; one that would protect the worker; one that would provide municipal services in all areas of the city rather than in the silk-stocking wards alone; one that would be active, energetic, elastic, and by all means personal. As Curley viewed the GGA, the typical structural reformer spoke for a limited group of downtown property owners, many of whom lived in the suburbs, and he turned the tables on his detractors. They, not he, were the spoilsmen. They, not he, stood for narrow class interests. Therefore, he taunted them as "hamstringers," "panderers," "flunkies," "lackies," and "toadies . . . of the economic royalists." The Municipal Statistics Department, run by prominent members of the GGA, existed "purely to satisfy the whims and fancies of a very few faddists."[57] Unpaid municipal boards—the Park Commissioners and Library Trustees, for instance—favored the wealthy: "their family lineage," said Curley, ". . . could easily have proven that they sailed with Captain Kidd or with some other man equally honest."[58] He tweaked their college—Harvard. On the day of his inauguration, he taunted them by threatening to sell the Boston Common, but not before installing a high-pressure pumping station. When the city's bankers, some of them members of the GGA, refused to contribute to his "Boom Boston" fund in 1914, he threatened to withdraw city deposits from their banks.

With members of his own party, he could be equally vitriolic. Some, he thought, were "lineal descendants of the notorious Biddy Moriarty," or they followed "the Dick Turpin method of finance," or they answered "the siren call of the corruptionists." One was a "flub," another a "fakir," a "skunk," a "wash-lady," a "wet nurse," a "chambermaid." When John A. Sullivan had chaired the Finance Commission, Curley had called him a man "of a loathsome character," a "pool shark," a man who maintained an interest in "at least five bar rooms in Boston." Nathan Matthews, Jr., was nothing less than "a door-mat thief." Curley claimed that one of his Democratic rivals had once served in the British army. Others were linked to the Baptist ministry, to corporate interests, to the Masons, to high living, to alleged corruption, and, in one instance, to birth control and abortion. In his campaigns, Curley developed an extensive bag of dirty tricks. In essence, his followers were told to ''Vote Early and Vote Often.''[59]

The direction in which Curley turned in his escalating struggle with reform elements, a struggle that began in earnest with his jail sentence, was probably not finally determined until rather late in his first term as mayor. There is no question that Curley had provoked Boston's Brahmin do-gooders, as well as the more affluent, better-educated Irish but they, in turn, had provoked him. Never did they let him forget his incarceration in the Charles Street jail, and when he won the congressional election of 1910, a concerned effort was made to bar him from his seat on the basis of his felony. During his first term in City Hall, GGA-endorsed City Council members opposed his quest for a lump sum budget and tried their best to prune allocations for projects of substantial merit. When Curley called for participation in a ''Boom Boston'' drive, they turned him down. It would not seem, as others have contended, that Boston's non-Irish notables had made things easy for an Irish mayor.

Then, in 1915, Curley suffered one of the most significant rebuffs of his career. The 1909 Charter contained a provision that allowed for mayoral recall: John F. Fitzgerald had had to face a recall election, and now the GGA targeted Curley for removal. For recall to occur, a majority of those *registered* to vote had to be achieved. Although this figure was not reached (57,000 would have been needed), 48,000 voters opted for Curley's removal, and only 35,000 supported him. Of the city's twenty-six wards, Curley carried but eight. Stung by this setback on November 2, 1915, but still in office, Curley swung ''the political broadaxe'' in a frenetic counterattack.[60] Given the psychological stakes that Curley had invested in office, and given his repudiation at the polls, he tried to recapture his following by proving himself. In this case, he directed his invective at the GGA-sponsored City Council candidates in December's municipal election, and his metaphors were tinged with suggestions of violence. Particularly vicious in his assaults upon the greatly admired James J. Storrow, Curley charged ''millionaire Storrow,'' as he liked to call him, with trying to purchase the election and corrupt the city through favors to his affluent friends:

The whipping post, the branding on the forehead, the cropping of the ears, the scourging at the cat's tail, are light punishments for the rich man who would debauch a State . . . If we cannot apply them literally and physically, let the aroused public sentiment of his countrymen pillory and brand and scourge the infamous offender. Leave him to his infamy. Let him be an outcast from the companionship of free men.[61]

Curley, however, was the one who was pilloried. In the election, a record-breaking turnout swept Storrow and three other GGA-endorsed City Councillors into office.

From that point on, Curley's first term as Mayor deteriorated into something of a nightmare. Anyone remotely associated with his enemies was dismissed, civil service regulations became meaningless, exacting standards of political loyalty were demanded of all contractors wishing to do business with the city, and a stalemate developed between Curley and the City Council over pay raises for the Mayor's allies. Sickened by these and other developments, John A. Sullivan let it be known that he planned to quit. Curley, threatened by abandonment, then fired perhaps the one man in Boston who could have exercised a restraining influence, who could have legitimated the Curley administration by virtue of the intellectual and political tradition he represented.

Fed up with these excesses, or perhaps a bit bored, the electorate turned James Michael Curley out of office, and in January of 1918, Andrew J. Peters, a graduate of St. Paul's and Harvard, was inaugurated. Pledging non-partisan government, he drew loud applause when he promised to liberate the "unhappy victims" of Curley's "pernicious, partisan and personal politics."[62] For the moment, Bostonians preferred a man who spoke for bureaucratic normalcy and who represented, by virtue of his background, a more traditional source of authority. Peters, however, had the bad luck to sit as mayor during the Boston Police Strike of 1919, and he also had the misfortune to preside during the serious recession of 1919 to 1921. As Joseph Dinneen once observed, there came a time when Peters, a thoroughly honest man, "looked around blinking, bewildered and uncomprehending, not knowing what had happened. He never did figure it out."[63]

Curley, however, always alert to the political possibilities of strife-torn eras, rode the economic slump into office, just as he would do again in 1929 when he won his third term as mayor, in 1945 when reconversion from a wartime to a peacetime economy helped him to a fourth term, even while under a federal grand jury indictment for mail fraud in connection with defense contracts: in times of distress, Weber reminds us, the charismatic leader will likely be summoned. The converse, of course, is that in more tranquil moments, he will be dumped. James Michael Curley would also experience defeat. To Bostonians, he never became a man for all political seasons.

The constraints of space permit only a cursory overview of this extensive period ranging from the 1920s into the 1940s, and yet these years were an amplification of the tendencies I have been delineating. With the firing of John A. Sullivan, Curley cut himself off once and for all from the possibility of consorting with the more reflective, less frenzied, more cerebral mode of leadership offered by those who, as of the 1920s, might have been called the ''Irish Brahmins''—those who had laid claim to the O'Reilly-Roche-Collins tradition. In the election of 1921, for instance, Curley opposed John R. Murphy, O'Reilly's son-in-law and ''a man of intelligence and integrity.''[64] Curley's campaign may well have been the absolute nastiest in the city's history, although he eventually ran others almost as demagogic. More and more, he resorted to a bruising personal style, to appeals based on ethno-religious claims. In the process, he offended the state Democratic organization of which David Ignatius Walsh served as nominal head, and he could not get along with the Democratic City Committee—''a collection of chowder-heads,'' as he liked to call them.[65] Unwilling to stay within the confines of ''exclusive functional jurisdictions,'' he shunned a political mode based on routinized procedures. Curley could agree that a man like Malcolm Nichols was ''the fifty-third card in a pack—a joker.''[66] Nichols, Mayor from 1925 to 1929 and a man we now remember as the last Republican to occupy the mayor's chair, had had elaborate plans for tunnel and courthouse construction. From Curley's vantage point, however, he could not get things done: he simply had no bugle in his voice. To Curley, a mayor like Frederick Mansfield (1933-1937), he of the Walsh-Joseph B. Ely faction of the Democratic Party, was in James Michael's words ''as spectacular as a four-day-old codfish and as colorful as a lump of mud.''[67] As Boston increasingly became a one-party city, political alliances tended to become either pro-Curley or anti-Curley. In local contests, then, the Boston electorate was seldom treated to campaigns in which ideological considerations counted for much. The virtual disappearance of the Republican Party[68] caused the Democrats to continue to be highly factionalized. What were the costs of

Democratic in-fighting and the political instability that resulted?[69] As I see it, the costs were substantial.

During the Great Depression, Curley's fractious approach to politics, as I have argued elsewhere,[70] carried a price. The first big-city mayor to come out for Franklin Delano Roosevelt, Curley nevertheless was not trusted by New Dealers. Curley, of course, expected patronage from Roosevelt, as well as a major appointment for himself. He received neither—unless one counts the offer of an ambassadorship to Poland, a possibility that inspired Boston's anti-Curley humorists into some of their better efforts: if Curley took the post, one wag proclaimed, he would pave the Polish corridor. Within the Roosevelt administration, too, Curley was a butt of frequent jest. When Andrew Peters visited Roosevelt to tell him that Curley should not be appointed, for instance, Roosevelt advised the former mayor not to worry. "What is there in Poland that Curley would want to steal?" the President asked.[71]

On a far more serious level, intergovernmental relationships worked much less well than they should have from 1933 until early 1937, by which time James Michael was out of office. For reasons much too involved to be treated here, conflict between Curley, the Roosevelt administration, and the political faction headed by David I. Walsh, Joseph B. Ely, and Frederick Mansfield cost Boston as many as ten thousand Civil Works Administration jobs, kept the city from getting a penny of Public Works Administration assistance until 1935 (when a meagre $680,000 was received), delayed the start-up of the Works Progress Administration by at least six months, made a shambles of federally-financed public housing in the city, and postponed by almost a year the payment of unemployment compensation provided by the Social Security Act of 1935. Having long advocated federal intervention in public works and relief, James Michael Curley could not effectively use help from Washington when it arrived. As we have seen in other contexts, his tendency to "breed turmoil,"[72] and his inability to share power, proved damaging.

In 1936, 1937, and again in 1938, the electorate let it be known that it had had enough: Curley in succession lost to Henry Cabot Lodge for a seat in the United States Senate, to Maurice Tobin for another term as mayor, and to Leverett Saltonstall for a second term as governor. A Lodge and a Saltonstall! Traditional legitimation, it seemed, still enjoyed currency. A Brahmin like George Read Nutter—son of Harvard, president of the Massachusetts Bar Association, and a long-time Curley nemesis in the GGA—must have rejoiced. To Nutter, Curley had always appealed only to the "excitable" Irish, to those with no idea "of moral values in politics." To Nutter, Curley "defiled everything political—in standards, in methods, in cheapness and vulgarity."[73] The validating gesture of recognition from the proponents of "good government" had eluded Curley once again. When Roosevelt looked to Boston for people he could trust to install the New Deal, he looked not to Curleyites but to his son, James; to Harvard professors and to graduates of Harvard like the Democrat, LaRue Brown, and like the Republican, Arthur Rotch; to A. Lincoln Filene and Edward A. Filene; to Louis Kirstein, David Niles and other liberals plucked from the Jewish community; to Congressman John McCormack to some extent; and to Irish "of the better sort" who steered clear of Curley.

At the same time, however, Curley was not by any means the sole cause of the New Deal's rocky moments in Boston. Indeed, I would argue that he was more of a New Dealer, at least more of an urban liberal in Joseph Huthmacher's sense of the term, certainly, than most of his opponents—this despite his all-but-formal break with F.D.R. in the mid-1930s. Both as mayor and as governor, Curley enlarged on the social justice package he had assembled in the first twenty years of his public life. Well before New Dealers invented the NRA, Curley was advocating a national industrial planning board along the same lines. Like several other big-city mayors, he called for a massive infusion of federal funds for public works. As mayor and as governor, thought Secretary of Labor Frances Perkins, Curley had made "a conspicuously clear portrayal of major social issues. . . ." He could in the process be outrageous but, as Marion Frankfurter put it, "the odor of sanctity" was so strong that the Commonwealth needed "a shock or two." Curley delivered the jolt.[74]

In contrast to Curley, his rival Democrats and the old structural reformers he had battled in the Progressive era did at least as much to hamstring the New Deal in Boston as did Curley. The City Council, for instance, scuttled PWA projects when the ward representatives decided they did not want to match federal funds. On other occasions, CWA, FERA, and WPA projects were aborted because the city council would not appropriate money for equipment and supplies. Downtown real estate interests, many of them veterans of the now-defunct GGA, helped block both PWA and United States Housing Authority projects and lobbied against accepting federal money if matching grants were

involved. When it came down to a contest between the tax rate and
projects for the unemployed with these people, the tax rate won almost
every time. Meanwhile, the anti-New Deal fulminations of William
Cardinal O'Connell, the anti-Roosevelt tirades of the followers of Father
Charles Coughlin, and the many Democrats who followed Joseph B.
Ely into the American Liberty League combined to give Boston a rather
conservative tone in the years of the Great Depression. Roosevelt several
times dispatched Joseph P. Kennedy to Boston to reassure the citizenry
that New Dealers intended no radical change: a dash of urban liberalism
of the type left over from the Progressive Era was widely held to be
sufficient. Partly because of reservations about the New Deal, and partly
because from mid-decade on the voters were also being influenced by
foreign policy considerations,[75] Bostonians gave Roosevelt a declining
share of their vote in 1936, and again in 1940, becoming, as one observer
put it, the "Democratic laggard."[76]

And what of friend Curley? What of the sense of having grown up
in a world where his legitimacy had always been in doubt, where his
sense of survival had been precarious? Reports of his political death in
the late 1930s proved premature. Was his miraculous levitation—two
more terms in Congress and another four years as mayor—in fact miraculous? I think not. Had the New Deal, as Edwin O'Connor argued
in *The Last Hurrah*, rendered men of the Curley type obsolete? Clearly
not. Had ethnic politics yielded to some new political form? That Curley
was able to rout John Kerrigan in 1945 by 54,000 votes, the largest
margin for any mayoral candidate up to that point, would surely suggest
that if a new political mode develped in twentieth-century Boston, the
change must have come at some point beyond Curley's fourth term—
with the election of Hynes and Collins, perhaps.[77] Moreover, there were
as many City Council members who were of Irish descent from 1935
to 1950 as there had been from 1920 to 1935. Afro-Americans remained
outside the charmed circle, and although an occasional Langone or
Bromberg might break through, the color of Boston politics remained
distinctly green, and Curley took advantage of that fact.

In scenes reminiscent of Curley's turn-of-the-century jailing, Curley
won a smashing electoral victory in 1945 even though under indictment.
His followers, those to whom he had addressed his mission, as Max
Weber would have put it, those to whom he had proved himself, once
more recognized him as their charismatically qualified leader. His send-
off to Danbury prison bore a familiar look, and so did his return five

months later. At South Station the band played "Hail, the Conquering Hero Comes," and in front of the House with the Shamrock Shutters another band played "Hail to the Chief." At the urging of Congressman McCormack, James A. Farley, and others, President Harry S. Truman had extended executive clemency.[78] So, quite obviously, had tens of thousands of his supporters—but in the same fashion that had always been the case. Farther than that his legitimation could not go.

The Curley story, I believe, argues for the continuity of Boston politics in the first half of this century—and with the mention of Harry S. Truman something he once said comes to mind. "The only thing new in the world," he observed, "is history you don't know."[79] In the Boston context, this is an appropriate "amen."

Notes

1. E. Digby Baltzell, *Puritan Boston and Quaker Philadelphia: Two Protestant Ethics and the Spirit of Class Authority and Leadership* (New York: Free Press, 1979), p. 373.

2. Ibid., p. 376, and Frederic Cople Jaher, "Businessman and Gentleman: Nathan and Thomas Gold Appleton—An Exploration in Intergenerational History," *Explorations in Entrepreneurial History*, 4 (Fall, 1966): *passim*.

3. Max Weber, "The Sociology of Charismatic Authority," in H.H. Gerth and C. Wright Mills eds., *Max Weber: Essays in Sociology* (New York: Oxford University Press, 1958), p. 245.

4. Ibid.

5. "Inaugural Address of Hugh O'Brien," Jan. 5, 1885, *Boston City Documents*, No. 1 (1885), p. 63.

6. Weber, "The Sociology of Charismatic Authority," pp. 245-47.

7. William V. Shannon, *The American Irish* (New York: Macmillan, 1966), p. 232.

8. "Rare Reminiscence: Beginning of St. Patrick's Fifty Years Ago," *The Highland Chronicle*, Parts 3, 4, Jan. 24, 31, 1885, St. Patrick's Church Records, Dudley Street, Roxbury.

9. Oscar Handlin, *Boston's Immigrants*, rev. ed. (New York: Atheneum, 1969), p. 72.

10. "Charities of Boston," *North American Review* 91 (July, 1860): 149-65.

11. Based on a sample of 643 names beginning with the letter "C" in "Admissions, 1824-1873," Records of the Overseers of the Poor, Massachusetts Historical Society, Boston, Mass.

12. "Index to Passenger Lists of Vessels Arriving at Boston, 1848-1891,"
Boston Public Library, microfilm, Reels 58, 115.

13. In 1890, 65 per cent of Boston's foreign-born Irish filled low-manual
occupations, 25 per cent held semi-skilled or skilled blue-collar jobs, 10 per
cent had edged into some sort of white-collar occupations, and a scant 0.013
per cent had made it into the professions. Stephan Thernstrom, *The Other
Bostonians: Poverty and Progress in the American Metropolis, 1880-1970*
(Cambridge: Harvard University Press, 1973), p. 131. The Curleys of Boston
showed almost identical occupational configurations in this same period, and
there were also Curleys who, as in Professor Thernstrom's study, momentarily
moved from blue-collar status to that of "proprietors," only to skid back. Part
of the reason may be attributed to their inability to obtain credit. A plasterer
named Michael Curley, who had set up his own business, was found by a credit
agent in 1874 to be "a steady, hardworking Man—but of no means." He had
accumulated a modest debt, was having difficulty with payments, and was
deemed "not desirable for credit." Two years later, the agent called on Curley
again and tersely reported: "Same, honest but poor." Seven months later, the
agent wrote the aspiring proprietor's economic epitaph: "out of bus[iness]."
"Early Handwritten Credit Reporting Ledgers of the Mercantile Agency—
Massachusetts," I.G. Dun & Co. Credit Ledgers, Baker Liberty, Harvard
Business School, VII, 345.

14. In Boston, almost half the deaths in the last fifty years of the century
claimed children of five or under, and the death rate for Irish mothers and their
offspring was more severe than that of other immigrant groups (63 per cent
higher, for instance, than the rate for those of German origin), more than triple
that of native Americans, and steeper than the rate suffered by Philadelphia's
Irish. In Boston, more Irish births were attended by midwives than in Philadelphia; population density, some 59 persons per residential acre in the Curley
neighborhood, was thicker; and a greater percentage of the city's Irish lived in
tenements than was the case in the City of Brotherly Love. Moreover, there
seemed to be a correlation between the altitude at which one lived and the death
rate (even a difference of six to eight feet above sea level could make a remarkable difference)—and in Boston, where pneumonia and consumption caused
an unusual number of Irish deaths, too many of the Sons of Erin, like the
Curleys, lived along tidal flats. John S. Billings, "The Health of Boston and
Philadelphia," *The Forum* 17 (July, 1894): pp. 595-602.

15. Handlin, *Boston's Immigrants*, p. 60.

16. Boston Catholic Cemetery Association, "Register of Interments, Calvary
Cemetery, September 1, 1884, to January 30, 1886," IV; "Plan of Mt. Calvary
Cemetery, Roslindale, Mass."

17. While the Yeoman and Dearborn School janitors were exclusively Irish,
only two of the twenty-seven faculty and staff had recognizably Irish names.

"Dearborn School Rollbooks, 1880-1890," at the Dearborn St. School; *Annual Report of the School Committee of the City of Boston*, City Document No. 27 (1880), pp. 292-93, 307.

18. James Michael Curley, "My Hopes and Memories," *Boston Sunday Advertiser*, Sept. 30, 1934.

19. *Mercantile Agency Credit Ledgers, Massachusetts*, XVIII, 67; The Mercantile Agency, *Reference Book and Key . . .* 48 (March, 1880) and 109 (July, 1895); Brock's Commercial Agency, Ltd., *Credit Guide* 37 (January, 1886); and the Bradstreet Company, *Bradstreet's Commercial Reports*, 116 (January, 1897).

20. *Boston Sunday Post* (Color Feature Section), Sept. 21, 1930; Curley, "My Hopes and Memories," *Sunday Advertiser*, Sept. 30, 1934; and Curley, *I'd Do It Again: A Record of All My Uproarious Years* (Englewood Cliffs: Prentice Hall, N.J., 1957), p. 33.

21. "Opportunity and Optimism," Address by Mayor Curley to the South Boston Council No. 78, Knights of Columbus, January 6, 1915, *City Record*, January 9, 1915, pp. 30-31. Throughout Curley's career, he reserved a special place for other prominent men who had either lost their fathers at an early age, or for men whose fathers had been so greatly reduced in circumstances that they could not protect their sons. Abraham Lincoln, not surprisingly, exemplified the former, while William Shakespeare was frequently used to illustrate the latter.

22. Michael Ward to James Roosevelt, Nov. 15, 1938, James Roosevelt Mss., Franklin D. Roosevelt Library, Hyde Park, Box 20.

23. It has been suggested that Curley's oratorical brilliance appealed uniquely to those who were Irish. Herbert Zolot, for instance, states that "a romantic conception of politics had long attracted popular sentiment in Ireland," and he quotes approvingly a passage from Nicholas Mansergh's *The Irish Question, 1840-1921* (Toronto: University of Toronto Press, 1956), p. 267: " 'The call' had not been 'for a Fabian policy with its dullness and solid achievement . . . [but] for charismatic leadership, for personality rather than principle, with faith in oratory rather than argument, in the picturesque rather than the precise, in the spectacular triumph rather than the steady advance.' " Yet another historian of Ireland speaks of the "gift for sparkling ridicule and deadly invective," for "quick impulses" that had never been "steadied by use of power." While these points are seductive, it is also the case that thousands of non-Irish also found Curley mesmeric. Herbert Zolot, "The Issue of Good Government and James Michael Curley" (Ph.D. diss., State University of New York at Stony Brook, 1975), pp. 228-30.

24. *City Directory* (1892). Not until 1894, three years after going to work at C.S. Johnson's grocery store, did he come clean and have himself listed in the *City Directory* as a clerk. Even this designation may have been a bit inflated.

25. Quoting the classics, one of Curley's forensic trademarks, does not appear in his public speeches until 1906. Had he acquired the mastery of literature he sometimes ascribed to his boyhood, it stands to reason that he would have employed literary quotations earlier in his political career. For a discussion of his oratorical style, see Zolot, "The Issue of Good Government," pp. 228-37.

26. Leon Edel, "The Figure Under the Carpet," in Marc C. Pachter, ed., *Telling Lives: The Biographer's Art* (Washington, D.C.: New Republic Books, 1979), pp. 24-25.

27. For a discussion of this pattern of leadership, see Sylvan Tomkins, "The Psychology of Commitment," in Martin Duberman, ed., *The Anti-Slavery Vanguard* (Princeton: N.J.: Princeton University Press, 1965), pp. 270-98.

28. This and subsequent quotations from the case are from Circuit Court and District Court indictments, transcripts, recognizances, and opinions, Federal Records Center, Waltham, Mass., File 82410, unless otherwise cited.

29. *Journal*, Sept. 25, 1903.

30. *Post*, Sept. 25, 1903.

31. Guild A. Copeland, "An Insolvent Utopia," Harper's *Weekly*, 44 (June 16, 1900): 549.

32. One of the "Creole Belles" was Mary Ellen Herlihy who, four years later, married Curley.

33. *Journal* and *Globe*, Nov. 7, 1904.

34. *Herald* and *Globe*, Jan. 7, 1905.

35. *United States* v. *Biggs*, 157 F. 264 (D. Colo. 1907).

36. The *Sacred Heart Review*, for instance, wrote that the only regret of discerning Catholics would be "that the punishment is altogether inadequate to the gravity of the offense." *Sacred Heart Review*, Jan. 14, 1905, clipping, Good Government Association Mss., Massachusetts Historical Society, Box 12.

37. Peter K. Eisinger, "Ethnic Political Transition in Boston, 1884-1933: Some Lessons for Contemporary Cities," *Political Science Quarterly* 93 (Summer, 1978): 217-39.

38. The distinction between social and structural reform is discussed at length in Melvin Holli, *Reform in Detroit: Hazen Pingree and Urban Politics* (New York: Oxford University Press, 1969), pp. 157-81.

39. Eric F. Goldman, *Rendez-vous with Destiny* (New York: Knopf, 1956; rev. ed., Vintage, 1960), especially pp. 66-81.

40. *Proceedings of the City Council of Boston*, March 26, 1906, pp. 324-25, hereafter cited *PCCB*.

41. Ibid., Feb. 3, 17, 1908, pp. 73-74, 137.

42. Ibid., May 4, 1908, p. 390.

43. Ibid., May 18, 1908, pp. 431-32.

44. This summary is based on a reading of all of his speeches recorded in the City Council *Proccedings*, 1900-1911, plus innumerable newspaper articles.

45. J. Joseph Huthmacher, "Urban Liberalism and the Age of Reform," *Mississippi Valley Historical Review*, 49 (September, 1962): 231-41.

46. These might include votes against transporting boxing films across state lines, attempts to control the manufacture and sale of liquor, and corrupt practices legislation.

47. *Congressional Record*, 62nd Cong., lst sess., April 20, 1911, pp. 516-17.

48. Ibid., May 3, 1911, p. 916.

49. Curley to Woodrow Wilson, March 25, 1913, Wilson Mss. (microfilm) Series 2, Reel 46.

50. *Congressional Record*, 62nd Cong., 3rd Sess., June 25, 1913, pp. 2032.

51. Ibid., 62nd Cong., 2nd Sess., Aug. 7, 1912, p. 10421.

52. Ibid., p. 10424. The literacy test, said Curley on another occasion, "makes provisions for the entry of the nonproducing class, preachers, teachers, and so forth, and aims to restrict admission of the producing class, despite the fact that the true source of national wealth and prosperity results from the work of those who toil with their hands and brains rather than brains alone." Ibid., 62nd Cong., 3rd sess., Jan. 25, 1913, p. 2031.

53. For the episode of the pen, see correspondence between Curley and Rudolph Foster, Feb. 15-20, 1913, William Howard Taft Mss. (microfilm), Series 6, Item 3686, Reel 446, and Series 8, Item 200, Reel 516. Two years later, though no longer a member of Congress, Curley rushed to Washington for a hearing in the East Room of the White House when the literacy test was again an issue. J.M.C. to Joseph Timulty, Jan. 6, 16, 17, 1915, Wilson Mss., Series 4, Item 292, Reel 251.

54. *Herald*, clipping filed April, 1914, James Michael Curley Scrapbooks, Book A-4, Dinand Library, College of the Holy Cross, Worcester, Mass., hereafter cited "JMC-SB."

55. *Journal*, March 7, 1914, clipping in *ibid.*, Book A-2. The *Herald* echoed this praise, finding "his general course" in his first month in office to be "astonishingly intelligent and unmistakably courageous."

56. Richard M. Abrams, *Conservatism in a Progressive Era, 1900-1912* (Cambridge, Mass.: Harvard University Press, 1980) p. 133. See also Richard B. Sherman, "The Status Revolution and Massachusetts Progressive Leadership," *Political Science Quarterly* 78 (March, 1963): *passim*.

57. *PCCP*, May 2, 1904, pp. 167-179.

58. Ibid., Oct. 5, 1908, pp. 643-644.

59. This portrait of Curley's darker side is based on all issues of the *PCCB*, 1900-1914, newspaper accounts, 1900-1913, and the Curley scrapbooks, 1914-1918.

60. *Boston Record*, Nov. 29, 1915, clipping, JMC-SB No. A-15.

61. *Post*, Dec. 6, 1915, clipping in *ibid*.

62. *PCCB*, Feb. 4, 1918, p. 3.

63. Quoted in Francis Russell, *A City in Terror: The 1919 Boston Police Strike* (New York: Viking Press, 1977), pp. 224-25.

64. Russell, *A City in Terror*, p. 224.

65. Shannon, *The American Irish*, p. 210.

66. *PCCB*, Jan. 4, 1930, pp. 428-29.

67. Curley, *I'd Do It Again*, p. 192.

68. By 1929, for instance, some 124,000—67 percent—of Boston's registered voters were Democrats.

69. By "political instability," I am referring to the fact that in the period from 1927 to 1931, the cumulative turnover rate in sixty-six ward contests for the city council amounted to 33 per cent, an extraordinarily high level when compared to a city like Chicago. In eighty-eight such races from 1933 to 1939, the cumulative turnover rate reached an astonishing 41 percent. From 1927 to 1939, seven ward elections were held to fill seats in the 22-member city council— a total of 154 contests. On the average, approximately 4.5 candidates could be found fighting it out in any given ward in any one of these races. Truly, the Democratic Party had become sprawling and inchoate.

70. Charles H. Trout, *Boston, The Great Depression, and the New Deal* (New York: Oxford University Press, 1977), especially pp. 147-72.

71. Robert Lincoln O'Brien, Columbia Oral History Collection, No. 81, p. 162.

72. Florence Brennan to Roosevelt, March 22, 1933, President's Official File No. 5434, Roosevelt Library, Hyde Park, N.Y.

73. George Read Nutter Diary, XXII, Oct. 9, Nov. 1-2, 1929, Massachusetts Historical Society.

74. Quoted in Trout, *Boston, the Great Depression, and the New Deal*, p. 282.

75. John F. Stack, Jr., *International Conflict in an American City: Boston's Irish, Italians, and Jews, 1935-1944* (Westport, Ct.: Greenwood Press, 1979), *passim*. Stack suggests that in the 1935-1944 period, ethno-centrism grew in Boston, a finding I extensively argued in *Boston, the Great Depression, and the New Deal*.

76. Robert K. Massey, Jr., "The Democratic Laggard: Massachusetts in 1932," *New England Quarterly*, 44 (December, 1971), pp. 553-74.

77. For an excellent discussion of this possibility, see Thomas O'Connor, *Bibles, Brahmins, and Bosses* (Boston: Trustees of the Public Library of the City of Boston, 1976), pp. 128-38. O'Connor argues that Bostonians, by rejecting Curley in the election of 1949, and by turning first to Hynes and then to Collins, were returning to leadership in the mode of Hugh O'Brien and Patrick A. Collins.

78. Harry S. Truman to James A. Farley, Sept. 26, 1947, Farley Mss., Library of Congress, lc, Box 25, and Truman Mss. on microfilm at the BPL.

79. Merle Miller, *Plain Speaking: An Oral Biography of Harry S. Truman* (New York: Berkeley Publishing Co., 1973), p. 70.

Part III
The City at 350: Pluralist or Fragmented?

8

Boston's Irish Mayors: An Ethnic Perspective

WILLIAM V. SHANNON

People of Irish birth and ancestry have played an important and often decisive role in the history of Boston over the last century in many different fields—in education, religion, business, in medicine and law, and most visibly and significantly in politics. The first Irish-born mayor of this city was Hugh O'Brien, who took office in 1886. The second was Patrick A. Collins, who was elected in 1901. Beginning with Collins, twelve men have served as mayor of Boston in the eighty years of this century. Nine have been of Irish ancestry. This Irish hegemony has been unbroken for the past fifty years.[1] No ethnic group in any other American city rivals this record of uninterrupted political influence although the Irish in Chicago have come close. (Chicago has had mayors of Irish ancestry for all but two of the last forty-seven years.) This essay will consider the part played by these American Irish mayors in the history of Boston and will view the office of mayor in an ethnic perspective.

It will be primarily concerned with the fifty years from 1910 to 1960, an era that began with the election of John F. Fitzgerald in 1910 and ended with the retirement of John B. Hynes in 1960. My decision to stop in 1960 is due to more than a diplomat's discretion in not commenting upon recent mayors who happily are still very much with us. There are also intellectually valid reasons for believing that these fifty years form a coherent period in the city's history, the era when the Irish alone had control of the politics of the city.

The period from 1880 to 1910 comprised the initial period of Irish participation in the political administration of the city. During the late nineteenth century the Irish held the mayoralty for only four years, but Irish representation on the huge City Council—it then had 75 members—

increased in size, and party bosses began to emerge at the ward level. In the first decade of the twentieth century, Irish contested with Yankees for the mayoralty while dominating the Common Council and the Board of Aldermen.[2] In 1910 John F. Fitzgerald won a narrow but decisive victory over James J. Storrow, Yankee banker and civic leader. That election, as two previous chapters by Blodgett and Burns make clear, was viewed by contemporaries—and it has been agreed by historians—marked a turning point.[3] Henceforth the Irish were to be in control of the politics and government of the city. Its destiny would be fought out within their ranks. How they would respond to that challenge would be the main thread in the political narrative for the next half century and beyond.

Although Fitzgerald's victory in 1910 marked the transition of political power, it was James M. Curley who dominated the era.[4] Curley's first city-wide victory in 1913 consolidated Irish control. Defeated in 1917 by opposition from other Irish political bosses, he triumphed again in 1921. The two decades following 1921 were the years of his personal supremacy. Throughout that period Curley was either in office as mayor or the most probable winner of the next mayoral election. The final decades from 1941 to 1961 represent the slow waning of Curley's power and the lingering aftermath of his departure from the place of leadership. Of the two mayors with whom he had principally shared power in those years, Maurice Tobin had been his personal protege while John B. Hynes had spent his entire previous career in the municipal bureaucracy in Curley's shadow. Curley's death in 1958 and Hynes' voluntary retirement a year later brought this period to a close.

This bare political chronology, however, does not do justice to the significance of the politics of these years. Politics is more than a matter of personalities and elections. It is one of the most important ways in which people work out their own sense of themselves as individuals and as members of groups. Are they, for example, hopeful about the future or pessimistic? Are they venturesome in their major decisions or conservative? The political setting in which they live helps shape their individual answers to these questions. Similarly politics determines not only how a city is governed but also, more profoundly, how its people think of their community. Are they proud to be Bostonians or apologetic? Do they look back upon their city's history with satisfaction or with anger? The way in which people participate in politics and the extent to which they believe themselves to be effective in influencing public affairs are important in determining whether they feel they belong in the city and the city belongs to them, or whether they feel the city is an alien and hostile environment.

The election of 1910 marked the transition of political power from Yankee to Irish, and it should not be surprising that it was not a smooth or trouble-free transfer: from Yankee to Irish, from Protestant to Catholic, from Brahmin aristocracy and business classes to working class, from 250 years of history to a new beginning: such changes mark an historic break in tradition as well as a transition of power. Viewed from a different perspective, of course, from that of world history, the transition was very smooth indeed. It was not accompanied by fascism or terrorism, by revolutionary violence or social turmoil that have accompanied social change in many countries. On the contrary the shift in power from Beacon Hill and the Back Bay to Roxbury and Dorchester, from men such as Josiah Quincy, George Hibbard and James Storrow to John F. Fitzgerald and James M. Curley was accomplished in free and peaceful democratic elections. But by the stricter standard, not of world history but of America's own democratic ideals, there was a shortfall in the performance in Boston in that period. The change was marked by a narrowness, a withholding of moral legitimacy toward the new regime by the dispossessed Yankees; it was marked by a politics of anger and catharsis on the part of the newly empowered Irish. This mixture of negative attitudes cast a long shadow over Boston for a half century and longer.

For fifty years the relations between the groups had been exacerbated by religious, ethnic, and cultural differences. Economic power and social prestige were very much in the hands of the city's Yankee elite.[5] Of course that would be true in almost every American city, for the Irish and other immigrants inevitably started out as client groups in an economically dependent position. Only in San Francisco were there American Irish entrepreneurs among the city's banking and business elite from the very outset.[6] But the dimensions of Boston's gap were unique. Perhaps most important of all was the cultural prestige of Boston's elite. They were, after all, the direct descendants of the people who had founded the city itself, who had founded Harvard College, who had organized the Boston Tea Party, placed the lanterns in Old North Church, fought the Battle of Bunker Hill, and put their John Hancock on the Declaration of Independence. In their great writers they had produced much of what could be called native American culture.

In more recent times Wendell Phillips and other Boston abolitionists had earned the glory of leading the fight to end human slavery on this continent. It would be a very long time before any member of the Boston Irish community could point to accomplishments of his own or his group to place alongside these mountain peaks of achievement— and both Yankees and Irish were aware of it. This sense of civic pride and achievement made Yankees reluctant to surrender political leadership in what Harriet Beecher Stowe had called "the sacred city" of New England Yankees.[7]

Boston, however, did not share directly in the great expansion of heavy industry that occurred in the United States in the late nineteenth and early twenteith century. It made its living from banking, commerce, shipping, and from service industries. The banks, insurance companies, and many other commercial firms quietly but persistently refused to employ Catholics for white-collar jobs. Even for ordinary jobs in manufacturing and domestic service there were still in the 1880s and 1890s the now-notorious advertisements, "No Irish Need Apply" or "Wanted— Young Ladies of Anglo-Saxon Parentage."

At the beginning of the twentieth century, the urban reforms of the Progressive Era culminated in the rationalizing, almost the depoliticizing, of city government. The mayor retained a critical role but one close to that of the executive of a large corporation. Yankees tended to regard city government as a machine for dispensing services to a city: policing its streets, putting out its fires, assuring its water supply, operating its rapid transit. The task of the chief executive was to see to it that these services were provided in a planned, orderly way at the lowest possible cost and in the most efficient manner. Ideally, politics had nothing to do with these tasks; it was a matter of engineers and managers, devoted to efficiency and sharing the core values of the Yankee group.[8]

For the immigrant poor who made up the majority in Boston and many other American cities in the late nineteenth and early twentieth centuries, their first political need was not the efficient, economical delivery of services, important and desirable as that was; rather their need was to be integrated into the larger community. They had to feel that Boston was really their city and that its government belonged to them. They had to close the gap between "we" and "they," between their sense of themselves as strangers, as powerless newcomers, and their sense of the government as something remote, as an instrument of power under the control of "them"—however "them" might be defined—and as an instrument which they feared would be unlikely to be used in their interest and might very well be used against them.

In addition to the perhaps inevitable sense of apartness that any immigrant group would have in a new city, the Irish also brought an awareness of the uses of politics. Most of them came from rural, western Ireland where local govenment was in the hands of an Anglo-Irish land-lord class backed by the British army and police. The political history of nineteenth century Ireland was essentially a struggle to break that monopoly. During that long struggle, the ordinary Irish people had shown formidable talents for political conspiracy and political agitation. They arrived in the United States a politicized people and they retain this characteristic. The Irish had been able to extract such concessions as they did in Ireland by community solidarity. As a result, their political culture puts a high value on loyalty and on strong leadership.

In their dealings with their rulers in "the big house" and in Dublin Castle, they had recourse to individual wiliness and verbal obfuscation. They became famous for their "blarney," their "soft answers" that made refusal sound like agreement, and for what one biographer of Daniel O'Connell termed "that most Kerryish form of silence: an excess of volubility." These highly developed verbal skills aided Irish poli-ticians in Boston and other cities in dealing with the heterogeneous circumstances of American life and in making the compromises and accommodations that are central to the reconciling tasks of politics.

But violence was also endemic in much of rural Ireland as tenant farmers and landless laborers struggled to overthrow the landlord sys-tem, and nationalist groups like the Fenians conspired to bring Ireland its freedom by the use of force. The Irishman as rebel is a tradition counterposed to that of the Irishman as politician. Professor Thomas Brown in a recent essay has vividly illuminated these two competing political traditions:

The Irish-American politician is an organization man . . . the ability to ac-commodate differences, to find when in office suitable compromises in moral and other dilemmas, is his particular function. The rebel is of a different order. He rejects compromise and pursues principles, even unto death. The moral distance between the rebel and the politician is immense: the rebel seeks justice, the politician is content with order.[9]

Since the Irish so quickly found their way into political power in the open American system, they had relatively little recourse on this side of the Atlantic to violence or to the moral absolutism of the rebel, but his romantic appeal lingered in the popular imagination. The verbal recklessness and swaggering style of James M. Curley evoke echoes of the rebel.

This then was the political background from which the Boston Irish derived their political values. Their immigrant-minority, rebellious, personalistic emphasis led to one kind of politics; the Yankee majority with their historical status, institutional orientation, stress on rationalization, led to rather another. Yet politics had been one of the significant means of bridging the gap between the two cultures. Leaders among both sections of the city were uneasily aware of the overriding priority to reconcile the diverging traditions and to build bridges between them. Among the Yankees, Nathan Matthews, Josiah Quincy, joined with such Irish as John Boyle O'Reilly and Patrick Collins to effect a politics of accommodation.[10] But the weight of history, the tensions of decades of Irish thrust and Yankee recoil, made a transition difficult. With the defeat of their "best" candidate, James J. Storrow, in 1910, the Yankees retreated to a position of a minority of moralizing critics; with the subsequent election of James M. Curley in 1913, the Irish turned to the politics of catharsis.

In 1910 John F. Fitzgerald was re-elected to an office from which he had been ejected three years before; his cries for "vindication" from the charges which had once defeated him had been answered. Returning to the mayor's office, he brought the talents of a showman. Genial, smiling, easily fluent, he was variously known as "the little general," "Honey Fitz," "Fitzy," or "John F." He began the custom of lighting a Christmas tree on the Common and he built the first bandstand there— two decisions of which the city's Puritan founders would surely have disapproved! He liked to sing and, although his repertoire was considerable, he became best known for his rendition of "Sweet Adeline." Fitzgerald was a booster and a salesman. He coined the slogan, "A Bigger, Better, and Busier Boston."[11]

Fitzgerald had an extraordinarily wide personal acquaintance and depended upon his personal friendships and alliances with ward leaders to win elections. In part because elections were non-partisan, control of the Democratic City Committee and the formal party organization counted for little. Every election was an internal "family fight" among Democrats. There was no party machine, no Boston version of Tammany Hall or the Cook County Democratic organization. Politics was intensely parochial as well. Although Boston is physically compact, it was still a big place to the ordinary voter of the period. His attachment was to his parish and his neighborhood. He thought of himself as, first of all, a resident of the North End or Charlestown, of South Boston or Hyde Park. Fitzgerald dealt with the city's problems in terms of these neighborhood loyalties, balancing a favor done for South Boston with a project for Dorchester. He walked the streets of Boston like the experienced monsignor of a large parish, able to greet constituents by name and tell where this one's father worked and what county in Ireland that one's mother came from.

When James Michael Curley became mayor in 1913 upon Fitzgerald's retirement, he continued this highly personal and feudal style of politics. But he brought a new rhetoric, a new ruthlessness, and a bravura personal manner. Curley clearly appealed to something deep in the makeup of the Boston community, since he had remarkable staying power. Thirty-nine years old when he was first elected mayor, he left office as mayor for the last time thirty-six years later in 1949, when he was seventy-five. He was defeated for re-election in 1917, coming in second in a field of four. The state legislature then changed the law to prevent anyone from serving two successive terms. Curley returned to serve as mayor from 1921 to 1925 and from 1929 to 1933. He served a single term as governor in the years 1934-1936, lost in his quest for a United States Senate seat in 1936, and returned to Boston for his political wars in 1937. He lost that year, but very nearly regained the office in 1941, and finally did so in 1945.

During the 1920s, Curley dwarfed his rivals. Fitzgerald, who had been a ward leader of "the dear old North End" was as mayor only a little more than first among his political equals, the other ward leaders. But by the time Curley had finished his second term in 1925, only the legendary Martin Lomasney still had an independent power base as a ward boss that was significant, and among potential candidates for city-wide office there was none who could match Curley's drawing power.[12]

Curley shattered the cultural consensus that had existed in Boston. Previous Irish mayors had appealed overtly or discreetly to Irish and Catholic group loyalties but they had not attacked the Yankee community or questioned its cultural preeminence and civic values. On the contrary, there had for decades been a conscious effort on both sides to reach across the cultural divide. Curley, however, derided the Yankee community and its most prestigious institutions, from Harvard College to Beacon Hill. In a letter to a member of the Harvard Board of Overseers, he wrote: "The Massachusetts of the Puritans is as dead as Caesar, but there is no need to mourn the fact. Their successors—the Irish—had letters and learning, culture and civilization when the ancestors of the Puritans were savages running half-naked through the forests of Britain. It took the Irish to make Massachusetts a fit place to live in."

He attacked wealthy Yankees as the descendants of scoundrels who "got rich selling opium to the Chinese, rum to the Indians, or trading in slaves."

On another occasion, Curley said, "The term 'codfish aristocracy' is a reflection on the fish."

He derided the Good Government Association as "Goo Goos," denounced the business leaders as "The State Street Wrecking Crew," and characterized bankers as "insolent, arrogant sharpies, swindling the city of all they could get away with, while at the same time prating about the high cost of Government."[13]

The details of Jim Curley's long and colorful career are well-known or readily accessible. Instead of reviewing those events, we might look rather at the needs of the people in the Boston community to which Curley's career was a response. He provided, first of all, the politics of catharsis. It was an emotionally wrenching experience to move from a tiny farm in Galway or Kerry to the commercial and industrial life of an American city. It was unquestionably a step forward to a better life for the immigrants and particularly for their children, but it was not a step forward into an easier life. On the contrary, rural life in western Ireland, although impoverished in a material sense, was a life lived to an undemanding pace in accordance with the slow rhythms of nature, in a mild climate, amid beautiful lake and mountain scenery, and under spectacular, rapidly changing northern skies. A man who made his living by driving a team of horses through narrow, traffic-choked Boston streets, or who did monotonous repetitive tasks in a noisy factory and who returned each night to a cold-water tenement might well ask himself whether he had gotten the better of the deal by exchanging life on the farm in the old country for life in the city in America. The big difference was hope; there was hope for better things here; there was little ground for hope in Ireland. But, as the Spanish say, hope makes a good breakfast but a lean supper. When there were severe economic hardships in Boston, when the local economy grew very slowly or failed to grow at all, when the Irish felt themselves patronized or looked down upon, when too many chairs at the banquet table of life bore a sign, "Reserved for Others," then the Irish immigrants or their sons and daughters could experience rage, resentment and frustration.

There might be little, in reality, that the head of the municipal government, be he Mayor Curley or anyone else, could do to alter these objective circumstances. But at least he could give vent to those emotions and act them out and, by doing so, make them legitimate.

Jim Curley, in his attacks on the "State Street Wrecking Crew" and the Brahmin aristocrats of Harvard College and the Back Bay, seems in retrospect to have been a demagogue of a fairly benign variety. His flights of rhetoric grew more gorgeous as the ostensible targets of his wrath diminished in power and, as a political force within the city, dwindled almost to the vanishing point.

In another, more positive role, Curley provided the politics of social service.[14] In an era when the federal and state governments had few programs to help the urban working classes to cope with the hazards of life, Curley, like major politicians in other big cities, provided through his own political organization some of the elements of a rudimentary welfare state. He helped unemployed men to find jobs, got drunken husbands and wayward boys out of jail, gave money or clothing to people hit by misfortune, and organized picnics, dances and outings at the beach. As Mayor, he invested municipal funds in the development of the City Hospital and of beaches, bath houses, playgrounds, and other recreation projects. He billed himself as "Mayor of the Poor" and this claim had some substance. The taxpayers' organizations and other enemies of Curley naturally stressed allegations of bribery in the allocation of contracts, of payroll padding, and of kickbacks. We can assume that these accusations were not without foundation, but it is also true that the facilities and public improvements that Curley constructed were needed and that the jobs that these projects generated were always welcome in a local economy that was chronically depressed. Moreover, when municipal bankruptcy is a real and present danger in New York and Cleveland as it was in Fall River fifty years ago, it is worth noting that, if Boston did not get everything it paid for, at least it paid for everything it got. Curley in his prime was an intelligent and forceful executive who conducted the city's business with vigor and competence.

Finally, Curley practiced the politics of entertainment. He was the

Mayor as Mythmaker, the colorful figure bigger than life. Our textbooks
do not prepare us to think of politics as a field of entertainment. Yet,
long before television, politicians recognized that in addition to other
attributes, it is useful to have what Noel Coward called "the talent to
amuse," and they developed mannerisms and props that became their
trademarks, such as Theodore Roosevelt's Rough Rider Hat and Al
Smith's Brown Derby and Franklin D. Roosevelt's cigarette holder. In
Boston politics, for forty years from the 1890s until the 1930s, ward
boss Martin Lomasney made the disclosure of his preferences in each
year's Democratic Party primary into an annual ritual. He held a meeting
of his supporters in his clubhouse the Sunday before the election and
harangued them for two hours or more. It was part of his routine that
he began by removing his suit coat, later discarding his tie, and finally
pulling off his detachable collar. His followers would have been dis-
appointed if he had made known his political views fully clothed or in
any faster time.

For most people even today in this relatively affluent and comfortable
age, life is a struggle, and in Curley's time, ordinary people found life
hard. Many turned to politics because they enjoyed politicking. As a
form of entertainment, politics is analogous both to a sporting competition on the field and to a melodrama on the stage. There are heroes
and villains, the thrust and parry of conflict, the rising tension of the
campaign reaching a clear-cut decision on election day.

In all ways that politics can entertain and beguile and divert, Curley
became a master. He dressed stylishly. He developed a resonant baritone
voice and became an accomplished orator. He could work his way across
the whole rhetorical range from savage, colloquial invective to formal
exhortation, adorned with Shakespearean quotations and historical al-
lusions. He could be defiant, insouciant, quick-witted. In a city that
loves politics as if it were a game, Curley was a great gamester, prolific
in devising ruses, planting divisive stories about the opposition, and
delighting in controversy and combat. In short, he was more interesting
to have around than most people are. Unwittingly, Curley's enemies
helped to prolong the appeal of his showmanship by enacting a law—
later repealed—that forbade mayors from serving consecutive terms in
office.[15] This meant that there was a new mayor every four years. In
what had become a one-party city, it achieved rotation in office more
effectively than a two-party system might have done. It served also to
renew Curley's appeal by giving him periodic seasons out of the limelight.

Andrew Peters who defeated Curley for re-election in 1917 was the last Yankee mayor elected on his own merits. When Curley retired in 1925 after his second term, Malcolm Nichols became mayor; but it was widely believed that his victory was due not to his own strength as a candidate, much less to that of the Republican Party of which he was a member, but to the covert assistance of Curley, who did not want a strong Irish mayor to succeed him. Peters and Nichols drew the votes not only of the dwindling Yankee element in Boston but also of the city's growing Irish middle class. Many voters in this latter group had never approved of Curley's aggression and flamboyance. They longed for another leader in the mold of Patrick Collins. When Curley retired from his third term as Mayor in 1933, these voters prevailed with the election of Frederick Mansfield, a conservative and respectable lawyer.[16]

When Curley sought to resume office in 1937, he was defeated by Maurice J. Tobin.[17] This was in part a generational change. Tobin was thirty-six and Curley sixty-three. Tobin had been a member of Curley's organization and was a personal protege, but now he and other younger men wanted to move into the places of leadership, supplanting Curley and his aging cronies. It was also in part a shift in rhetoric and political base. Tobin appealed to those members of the Irish community who in increasing numbers were developing a new outlook. Tobin put together an alliance of middle-class Irish, Yankee aristocrats, and a majority of the Jewish community. He substituted conciliation and consensus for Curley's confrontational style. An exceptionally handsome man and an increasingly good public speaker, he projected an attractive personal image. He won in part, however, for other reasons: the lowest income groups, which had always been the hard core of Curley's strength, were disillusioned with his gubernatorial failure to solve the unemployment problem and had hopes that Tobin would be more effective in getting federal money. When the hope was not fulfilled, Curley recaptured this strength in subsequent elections. Although the state legislature changed the law to make him able to seek a second consecutive term in 1941, he was barely able to beat back Curley's challenge. The recession of 1937, which persisted in Boston until the outbreak of World War II, convinced the least well-off segment of the Boston Irish of the truth of the old adage Curley and his adherents assiduously promoted for decades, ''Curley spends money and that means jobs.''

The election returns of 1941, 1945, and 1949 reflect this attitude. Of the city's twenty-two wards, the first eleven (with the exception of

Wards 4 and 5, which are the Republican Back Bay–Beacon Hill area)
are the worst parts of the city in terms of income and housing. Here
Curley ran well: Charlestown, East Boston, South Boston, the North
and West Ends, and Roxbury. The wards from 12 through 22 represent
the more affluent parts of the city. Here Curley, except in one or two
neighborhoods, did poorly, but "affluence" is only a comparative term.
There were many workingmen and their families and many poorly paid
schoolteachers, salespeople, and clerks living in these wards. The cleavage was cultural as much as economic, and it was producing a growing
incomprehension between the two parts of the city.

When Tobin was elected governor in 1944, John Kerrigan, president
of the City Council, became mayor and served the remaining year of
Tobin's term. In 1945, Curley was elected to his fourth term, his first
return to the mayor's office since he left it a dozen years before. Midway
in his term, in July 1947, he confirmed all the worst assumptions of
his opponents when he was convicted of conspiracy in connection with
World War II military contracts and departed to serve five months in
federal prison. It was impossible to allow the President of the City
Council to serve as acting mayor in Curley's absence because he, too,
was under investigation in a different scandal. As a result, the state
legislature authorized the City Clerk to serve as temporary mayor. The
clerk was John B. Hynes. Hynes administered the city's routine affairs
in a competent, unspectacular fashion for the five months that Curley
was away. After the five-month incarceration was over Curley returned
to the mayoralty and the cheers of his followers and Hynes returned to
his job as City Clerk.[18]

In the absence of any prominent politician well positioned to challenge
Curley in 1949, Hynes was the choice of the same coalition that had
elected Tobin. Hynes won in a close race with 138,000 votes to Curley's
126,000. But he did not poll a clear majority because two other candidates drew off a small number of votes. The more notable of the two
was Patrick J. "Sonny" McDonough whose appeal was to the Curley
constituency. The closeness of the vote underlines the durability of
Curley's appeal to Bostonians who felt themselves best represented by
his neighborhood-oriented politics and by his disdain of the more cosmopolitan attitude.

Because of another change in the charter, Hynes's first term was
shortened from four years to two.[19] He was re-elected to full terms in
1951 and 1955, thus serving a full decade in office. Hynes's record in

his five months as temporary mayor turned out to be a good forecast of the ten years he served in his own right. He was an administrator, not an innovator. It could hardly have been otherwise. If one were looking for imaginative leadership to map out new directions for the city, one would not be likely to look for such leadership from a man who had spent twenty-nine years slowly progressing through the ranks of the civil service.

During the decade from 1950 to 1960, the city's population declined by over 100,000 persons. Large sections of its business district became shabby and unkempt. Some inner city neighborhoods were slowly decaying into slums. As the decade ended, Boston seemed set in a downward drift. Neither the Curley style of confrontation nor the alternate politics of accommodation as practiced in these years seemed to point a satisfactory way toward addressing the problems of the future.[20]

The election of John F. Kennedy to the Presidency in 1960, although it had nothing directly to do with the municipality, proved an important psychological event for Boston and its citizens, particularly the Irish. For a people so preoccupied with politics, the election of one of their own to the highest political office was a dream come true. It seemed to do away with any lingering sense of inferiority; it liberated energy and idealism among the young. The fact that Kennedy was the grandson of two turn-of-the-century ward bosses, "Honey Fitz" and P. J. Kennedy, cast a glow over the parochial battles of that earlier generation and retrospectively legitimated the political takeover of the city by the Irish. As the new president reached out to surround himself in Washington with McGeorge Bundy, Archibald Cox, Arthur Schlesinger, Jerome Wiesner and other leading figures from the faculties of Harvard and MIT, the old cultural divisions between Irish and Yankee were bridged and transcended in a way that could not have been foreseen in the generation of Josiah Quincy and John Boyle O'Reilly.

From within its own ranks, meanwhile, Boston in the same year began to find under the leadership first of Mayor Collins and later of Mayor White the capacity to renew itself, with politics as the catalyst of that renewal.

Notes

1. A most useful source for any study of urban politics is *The Biographical Dictionary of American Mayors, 1820-1980*, ed. Melvin G. Holli and Peter

d'A. Jones (Westport, Ct.: Greenwood Press, 1981), hereafter referred to as BDAM.

2. *A Catalog of the City Councils . . . and the Selectmen of Boston* (Boston: City Printing Department, 1909). This listing shows the gradual but inexorable growth of Irish strength in the city, from 1860 when they dominated two wards of the city's twelve to 1900 when they dominated a majority of the larger city's twenty-five wards.

3. Geoffrey Blodgett, "Yankee Leadership in a Divided City 1860-1910," in *Boston 1700-1980: Evolution of Urban Politics*, ed. Ronald P. Formisano and Constance K. Burns, (Westport, Ct.: Greenwood Press, 1984), and Burns, "The Irony of Progressive Reform," in Formisano and Burns, *Urban Politics*.

4. There is no adequate biography of Curley. For the chronology, *BDAM*; for anecdote and color, James M. Curley, *I'd Do It Again; A Record of all My Uproarious Years* (Englewood Cliffs, N.J.: Prentice Hall, 1957), and Joseph F. Dinneen, *The Purple Shamrock* (New York: Norton, 1949). William V. Shannon offers an interpretation of Curley's life and place in the city in *The American Irish* (rev. ed., New York: Macmillan, 1964), pp. 182-232; Herbert Zolot has written of Curley's early years in "The Issue of Good Government and James Michael Curley" (Ph.D. diss., State University of New York at Stony Brook, 1975).

5. Boston's noted nineteenth-century elite, The Brahmins, has been much examined. Several recent valuable studies include Frederic Cople Jaher, *The Urban Establishments: Upper Strata in Boston, New York, Charleston, Chicago, and Los Angeles* (Urbana, Ill.: University of Illinois Press, 1982), pp. 15-156; and Ronald Story, *The Forging of An Aristocracy: Harvard and the Boston Upper Class 1800-1870* (Middletown, Ct.: Wesleyan University Press, 1980). Unfortunately there have been no studies of the traditional Yankee or the new cosmopolitan elites in the twentieth-century city.

6. James P. Walsh, "The Irish in New America: Way Out West," in *America and Ireland, 1776-1976*, ed. David N. Doyle and Owen D. Edwards, (Westport, Ct.: Greenwood Press, 1980), pp. 165-76, gives the setting and contains a useful bibliography. Shannon's chapter on "The Gold Coast" in *The American Irish*, pp. 86-94, is an account of some of the more famous of these people.

7. Harriet Beecher Stowe, *Old Town Folks*, ed. Henry F. May (Cambridge: Belknap Press of Harvard University Press, 1966; originally published, 1869), p. 346.

8. Such goals were common to middle class reformers and administrators across the nation. Two views of the structural reformers and the professional administrators who espoused such views are seen in Kenneth Fox, *Better City Government: Innovation in American Urban Politics, 1850-1977* (Philadelphia: Temple University Press, 1977), and Melvin G. Holli, "The Varieties of Urban

Reform," in *Reform in Detroit: Hazen Pingree and Urban Politics* (New York: Oxford University Press, 1969), pp. 161-81.

9. Thomas N. Brown, "The Political Irish: Politicians and Rebels," in Doyle and Edwards, *America and Ireland*, pp. 133-50.

10. Blodgett, "Yankee Leadership," and Thomas N. Brown, "The Irish and the Politics of Accommodation 1876-1905," unpublished paper, 1980.

11. For Fitzgerald, *BDAM*. There is no serious work on his career.

12. Lomasney, a ward boss with city-wide stature, is the subject of two articles: John D. Buenker, "The Mahatma and Progressive Politics: Martin Lomasney as Lawmaker, 1911-1917," *New England Quarterly* 44 (September, 1971): 397-419; and Albert D. Van Nostrand, "The Lomasney Legend," *New England Quarterly* 21 (December, 1948): 435-58.

13. Examples of Curley's deliberately outrageous anti-Yankee remarks are scattered throughout the works on him. See, for example, Curley, *I'd Do It Again*, pp. 2, 114, 117; Shannon, *American Irish*, p. 216; Zolot, "Curley," pp. 531-38. Such remarks were part of his larger rhetorical style; his attacks on Irish opponents were as vitriolic.

14. There is no study that details Curley's formal activities as mayor, either as the dispenser of public welfare or as builder of public facilities. Charles H. Trout in *Boston, The Great Depression, and the New Deal* (New York: Oxford University Press, 1977) does deal with Curley's important third term (1929-1933) but as a precursor of the New Deal rather than as a city executive in his own right.

15. Mass. Acts and Resolves, 1918: ch. 94 (March 25, 1918); Mass. Acts and Resolves, 1939: ch. 300 (May 10, 1938). For the popular referendum approving the 1938 change: Annual Report of the Board of Election Commission for 1939 (Boston, 1940).

16. For Peters, Nichols, Mansfield, see *BDAM*.

17. Tobin: *BDAM*. Also, Vincent Lapomarda, "Maurice J. Tobin, 1901-1953, A Political Profile" (Ph.D. diss., Boston University, 1968); Trout, in *Boston, The Great Depression*, describes Tobin in his relation to federal efforts to deal with the Depression in Boston.

18. The Boston press from January 15-25, 1946, deals with his conviction and triumphal return to the city. Subsequent events in the drama of this second conviction are his sentencing on June 26, 1947, and his pardon and return to the city on Nov. 26, 1947.

19. William Marchione, "The 1949 Boston Charter Reform," *New England Quarterly* 49 (September, 1976): 373-98.

20. Nor did the business/professional sector of the city have any answers for Boston's blight. Walter Muir Whitehill in his classic *Boston: A Topographical History* (Cambridge, Mass.: Harvard University Press, 1968), p. 284, began his last chapter on "A Decade of Renewal" by speaking of the cynicism held

by the cosmopolitan sector of the city about any possibility for change in the city more than a decade after the ending of World War II. Studies documenting the stagnation and the apparent need for governmental intervention include, for example, The Greater Boston Economic Study Group's "Report on Downtown Boston" (Boston: GBESC, 1959) and The Municipal Research Bureau's "Charting the Future of Urban Renewal" (Boston: MRB, 1959).

9

Boston's Kevin White: A Mayor Who Survives

MARTHA WAGNER WEINBERG

While the 1960s might be described as the years of expansive hopes for political leadership, the 1970s could be characterized as the years of despair. Opinion polls showed that in unprecedented numbers Americans began to express skepticism about the motives and talents of political leaders. Scholars have shared in this skepticism. The most thoughtful and provocative literature on elected chief executives during the early 1960s focused on analysis and definition of successful leadership strategies.[1] But as the decade of the 1960s approached a close, optimistic predictions about the possibility for enlightened leadership gave way to tough and bitter critiques of political leaders and the institutions that were supposed both to support them and to check them in their excesses. In the aftermath of the Vietnam War and in the wake of Watergate, despair and increasing concern about whether government was ''governable'' began to characterize analyses of American politics.

Nowhere was this change more evident that in the literature on mayors and urban politics. The most widely read and important analyses of mayoral leadership written in the early 1960s explained how Richard Daley of Chicago, Richard Lee of New Haven, and even John Reading of Oakland managed and directed their cities.[2] By the end of the 1960s, however, scholars described many of the big-city

Chapter 9, ''Boston's Kevin White: A Mayor Who Survives,'' by Martha Wagner Weinberg was previously published in the *Political Science Quarterly*, vol. 96, no. 1 (Spring 1981), pp. 87-106. Reprinted with permission. The author is grateful to Walter Dean Burnham, Frank Levy, Michael Lipsky, and Robert Weinberg for their helpful comments. An earlier version of this article was presented at the annual meeting of the American Political Science Association in September 1979. In June 1983 Kevin White decided not to run for mayor again, and 1983 was his last year in office.

mayors who had risen to prominence in the mid-1960s as being at best unable to manage unmanageable jobs, at worst, as inept. John Lindsay, in many ways the symbol of the new mayors, served only two terms, at the end of which he was scorned by many who had once looked to him to champion the cause of the cities. Carl Stokes and Thomas D'Alesandro, battered by the demands of the job, chose not to run for reelection. Many mayors began to talk about the impossibility of their jobs.

A new body of scholarly literature reflected this pessimism about mayoral leadership of cities. One astute analyst of urban politics described cities as "ungovernable."[3] Another argued that the popular hope for mayors to be forceful crusading leaders was misplaced and that, at best, mayors could be umpires.[4] Others suggested that, with the demise of old-style political machines and their replacement with the "new machines" of professionalized administrative agencies, the power of the mayor would decline, leaving cities "well-run but ungoverned."[5] In one of the most incisive analyses of the problems facing big-city mayors, James Q. Wilson suggested in 1969 that at the root of their difficulties were problems of demography and authority. Wilson singled out several potential sources of these problems including the continuing influence of liberal voters who had moved outside the city without relinquishing their share in governance; the strength of devices such as civil-service and employee organizations that insulated urban bureaucracies from mayoral control; the decay of political parties; and the demands of the electorate that mayors deal with issues such as crime and racial conflict that they were unable to manage.[6]

But not all big-city mayors have fallen victim to the sad fate predicted by social scientists. On 7 January 1980, Kevin White was sworn in for an unprecedented fourth four-year term as mayor of Boston, the sole survivor of the group of bright, young, charismatic 1960s mayors. By examining the causes and significance of White's survival, this article attempts to extend the analysis of the possibilities for and obstacles to mayoral leadership. Four questions are particularly relevant. First, how have White's own personality, style, and "statecraft" helped him achieve electoral success?[7] Second, how have environmental conditions affected White and his ability to be reelected? Third, which of the threats to White's survival are not unique to him or to Boston, but face all big-city mayors as they enter the 1980s? Finally, what are the costs of electoral survival both for mayors such as White and for the cities they govern?

The Strategy and Style of the Mayor

Though Kevin White was only thirty-seven years old when he was first elected mayor of Boston in 1967, he was not a newcomer to politics. The son and son-in-law of two prominent Boston politicians, White had run successfully on the Democratic ticket for Massachusetts Secretary of State in 1960 and had been reelected in 1962, 1964, and 1966. In his first attempt to gain city-wide office, he was widely regarded as the moderate alternative to school committee member Louise Day Hicks, whose ominous "you know where I stand" statement in response to questions about her position on integration made her the target of a widespread coalition of liberals and racial moderates. White defeated Hicks by 12,000 votes, a margin that he widened to 60,000 votes when he ran against her once again in 1971. In 1975 he ran for a third term, defeating State Senator Joseph Timilty by 7,000 votes after a bitter campaign in which charges of corruption were leveled at White. In the 1979 election, White again defeated Timilty, extending his margin of victory to 14,000 votes and broadening his base of support to win in many sections of the city in which he had previously lost.

Though Kevin White has been elected to four terms and has brought to the job a certain set of personal traits and attributes that have allowed observers to generalize about his personality and style, it would be a mistake to talk about the job of mayor during the White administration as if White and his style of leadership had remained static. To understand White's tenure as mayor, one must look beyond the length of time he has held office and the vote totals he has amassed to the eras he has spanned and to the changes in his own political amibitions. As he announced his candidacy for reelection in 1979, the Boston press and many local observers suggested that the voters were faced with a "new" Kevin White, a man very different from the progressive moderate who had first been elected in 1967, a man obsessed with bringing old-style machine politics to Boston. Whether White himself has changed is an issue of debate among those who understand and care about Boston politics. But it is clear that White's political ambitions and fortunes have shifted since he was first elected and that it is important to understand how these changes have affected White's fortunes and strategy.

The "eras" of Kevin White have been shaped by his ambitions. From 1967 until 1970, White, while mayor, had one eye on the governor's office for which he announced his candidacy and received his party's nomination in 1970. In the 1970 election he was soundly defeated by Republican Francis Sargent. This loss was especially humiliating to White because he was defeated by Sargent in the city of Boston. But 1970 did not mark the end of White's ambitions for higher office. In 1972 George McGovern notified White that he was seriously considering asking him to be his running mate on the Democratic ticket. Though ultimately White was not named the experience whetted his appetite for pursuing national office, and from 1972 through 1974 he devoted a great deal of energy to nurturing and fostering a national reputation. Though from 1967 through 1974 White by no means ignored his constituency, he spent a good deal of time preparing himself to run for higher office and maintaining a network of contacts with a national audience.[8]

By 1975 this era of Kevin White's ambitions had ended rather abruptly. Though White defeated Timilty in the 1975 election, he did so by a very narrow margin. During the course of the campaign, for the first time in his political career White had to face charges that he was personally corrupt. According to observers and to White himself, the shock and bitterness that White felt about the campaign left him a changed man, a man who did not want to have to depend again on the judgment or good will of the press or of political mediators ever again. At the same time, White was faced with the job of implementing the 1974 federal court order mandating school busing in Boston, an order that threatened to divide the city. In a very short time, White had watched his reputation change from that of a rising national figure to an embattled mayor fighting for his political life. In 1975 Kevin White seemed to have settled for being mayor and to have begun to make every effort to strengthen and insulate himself in that position.

Yet despite the fact that White's ambitions and, consequently, his handling of the job of mayor have changed during his tenure in office, it is possible to trace the consistencies in White's administration and, in doing so, to identify a style, a strategy, and a brand of politics that have allowed him to survive. Thus, it is essential first to understand something about White himself, for the style and personal qualities of political leaders have a great deal to do with the success or failure of policies and with the tone of an entire administration.

Scholars often judge political leaders by assessing how well they fit the norms and characteristics of the climate in which they operate. They cannot simply lead by being distinctive individuals. They must also be recognizable products of the followings which they lead.[9] White's own style blends well with the dominant political ethos in Boston. Boston is both a traditional and a cosmopolitan city and White is a product of both cultures. His father, Joe White, was an influential Boston politician, and White grew up in a family that understood and respected the rules of Boston politics. Although he spent his youth in the midst of an Irish neighborhood, he has also been part of the world of cosmopolitan Boston. He was educated at a private preparatory school and at Williams College and has lived on Beacon Hill for twenty years.

White has benefited enormously from the fact that he is a political hybrid. His personal strengths mesh well with the traditions and style of the city. He enjoys and takes great pride in being able to talk easily with many groups of Boston's diverse population and in being able to put together unlikely coalitions. One of his oldest associates describes the relish with which White undertakes this task: "Kevin's idea of a great time is to invite the Aga Khan, Johnny Powers (the former president of the Massachusetts Senate), the cardinal and a couple of professors over to the Parkman House for dinner, draw them into a discussion, and have the evening end with all of them agreeing that they have a great deal in common."[10]

This is not merely to say that White is a good politician. It is also to acknowledge a crucial personal skill that the mayor of Boston must possess to be able to govern and to be reelected, for Boston is a heterogeneous city, a city of neighborhoods and tightly knit ethnic groups. Political followings have historically been personal followings and have lasted only as long as individuals have been able to hold them together. Though a majority of voters registered in Boston are nominally Democrats, the Democratic party in Massachusetts is so badly fragmented that the party has meant little as a stimulus to organizing voters, especially in nonpartisan city elections. No single organized group or economic organization dominates Boston politics. The business community does not speak with a single voice on political issues.[11] Unions, though organized, have not been monolithic on political issues nor have they dominated the political landscape. In short, the politics of Boston has always been coalitional politics, but a coalitional politics whose stability has depended on the talents and skills of individual politicians rather than on the strength of ongoing loyalties or organizations.

Kevin White's political style and strategy as well as his personality have been suited to the particular demands of Boston politics. Boston is a "strong mayor" city, and White has used the formal authority of the mayor's office.[12] But he has also had to fashion and hold together a group of followers who have reelected him four times. Any mayor of Boston must appeal to a broad range of voters and must tailor a strategy that allows him to build a winning coalition. White has fashioned such a coalition and has held it together over time. It is well to look at how he has done this, for it tells us a great deal not only about the career of Kevin White but also about how elected officials must use strategies that are highly sensitive to the climate and characteristics of the environment in which they operate.

Coalitional Politics and Constituent Support

When he first ran for office in 1967, White garnered the support of liberals, blacks, and Italians, and it is these three important constituencies who have remained at the heart of White's political coalition in all elections. In 1967, 1971, and 1975 White received 80 percent of the black vote, approximately 70 percent of the liberal vote, and approximately 60 percent of the Italian vote, a total which, when summed, equals 40 percent of Boston voters.[13] In addition, by 1975, White had begun to enjoy popularity among a fourth group, the elderly. In 1979, many black voters supported black mayoral candidate Mel King in the nonpartisan "preliminary" election, and there was widespread speculation that White would lose a substantial percentage of black votes in the final race against Timilty. But despite these predictions, White maintained his strong standing in the black community, winning 74 percent of the black vote while making substantial gains among the Irish in white, antibusing South Boston.[14]

The most interesting thing about this winning coalition is not that it ever existed but that it has remained stable over time. White's politics has been first and foremost a politics of coalition building among constituency groups. As he himself has summed it up: "I can't think of any group in Boston that says, 'If Kevin White is in, we're in.' On the other hand, nobody says 'we're out.' That's not my brand of Boston politics. I can't win that way."[15]

White has held his coalition together through use of both symbolic and material rewards. He came into office prepared to respond to the policy concerns of his constituencies, though he had not yet identified what manifestations these would take. But he did something else, equally if not more important, to win and hold the loyalty of his constituents—he opened city government to them, both by giving them jobs and by providing them with access to him and his administration. Until White became mayor, Boston City Hall was an almost entirely Irish, white male enclave. "The walls in Old City Hall were even painted green," recalled one observer of Boston politics in talking about the absence of non-Irish in the government. "And look at the airport," he continued. "There it was in the middle of Italian East Boston, and they name it and the tunnels connecting it to the city after Irishmen."[16]

Having become mayor of an ethnic city at a time when citizen groups were becoming an important voice in the political process, White strengthened his ties to his constituencies by careful use of one of the most important resources of his office, his appointment powers. His first cabinet included two blacks, three Italians, and many professionals with impeccable liberal credentials. One of his most important appointments, symbolically, was that of an Italian, Robert DiGrazia, to be commissioner of a police department that had always been dominated by the Irish, but which under White began to recruit Italians and blacks.

The appointment of a heterogeneous group of officials to highly visible high-level jobs in the government was important in cementing White's constituencies to him. But just as important were the lower-level jobs that he opened up to his constituents. In 1967, at most 6 percent of city jobs were held by members of racial minorities. By 1979, minorities constituted 18 percent of the city's workforce, and 18 percent of those earning $15,000 and above were members of racial minority groups.[17] Although employment data are not kept or broken down by ethnic groups, most observers feel that during White's terms in office Italians have entered the city work force in record numbers. At the same time, many young professionals, the favored employees of the liberals, became visible presences in city agencies and departments. One observer has commented: "Before Kevin White the only agency that had people with college degrees on the staff was the BRA (Boston Redevelopment Authority). All that changed under White. The liberals knew that there was a new managerial class all throughout the government."[18]

White tied his constituencies to him by delivering not only a share of the symbolically important, high-level, visible jobs, but also by opening up large numbers of jobs at all levels of government that had previously been inaccessible. Although by doing this he slighted many of the old-line Irish who had predominated in City Hall, he added personnel at a time when local government was booming; therefore in most cases he did not add injury to insult by firing longtime civil servants and avoided creating an ''us-against-them'' climate.

Neighborhood Linkage and Community Advocacy

White did not rely on his hiring policy as his sole means of appealing to his constituents. Boston constituency politics is also neighborhood politics, and White concentrated on policies that would reinforce his ties to his constituents in their communities. Perhaps the most important step he took in linking the neighborhoods to City Hall was his establishment in 1968 of the ''Little City Halls'' program.

In his 1967 campaign White had pledged to bring government back to the people and had said that if he were elected, he would set up a mechanism to link City Hall with neighborhood concerns. ''Neighborhood government'' was a good issue in the late 1960s and perhaps no city was naturally more receptive to it than Boston with its well-established neighborhood base and its strong mayor government. No politicians could afford to be against neighborhood government, and by 1971, the Mayor's Office of Public Service had established fourteen Little City Halls. Their staffs were charged with following up on local complaints and with expediting the delivery of city services. In addition to performing these functions, the Little City Hall managers became important links between the mayor's office and the neighborhoods, often performing as neighborhood and community advocates and achieving high visibility in the community.[19] In most cases, White was able to benefit from the Little City Halls as a political and organizational base for his administration without having to pay the cost of creating from scratch the whole series of social, religious, and community ties necessary to make such a neighborhood-based organization work.

The policies of White's administration have been tailored to the coalitional nature of his constituency and to the groups that make it up. Many of the policies for which he is best known, such as his challenges to the expansion of the airport in East Boston and his opposition to the extension of the interstate highway network through established Boston neighborhoods, have been direct responses to galvanized communities and have been fashioned by staff members who advocate sensitivity to community concerns. Other issues for which White has become well known include his attack on tax-exempt institutions and his efforts to stop revaluation of residential property, both issues of concern to taxpayers.

Though many of these policies have not been formulated as part of a grand plan and often have been responses to pressure from groups outside City Hall, there are some general themes of the administration's policy that have remained consistent over time. White and his staff have been both diligent and adroit at capitalizing on issues that involve answers to the question "who owns this city?" Much of the energy for taking on these issues has come from White and seems to be based on his genuine personal conviction that on some issues the rights of citizens of Boston should not be encroached upon by outsiders who stand to make money or gain political influence at the expense of the city. But perhaps more important, focusing on these kinds of issues provides tremendous political capital for an astute mayor who knows that he must bring together a diverse coalition of groups around issues on which they can agree. Like Mayor Daley of Chicago and Mayor Lee of New Haven, White has a shrewd eye for the issues that will unite his constituencies or issues that at least will not pit one constituency against another.[20]

Analysts of cities have suggested that an overwhelming problem for mayors is the considerable influence wielded over urban affairs by those who do not live in the city but who remain a crucial "audience."[21] While White has always had to be aware of the attitudes and concerns of those who control state and federal power, he has also often managed to use Boston's chauvinism and parochialism to his political advantage by uniting his diverse constituencies on issues that pit Bostonians against "outsiders." This has been true especially since 1975, when White abandoned his enthusiastic quest for higher office and eliminated the corresponding need to court the support and votes of a broad national audience.

Like all mayors, White has had to face what Douglas Yates has called "street fighting pluralism," the free-for-all conflict among diverse groups who live in cities and who look to City Hall for satisfaction of their demands.[22] In his attempts to avoid this kind of internal division of his coalition, White has benefited greatly from the fact that Boston is a decentralized city of often insular neighborhoods, a city in which many issues can be handled in neighborhoods without causing city-wide repercussions. White has capitalized on this geographic and historic feature of the city. In many instances, he has deliberately avoided using the city-wide media to make announcements of programs or policies that benefit certain sections of the city.[23] Instead he has made his policies known through neighborhood channels of communication like newspapers, Little City Halls, and city workers, thus reaping the benefits of having helped one group of constituents without having to face the demands of other groups in the city who want to know what White is going to do for them.

Subcultures of Political Participation

For White, as for any other chief executive, the battle to survive depends not only on making individual decisions about policy or personnel, but also on maintaining an ongoing group of supporters who are willing to be active and vigilant in his behalf. Unlike elected officials who deliberately segregate their electoral organizations from their staffs and from those who perform the ongoing functions of government, White has always considered members of his administration and of his electoral apparatus to be part of one organization. In so doing, he has avoided many of the problems and costs associated with maintaining two staffs that often compete and operate at cross-purposes. But he has had to deal with the problem of blending into one organization individuals with widely varying motives and with extremely diverse backgrounds, training, and skills.

There are at least three different subcultures of political participants in the White administration, and White has offered strong incentives to each to work in his organization. First, there are the "policy professionals," the members of the organization whose primary incentive for participating is a desire to influence policy. Second, there are the "meal-ticket" seekers, who support White in return for salaried jobs and other material rewards. Finally, there are the "team players," who consider the game of Boston politics a way of life and who feel that they must be part of one organization or another to be able to play.[24] White has attracted members of each of these groups and, in return, counts on them to be active participants in his organization and to link his organization and City Hall with constituencies around the city.

Throughout his years as mayor, White has surrounded himself with a group of policy professionals—bright, usually young, usually mobile people who have been attracted to him because of his reputation as an intelligent and progressive mayor who cares about policy. Though individual policy professionals tend to stay with White for a relatively short period of time and though their numbers have decreased since the 1975 election, the White administration has been known around the country as a training ground for young public servants who want to pursue careers in government. White has attracted many of these individuals to his personal staff by offering them several attractive incentives. First, the mayor delegates considerable responsibility to them and, characteristically, has done so without second-guessing them. As one longtime staff member suggests: "Kevin was never one to review fire hydrant designs. He lets you do your job without interfering."[25] White also spends time educating the policy professionals about politics and helps provide them with a road map of the often unfamiliar terrain that will affect the outcome of the policy they make. Third, he acknowledges their professionalism by backing their decisions. Barney Frank, once a key aide and now a frequent critic of White, has suggested that White's greatest strength as a manager is that "he doesn't overrule people. He knows he's a delegator and understands that that implies letting people know you're not going to second-guess them."[26] Finally, White attracts many capable young public servants because he has demonstrated his willingness to respond to substantive policy concerns and, at times, to take risks. For many of the young liberal professionals who have worked for White, the most important remuneration for their efforts is their sense that they are part of a good cause. White's controversial opposition to the expansion of the airport and construction of the interstate highway network gave him a reputation as a politician who was willing to take a long, hard look at public policy—a reputation that survived much of the criticism leveled at him in his later terms in office as an opportunistic politician.

White has held the meal-ticket seekers in his organization by extensive use of material rewards and jobs. Unlike many other politicians with an interest in the substance of policy, White has never shied away from manipulation of jobs, favors, and contracts. Raymond Wolfinger has pointed out that machine-style politics often exists in cities where there is no political machine and that "the rewards of machine politics are essentially issue-free in that they flow regardless of what policies are followed."[27] White understands that he controls a series of desirable rewards and has always used material incentives. His patronage and personnel offices have kept close track of job placements in the White administration. He has appointed many members of boards, commissions, and authorities on "holdover" status, in effect making it clear that they serve at his pleasure. In addition, before each election in which White has run as an incumbent, the number of persons holding city jobs has increased dramatically. After each election there have been layoffs.[28] Many workers in his campaign organizations are also on the city payroll, and especially since 1975, have been rewarded for active participation in campaigns by increases in pay and by promotions.

The team players also receive support from White. Boston is a city that takes its politics seriously, and for many of the city's residents politics is a way of life. For these team players, politics is the basis for a network of friendships and other rewards, such as access to City Hall, public recognition of their contributions, and acclamation that they are important links to their friends and neighbors.[29] White has always observed the traditions and the rules of the game of Boston politics. His father and his father-in-law were influential politicians, and many of the team players support him because he is a product of an old Boston political family. But, most important, White is the mayor, a demonstrated winner.

In return for these rewards, White commands a price. All members of White's organization are expected to work in his campaigns, and many are asked to contribute money. The campaign apparatus and the White administration are folded into one large organization, and members are expected to be loyal to the person who heads that organization. Employees understand that they work for White and that part of their job is to keep him in the mayor's office. Political organizations in Boston have traditionally been highly personalized. White has reinforced the loyalty of his personal following by his careful use of tangible and intangible rewards and punishments.

In 1963 Edward Banfield and James Q. Wilson described the political sphere of Boston as decentralized, arguing that "the city is nonpartisan, and no politician or possible combination of politicians has enough prestige, or enough organization to dominate the city."[30] Though it is still true that Boston is not susceptible to any one politician's total domination of the political terrain, White, through careful use of the powers and resources of his office, has built a tight, personal organization geared toward building support for ongoing policy initiatives, turning out a substantial number of White voters in the primary, and providing a formidable electoral organization and base in the general election.

The Political Environment

Kevin White has enhanced his chances of being a mayoral survivor by capitalizing on those elements of his own personality, style, and political skill that mesh especially well with the political ethos and style of the city he governs. But for any mayor, skill and adroitness, even when carefully attuned to the style and demands of those he represents, are not enough to ensure survival or success. All chief executives depend on a favorable climate in which they can ply their trade.[31] Because scholars and political analysts seek categories that describe the behavior of many persons, they most often focus on those attributes that members of these categories share. Thus, many scholars have written about the problems and characteristics that mayors have in common. But in attempting to answer the question of why a mayor is able to survive, it is important to understand not only the particular qualities and talents he brings to the job, but also the particular characteristics of the political environment that he faces that are favorable to his survival.[32] It is well to ask, then, what structural and environmental conditions have been important to White's success, and what major, potentially catastrophic problems he has not had to face. Of these, three are especially significant: the absence of issues so intractable that no mayor could manage them; the lack of significant independent agencies or employee unions; and the absence of powerful challengers.

In the last ten years, there have been two major issues that have had the potential to fly out of control in Boston, and, in the process, to destroy White: the racial problems that erupted with court-ordered busing, and the city's financial problems during the mid-1970s. Though dealing with each strained both White's capacity and luck, neither made him unelectable.

In 1974, a federal district court judge handed down an edict ordering the integration of the Boston schools by means of busing. Many observers felt that the widely unpopular plan would split the city, heighten racial confrontation, bring violence to the city, and cause the defeat of all politicans who had to deal with it.[33] Though the years following the busing order were not easy ones for Boston or for White, the issue did not terminate his career. There are at least three explanations for this.

First, though White was mayor, he was not legally responsible for the schools. Boston has an independently elected School Committee, and much of the citizen disenchantment with and anger at busing was directed at School Committee members. Second, because the order had been handed down by a federal judge, there was a widespread feeling that no single person within the city could control the issue. Finally, and perhaps most important, White focused his attention and his energies on the one issue in the controversy on which all could agree and over which he had jurisdiction—the safety of school children. Though there were violent incidents involving blacks and whites in the schools, they were sporadic and scattered around the city. By 1978 South Boston High School, the center of resistance to busing, had been removed from court receivership, many white students were attending private schools, and the potential for political disaster for White as a result of the busing issue seemed to have passed.

Racial tension in the city surfaced again immediately before the 1979 election when Daryl Williams, a black high-school football player, was shot during a football game in Charlestown, a white, Irish section of the city. Angry groups of white and black citizens held meetings and rallies, and the city seemed once again to be dominated by racial tension. White's popularity in the polls began to dip.[34] But White was lucky. Though the city remained tense, there were no major racial incidents in the week before the election and White swept to victory, avoiding mention of the issue that he and other astute observers knew could cost him the election were it to fly out of control.

Another issue that would almost certainly have caused White's downfall was the escalation of the city's fiscal crisis of 1976 to a full-scale collapse. This collapse was narrowly averted. In the 1976 fiscal year the city spent $70 million more than projected, with most of these unanticipated costs attributable to the costs of school desegregation and election-year budgeting designed to ensure no increase in property taxes. At the same time the city was in the midst of several capital-building efforts including the $108 million school-building program. With the collapse of credit markets in 1975, Boston, like most other major cities, faced a financial market access problem. As in other cities, elements of the banking and financial communities felt that the city should be allowed to go bankrupt.

Boston's finances did not collapse. Part of the explanation for this concerns the timing of the problem. The climate for borrowing changed at the crucial time for Boston. But part of the explanation concerns actions taken by the White administration. White had in place a small but extremly competent staff of fiscal advisers who saw the crisis coming. By the time the financial community began to exert pressure, White's fiscal staff had already begun to take action to shore up the city's reputation and to put the city back on a sound footing. By increasing taxes, decreasing expenditures, and bringing in Morgan Guaranty Trust Company to be chief underwriter of their bond issue and to increase confidence, they began to bring the city's finances back into line, narrowly averting a fiscal collapse and the political disaster for White that would have accompanied it.

Both Theodore Lowi and James Q. Wilson have suggested that independent city agencies and organized groups of city employees pose threats to mayoral control of city governments.[35] But for White neither has threatened to cause him to lose his grip on the apparatus of government or on his job. Though public employees are well organized in Boston, they have never squared off for a major confrontation with White. There are several reasons for this. First, the climate in Boston has been favorable to organized labor. The city has traditionally had high taxes and a correspondingly high level of services. There has not been a fiscal crisis, nor have there been large numbers of layoffs. Moreover, union leaders have been able to negotiate successfully with the city. City employees' wages compare favorably with those of public employees in similar jobs around the country. Finally, there is a sense of mutual respect that has grown between the unions' leaders and the vice-mayor of Boston who is in charge of labor negotiations.[36] The climate of distrust and mutual hostility that has characterized the dealings between the unions and the city government in so many cities has never materialized in Boston. As a result, though the unions have not always gone out of their way to help White, they have never made him their target.

Independent, autonomous city agencies have also never posed a real threat to White. This is not to suggest that he has complete control over all policy made by the bureaucrats in agencies he nominally controls. There are several line agencies such as the Real Property Department, the Building Department, and the Assessing Department that White has avoided changing, either by ignoring them or, at the very least, by naming to key positions loyalists who have not forced White to think about reform. As one staff aide put it, "He's terrified of turning over the rock and finding all sorts of ugly creatures he'd have to deal with."[37] But there are a few agency heads who have moved their organizations in a direction out of White's control, and these few, such as Commissioner Robert DiGrazia of the Police Department and Robert Kenney of the Boston Redevelopment Authority, have been dismissed with dispatch.

White has several important sources of control over agency activities. Perhaps the most important of these is the sheer number of appointments he has been able to make in his twelve years as mayor. He has kept a careful eye on the loyalty of all mayoral appointees, has converted many of the appointments to independent boards and authorities to holdover status, and has not hesitated to remove those who appear to be straying from the White fold. In addition, the budgetary powers of the mayor are considerable. Central control over agency budgets and purchasing is situated in White's office and gives him substantial leverage in negotiating with agencies. Finally, White has become increasingly invulnerable to the great weapon of bureaucrats, the sense that they can outlive any chief executive. Many of the agency personnel who early in White's career as mayor treated him as a temporary nuisance have had to make peace with him, for they have come to recognize that a four-term mayor can, if he wishes, exercise a great deal of control over the quality and even the existence of their jobs.

Of all the questions that could be asked about the political environment in Boston during White's tenure, perhaps the most crucial is the question of why White has not had to face more formidable opponents, opponents who by force of their own political skills would be able to wrench the mayor's job away from White. There are several reasons for the scarcity of powerful challengers. First, unlike some other large cities, Boston has no stepping-stone institutions that lead naturally to the mayor's office. There is no single congressional district. Members of the City Council and the School Committee are elected every two years in city-wide elections, but both organizations have limited power and visibility and are overshadowed in power and authority by the mayor's office. In addition, members of these bodies, and indeed city politicians in general, have traditionally been held in low esteem in Boston.[38] In contrast, during White's tenure in office, citizens have viewed both White himself and the office he holds with respect and, often, affection.[39]

Election to Boston political office, moreover, has always required a personal organization, something that is difficult to build in the face of a powerful and well-organized incumbent. Historically, political loyalty has not been transferable from one person to another in Boston.[40] There are no tightly knit party organizations in the city. More importantly, Boston mayoral primaries and elections are nonpartisan. Incumbents such as White benefit from having a tightly organized cadre of activists who vote in the preliminary election and who serve as an already established electoral organization to work in the short period between the September preliminary election and the November final election. It is difficult for challengers with no electoral base to build such an organization and to raise the money and attract the staff necessary to defeat an incumbent.

Finally, one can argue that there have been no powerful challengers to White because the demands of Boston's coalitional politics are difficult to meet. Because of the diversity and heterogeneity of the city, it is impossible to win the election with the support of only one group. The kind of coalition building at which White has excelled is complicated in the best of circumstances and extremely difficult to manage in opposition to an incumbent mayor who has won and held the loyalty of a winning electoral coalition. Many of the most astute observers of Boston politics have argued that a successful challenger would have to look very much like White himself. The likelihood that someone of this ilk will challenge White is small, both because most of the credible challengers who fall in this category are White supporters and because, even if they were to become disaffected, they would have to overcome the tremendous advantages of incumbency and long-term loyalty that White enjoys.

The Threat to Mayoral Survival

Kevin White has managed to survive and, even, it would seem, to prosper at a time when many analysts of cities predicted that big-city mayors would falter. He has been elected four times. Throughout his years as mayor, public-opinion polls have shown him to be extremely popular.[41] The city of Boston has survived a financial crisis, and its financial condition seems healthy. The flow of persons moving into the city is steadily increasing, and public-opinion polls indicate that residents of the city feel more optimistic about its future than they have felt in many years.[42]

Yet as White ran for his fourth term in office, his whole style of campaigning and politicking seemed to have shifted dramatically from his style in earlier elections. In each of his mayoral campaigns White has maintained a tight electoral organization, but in 1979 he seemed determined to flaunt it, to work both in public and in private to centralize electoral and political control of the city in his own hands.

As early as 1977 White had seemed to feel that one of his most pressing problems was that of centralizing power. Accordingly, he proposed that the city charter be changed to increase the powers of the mayor. After a protracted battle in which his opponents characterized his efforts as a power grab and as a selfish attempt to achieve personal gain, White's proposal was defeated.[43] But this defeat did not stop him from focusing on his attempt to centralize power and authority. In his 1979 campaign he made an undisguised effort to create a tight political organization, an organization manned by city workers who knew that pay increases and, in fact, their very jobs might depend on their success at working in precincts and wards.

White's strategy and actions were neither uncalculated nor careless. For White, the survivor of the politics of the late sixties and early seventies, had come to believe that the terrain of mayoral politics had shifted, that the major concern of the voters was that chief executives be strong leaders and that, therefore, the major threat to mayoral survival was to fail to pull together enough power to satisfy the public's increased craving for strong leadership. As White himself put it:

The issue of the political machine, the "imperial mayoralty," is no longer dominant. People want leadership, but they're demanding it at a particularly difficult time.

The rule used to be that he who won had the right to govern. But since 1970, there's been an unstructured assault on the political profession's right to govern, to lead. Until we recapture a very diffuse political process, nobody can do anything.... When I'm faced with this kind of situation, you bet your life I'm going to pull together all the scraps of power I can assemble.[44]

White is not alone in seeing dispersion of authority as the central issue that elected chief executives face. As early as 1965, Banfield and Wilson pointed out that one of the results of the reform movement in cities was to increase the trend of decentralization of power and to decrease the power of the politician. The reform movement compensated for this to some extent by increasing (the politician's) authority. . . . But, because the increase in authority was usually not enough to make up entirely for the loss of power, the politician's total influence declined. While this was happening, more and more accomplishment was being expected of public officials (i.e. politicians in office); both the quantity and quality of public services being demanded increased. This left elected officials in a difficult position: as their need for influence increased, their supply of it declined.[45]

Walter Dean Burnham has argued that the collapse of political authority is characteristic of all levels of government and that there is an ever-increasing tendency toward dispersion of political authority. His argument for the need to centralize authority sounds much the same as White's when he writes: "In the American system, above all, the price for creating the support of mass electorates and cadres of activists—a support essential to the accumulation of power resources by executives—is the existence of some organized force able to overcome the fragmenting which the institutional structure mandates."[46]

But to recognize that chief executives need to be leaders in a system characterized by increasingly dispersed authority is, for mayors, only to begin the battle. By acting on his belief that centralization of power in himself was the single most important issue he must face, White took an enormous gamble, a gamble that many chief executives must face. He gambled that he could actively and publicly seek to win power both for himself and for his office, without being thrown out of office by an electorate fearful of and angry at a politician hungry for power. White had to gamble on striking the correct balance between assembling enough power to satisfy the public's craving for leadership and remaining aloof enough from pursuit of power to survive the public's enduring suspicion.

Kevin White won his gamble in the 1979 election. He placed his bets on assembling power visibly and on risking the electorate's perception of him as a strong, if at times unscrupulous, leader and, once again, survived. One might well argue that White's victory is a true example of mayoral success, both for those who have supported him in the past and for those whose primary concern is that the mayor, any mayor, be able to govern. For if White is correct in his assessment that authority is becoming more and more fragmented, defeat for White, a mayor who has marshalled considerable resources and authority, would only have ensured further fragmentation and decentralization of political power.

One might also argue that without the leadership of someone such as a Kevin White, someone able to glue together a diverse and hetero-geneous coalition, the Boston electorate might well choose a series of one-term mayors, each elected by ad hoc coalitions formed around the issue of throwing the incumbent out or held together by promises of rewards that mayors have a great deal of difficulty delivering. In such a situation, all of the forces that analysts have argued make cities ungovernable could easily come into play.

But there are also costs and risks attached to survival in mayoral politics in the current era, and these affect mayors, active constituents, and members of the electorate who care about the substance of public policy. For Mayor White, the cost associated with his most recent victory may be an increasing reluctance to pursue any goals other than those associated with building his own power and with keeping his naturally fragmented house in order. The risk of this for those who care about the quality of policy the administration makes is that White may come to believe that the job of the elected politician is to seek power for its own sake and to dismiss policy and programs as irrelevant. For those who have worked for White or who have supported him because they believe he has stood for the right issues, the costs of his winning and governing as if the accumulation of power were his central concern may be very great.

The citizenry of the city may pay a great price for the current state of mayoral politics. For all mayors, even adroit survivors such as Kevin White, may have to pay so much attention to amassing power to ensure survival that they are unable to ask themselves what beyond survival they want to achieve. The great obstacle to true mayoral leadership may be that even the survivors must focus on the mechanics of organizing power to the exclusion of caring about the substance of policy.

In his fourth inaugural address, White announced that ''racism in any and all of its ugly manifestations won't be condoned and will be confronted directly and aggressively by this government.''[47] His promise to deal with a complicated and emotional issue of public concern may or may not bear some relationship to his announcement during his campaign that he would not run again for the job of mayor. Skeptics have argued that White's commitment is largely rhetorical or simply a fleeting fancy. Even those who accept White's sincerity and commitment suggest that Boston's racial problems can only be attacked by a mayor who will not seek reelection, but many of these same individuals argue that a mayor who is not constantly tuning an electoral machine has very little chance of making sweeping reforms. Whatever White's motivation for singling out racial tension as a problem that his administration must face, it is clear that in dealing with it he will face a stern test of mayoral influence and strength.

The story of White's successes or failures in his fourth term almost certainly will not tell interested observers all they would like to know about mayoral leadership and public policy. But it may suggest something about the limits of and possibilities for executive leadership on issues of public concern. Kevin White has proven that under some circumstances big-city mayors can survive and, in so doing, has defied many of the obstacles to survival identified by social scientists. Now that White has survived and has paid the attendant costs of survival the more interesting questions become whether he wants to affect and shape public policy and if he does, whether or not he can succeed.

Conclusion

What are the lessons to be learned from this discussion of Kevin White and his career as mayor? The first is perhaps the most obvious, that personality and leadership style are important factors in determining mayoral success, though probably not in as straightforward a way as much of the literature about chief executives written in the 1960s would lead readers to believe. Organization charts are misleading in depicting executive influence: mayors are not dominant simply by virtue of their position in the formal structure of government; therefore an engaging personal style and a will to achieve power are not in themselves sufficient to ensure success. An individual's personality and style must mesh with the characteristics of the particular environment in which he plies his trade. Kevin White's personality and style fit with Boston's political and cultural environment, and this fit provides him with strength. But to argue on the basis of this that White's same style or traits would be effective in New York or Atlanta or San Francisco would be totally misleading. Generalizations about leadership style are useful only to the extent that they are coupled with an understanding of the particular context in which the leader operates.

The second lesson is closely tied to the first. To be successful, a mayor must be not only skilled and intelligent, but also lucky. He must govern in a favorable environment, the elements of which he cannot

control. Not even the strongest mayors are powerful enough or influential enough to survive all the kinds of racial, fiscal, or other crises
that the contemporary American city almost routinely faces. Kevin
White's success, to a certain extent, is a result of the fact that he has
led a charmed life. Without a favorable political climate, no mayor can
succeed, no matter what his talent or skill.

The third lesson to be learned from the story of Kevin White is that
in contemporary urban politics skills and a favorable environment are
necessary but not sufficient to ensure a mayor's electoral success. For
even the most powerful and long-lived mayors must attempt to assemble
influence in a political system in which power is increasingly dispersed.
In so doing, they must face the ambivalence of an electorate that is
increasingly skeptical of those who seek power for its own sake but
one also anxious for strong political leadership. Because mayors are no
longer automatically perceived as having a legitimate right to govern,
they must constantly assemble power and appear strong; at the same
time, they must publicly deny their quest to be powerful. One might
argue that this is the greatest obstacle mayors face, for they must perform
this delicate balancing act not only at election time, but, increasingly,
throughout their term of office.

The final lesson to be learned from the story of Kevin White is that
even mayoral "success" in the contemporary environment is not without
costs. For even the most electorally successful mayors must develop an
obsession with holding enough power together to continue to win. When
this obsession becomes firmly entrenched, the choice of policy directions
and commitments to programs may remain instrumentally important but
is unlikely to dominate the mayor's agenda. The price of this success
may be high. Even though the electoral success of mayors such as Kevin
White may bode well for the possibility of stability in governance in
large American cities, it bodes poorly for the possibility of commitment
to programs and of strong leadership in solving the most pressing problems that urban residents face. The success of Kevin White may seem
to mute Lowi's warning that cities may be "well-run but ungoverned."[48]
Instead the major dilemma for cities in the 1980s with electorally successful mayors may be that they are governed but poorly led.

Notes

1. See, for example, Richard Neustadt, *Presidential Power* (New York:
John Wiley and Sons, 1960), Robert Dahl, *Who Governs?* (New Haven, Ct.:

Yale University Press, 1961), and James Sterling Young, *The Washington Community, 1800-1828* (New York: Columbia University Press, 1966).

2. In *Political Influence* (New York: Free Press, 1961), Edward Banfield analyzed Mayor Daley and Chicago. Robert Dahl discussed Richard Lee in *Who Governs?*; Jeffrey Pressman compared Mayor Reading to his predecessor John Houlihan in "Preconditions of Mayoral Leadership," *American Political Science Review 66* (June 1972): 511-24.

3. Douglas Yates, *The Ungovernable City* (Cambridge, Mass.: MIT Press, 1977).

4. Roger Starr, "Power and Powerlessness in a Regional City," *Public Interest 16* (Summer 1969): 3-40.

5. Theodore Lowi, "Gosnell's Chicago Revisited Via Lindsay's New York," foreword to the second edition of Harold Gosnell, *Machine Politics, Chicago Model* (Chicago, Ill.: University of Chicago Press, 1968).

6. James Q. Wilson, "The Mayors vs. the Cities," *Public Interest 16* (Summer 1969): 33.

7. The term statecraft is Young's, *Washington Community*.

8. For a discussion of the difference between constituency and audience, see Wilson, "Mayors vs. Cities," p. 28.

9. For an excellent discussion of this aspect of political leadership, see Murray Edelman, *The Symbolic Uses of Politics* (Urbana: University of Illinois Press, 1964).

10. Interview with a former member of Kevin White's staff, 25 April 1979, Boston, Mass.

11. Edward Banfield and James Q. Wilson have found influence to be decentralized in the Boston business community. See Edward Banfield and James Q. Wilson, *City Politics* (Cambridge, Mass.: Harvard University Press, 1965), p. 275.

12. For a description of Boston's strong mayor government, see Philip Heymann and Martha Weinberg, "The Paradox of Power: Mayoral Leadership on Charter Reform in Boston," in *American Politics and Public Policy*, eds. Walter Dean Burnham and Martha Weinberg (Cambridge, Mass.: MIT Press, 1978), p. 292.

13. Data presented by John Marttila, White's campaign organizer in 1971 and 1975, in an interview, 1 June 1979, Boston, Mass. See also "How Boston Votes: A Graphic Profile of the City's Electorate," Boston *Globe* Magazine, 4 November 1979.

14. "Why White Won Black Vote," Boston *Globe*, 9 November 1979.

15. Interview with Kevin White, 4 June 1979, Boston, Mass.

16. Interview with Frederick Salvucci, 21 May 1979, Boston, Mass.

17. These estimates were supplied by John Ahern of the Massachusetts Council Against Discrimination (MCAD). MCAD did not exist in 1967, nor

were there records kept of minority employment. On the basis of Ahern's research, he suggests that 6 percent is the highest that the percentage of minorities working for the city of Boston could have been. By 1973, when MCAD began to keep accurate records, the minorities accounted for 9.3 percent.

18. Interview with Frederick Salvucci.

19. For an excellent description and analysis of the Little City Hall program, see Eric Nordlinger, *Decentralizing the City: A Study of Boston's Little City Halls* (Cambridge, Mass.: MIT Press, 1972).

20. See Banfield, *Political Influence*, and Dahl, *Who Governs*?

21. Wilson, "Mayors vs. Cities."

22. Yates, *Ungovernable City*, p. 34.

23. Both Frederick Salvucci and Gail Rotegard, two former members of the mayor's staff, made this point in interviews with the author.

24. These three categories of participants correspond to the three different kinds of incentives explained by James Q. Wilson in *Political Organizations* (New York: Basic Books, 1973).

25. Interview with James Young, 2 May 1979, Boston, Mass.

26. Interview with Barney Frank, 27 April 1979, Boston, Mass.

27. Raymond Wolfinger, "Why Political Machines Have Not Withered Away and Other Revisionist Thoughts," *Journal of Politics* 34 (1972): 377.

28. After his 1975 election White laid off 1209 employees. Shortly after election to his fourth term in 1979, White's budget director predicted that White would soon lay off 1600 employees. See "1600 Face Hub Layoffs," Boston *Globe*, 27 November 1979.

29. For an especially good description of the rewards offered by political organizations, see Wilson, *Political Organizations*, p. 33.

30. Banfield and Wilson, *City Politics*, p. 275.

31. James Sterling Young has made this point very well in his analysis of post-Jeffersonian Washington. See Young, *Washington Community*, p. 206.

32. It is unfortunate that so little scholarly attention has been devoted to analyzing how context affects policymaking. Two exceptional studies that raise the issue of context are Richard DeNeufville, *Airport Systems Planning* (Cambridge, Mass.: MIT Press, 1976), and James Q. Wilson, *Varieties of Police Behavior* (New York: Atheneum, 1972).

33. For an excellent account of busing and White's involvement in it, see Alan Lupo, *Liberty's Chosen Home* (Boston, Mass.: Little, Brown and Co., 1977).

34. "Why White Won Black Vote," Boston *Globe*, 9 November 1979.

35. Lowi, "Chicago Revisited"; and Wilson, "Mayors vs. Cities," p. 33.

36. Much of this discussion is based on a 6 June 1979 interview with Abraham Siegel of MIT's Sloan School of Management who has for many years been the negotiator between the fire fighters and police and the city of Boston.

Some analysts would dispute Siegel's contention that the relationship between city and union officials has been characterized by mutual respect and cordiality. See "City, Unions Not the Best of Friends," Boston *Globe*, 4 October 1979. Most analysts of city–union politics, however, would agree that the relationship has never been characterized by irreparable strain.

37. Interview with a longtime aide of White, 25 April 1979, Boston, Mass.

38. In 1960 Murray Levin found widespread distrust of politicians. See *The Alienated Voter: Politics in Boston* (New York: Holt, Rinehart and Winston, 1960), esp. p. 61. In 1970, Eric Nordlinger found that 51 percent of Boston residents expressed extreme disaffection with public officials as a class. See Nordlinger, *Decentralizing the City*, p. 79.

39. This is reflected in polls taken by John Marttila from 1970 through 1975.

40. Even James Michael Curley, the legendary Boston political boss, ran the city through a personal organization. For a thoughtful analysis of the Curley organization see Paul Grogan, "James Michael Curley: The Machine Politician as Maverick" (Cambridge, Mass.: MIT Department of Political Science).

41. According to John Marttila, White's campaign organizer in 1971 and 1975, White's "favorable" ratings in polls remained a consistent 60 percent (with a 20 percent "unfavorable" rating). Though White's "unfavorability" rating increased after the 1976 tax increase, it remained well below the 35 percent figure that is more typical of elected chief executives in office.

42. See "Report of Findings: A 1978 Survey of Boston Resident Attitudes Toward Their City, Their Neighborhoods and its People" (Paper prepared for the City of Boston Office of Program Development by Consensus, Inc., Boston City Hall).

43. For a detailed account of the charter battle, see Heymann and Weinberg, "Paradox of Power."

44. Interview with Kevin White, 4 June 1979.

45. Banfield and Wilson, *City Politics*, p. 336.

46. Walter Dean Burnham, "The 1976 Election: Has the Crisis Been Adjourned?" in *American Politics*, Burnham and Weinberg, p. 22.

47. "Text of Mayor White's Inaugural Address," Boston *Globe*, 8 January 1980.

48. Lowi, "Chicago Revisited."

10

All in the Family: The Dilemmas of Busing and the Conflict of Values

J. ANTHONY LUKAS

My text for this chapter comes from the best novel I know about Boston politics, Edwin O'Connor's *All in the Family*. Overshadowed by his more popular *The Last Hurrah*, less honored than his Pulitzer Prize-winning *The Edge of Sadness, All in the Family* is the story of the Kinsella family, a big, tightly-knit, fiercely competitive clan of Boston Irishmen, led by a millionaire patriarch, one of whose sons goes on to become the dominant political figure in the state and, ultimately, per-haps, in the nation. That may sound familiar.[1]

Towards the end of the novel, Charles Kinsella, now the state's governor, has a bitter falling out with his brother, Phil, a modern man who has emancipated himself from both the time-honored mores of state politics and the claustrophobic loyalties of the Kinsella clan. When Phil threatens to expose his brother's shady dealings with political hacks, Charles moves to have Phil committed to a mental hospital. This pro-vokes a climactic family conference in which Jimmy Kinsella, the aging patriarch—obsessed as always with the family's need to stand together against the outside world—rages at his disloyal son:

You turned on us, Phil. You tried to blow us sky-high and to smithereens. You tried to do that to your own family! You tried to do it to Charles! And, by God, you tried to do it to me! And now you've got the guts to sit here and look at me and ask me if I think you're crazy. All right. You want an answer, so I'll give you one. You bet your ass you're crazy. Believe it or not, you're as bughouse as they come.

This, in turn, brings a bitter tirade from Phil's wife, Flossie. "You're a horrible old man," she shouts at her father-in-law.

Really horrible. For anyone like you to say what you've just said to someone like Phil, you ought to be knocked down and beaten ... you're a dreadful, horrible, insensitive, vulgar, stupid little tyrant ... I don't pray much, but tonight I'm going to get down on my knees and pray that after tonight neither one of us will ever be bullied by you or even talk to you or even so much as catch sight of you ever again.

A moment later, as Phil and Flossie leave the room, the bewildered old man cries after them, "What the hell has happened? What the hell has happened to my family?"

And Phil, from the doorway, responds, "I don't know, Pa. I guess we all grew up."[2]

I suggest that O'Connor is writing here less about any particular family of politicians than about the whole world of the Boston Irish and, more broadly still, about what has come to be called "ethnic politics." When Jimmy Kinsella talks about his family—that tight little grouping which is linked not only by blood but by self-interest, turf, ideology and sentiment—he is talking about something more than mere biological family. He is talking about the whole nexus of neighborhood, church and family which for more than a century made up the traditional world of the urban ethnic.[3]

And when Phil Kinsella breaks with those old loyalties to point the finger at corruption in his brother's administration, he is invoking a larger ethos: of political morality, social justice, efficient government, in a word—of reform. In Massachusetts, of course, that is an ethos long associated with the Yankees, the Mugwumps, the "Goo-Goos," who deserted the city in the late nineteenth century for the more salubrious climate of Dover, Beverley, Winchester and Newton.[4] But, by the era O'Connor is describing, it had been inherited by a new generation of middle-class Irish, the Phil Kinsellas of this world. And that, in turn, led to bitter vendettas in which both factions, old and new, felt stabbed in the back.

It was O'Connor's special contribution to see that this had all the markings of a family feud—the intensity bred of long, close association; the combustible mixture of pride and envy; the acute sense of betrayal. Our deepest antipathies, of course, are reserved for our own kind, those whom we expect to support us, no matter what. Such acts of disloyalty— between father and son, brother and brother, sister and sister—are the stuff of classical tragedy.

And I would extend O'Connor's metaphor to argue that this is the kind of tragedy which Boston has been experiencing in the last decade, from which it is still suffering today.

It is a special tribute to O'Connor that, writing in 1964, he had an intuition that the city's next great testing ground would be the issue of race. And, as all Bostonians now know, school desegregation has divided this city as rarely before. The desegregation fight is usually seen as a battle between the races and, of course, to a large degree it is. When white youths spear a black lawyer on City Hall Plaza with an American flag; when blacks in Roxbury beat a white worker so badly he lives out the rest of his short life in a coma, then certainly the city is experiencing a war of the races.

But the struggle has other dimensions too—among them, that of economic and social class. Those Bostonians who can afford to live in suburbia or who have the resources to send their children to private or parochial schools are exempt from the court order. Thus, the burden of desegregation here—as elsewhere—falls on the disadvantaged, an inequity of which they are acutely aware.[5]

I have been working on a book about the lives of three Boston families during the decade following Martin Luther King's assassination: an Irish-Catholic widow and her six children who live in the Bunker Hill housing project in Charlestown; a black woman and her six children who live in a subsidized housing project in the South End; and a Harvard-educated Yankee lawyer and his wife, who grew up in Lexington, moved into the South End following King's death and then out to Newton eight years later. These are three real families whose lives I have followed for much of that period. Although it is not a book about school desegregation, the busing battle is one of the principal cockpits in which the interests of the three families collide. The eldest daughter of the black family was bused into Charlestown High where she found herself in the same class as the eldest daughter of the Charlestown family.

The Charlestown family is very angry about busing. But when I talk with them, the principal focus of their anger is not blacks, not Yankees, not Jews—as some of the textbooks would suggest. Their anger is directed principally at other Irishmen. The names that come up most often in our conversations are W. Arthur Garrity, Ted Kennedy, Kevin White, Tip O'Neill, the hierarchy of the Catholic Church (under Cardinal Medeiros), even Bob Healy of the *Globe*.

And that, I think, is an accurate perception. For it was not Yankees who imposed busing on Boston—except for a few bankers, professors or newspaper editors, Yankees don't count for much in 1980s Boston. Nor was it the Jews; now that Charlie Wyzanski has largely retired from the bench and Eli Goldston is dead,[6] Jews don't cut much of a swath east of Waltham. Blacks, to be sure, took the initiative in the fight to desegregate Boston's schools. Ruth Batson and Ellen Jackson, Jim Breeden and Mel King fought the good fight for years and ultimately it was the NAACP's suit which prevailed in Federal District Court.[7] But with barely twenty percent of Boston's population, and far less than their share of political office holders and business leaders, blacks have little clout in the city.

No, it was the Irish who introduced and enforced busing in Boston—if only because it is the Irish who now hold virtually every position of political or governmental leverage in the city.[8]

First among them, of course, is Judge W. Arthur Garrity.[9] There is, to be sure, a debate about Arthur Garrity's Irishness, a debate which itself tells us something about contemporary Boston. I don't mean that his ethnic origin is in doubt. We know that his great-grandfather emigrated from County Sligo to Boston in 1850, later settling in Milford, New Hampshire. But Garrity's critics contend that he has long since lost his Irishness, or at least the stigmata deemed to identify an Irishman in today's Boston. They point to his longtime residence in Wellesley, his law degree from Harvard, but especially his spare, austere, almost ascetic style—fourteen hour work days, a sandwich and an apple for lunch, Royal Canadian Air Force exercises on his office floor. Some go so far as to label him a "hoper"—Boston's language for "a man who goes to bed Irish and hopes to wake up Yankee."

It is an old form of denigration among Boston's Irish. What is most intriguing, though, is how many of Garrity's defenders choose to fight on the same battleground. They invoke his faithful attendance at the Clover Club, that grand old marching and chowder society whose members, at their gatherings, wear clover medallions on green ribbons around their necks, smoke Irish tobacco out of clay pipes and dine on "catch of the Irish sea," "Mulligan's spinach stew," and "Irish soda bread." (Is there perhaps a wistfulness in all this frippery, as if the diners were trying to reassert their Irishness in the face of relentless assimilation?) Or they cite Garrity's love of song and dance. His sister remembers how Arthur loved to sing around the piano at home, particularly the old-time tunes like "How You Going to Wet Your Whistle When the

Whole Damn World Goes Dry?'' "I can't think of a person I'd rather go to a party with,'' recalled Kenny O'Donnell,[10] "He sings and dances. He's very convivial.'' Translation: hoper, hell: he's as Irish as you are.

Garrity is, of course, quite as Irish as most fourth-generation Irish-Americans. His style is not so much Yankee as middle-class, the assimilationist mode of countless immigrant families who have made it into mainstream America. Such families abound in the suburban communities surrounding Boston. Much has been made of Garrity's residence in Wellesley. Once that comfortable town was overwhelmingly Yankee, but now it is nearly a third Catholic and perhaps a fourth Irish. Within a few blocks of the Garritys lives the Murphys, the Looneys, the Carens, the Quirks, the Lynches, the Curtins, the Cullens, the Haleys and the Fays. On their street alone are two Kellys, whom the neighbors distinguish as the "Red Kellys'' and the "White Kellys'' after the color of their houses.

Perhaps significantly, Garrity chose a host of Irishmen to enforce his order: Marty Walsh, Regional Director of the Justice Department's Community Relations Service; the late Arthur Gartland, longtime School Committee member and devout Catholic, who served as first chairman of Garrity's Citywide Coordinating Council; Father Michael Groden, first Executive Director of the Coordinating Council; and many others, Frank Harris, Jack Driscoll, Bill Looney.[11] Or, among more reluctant draftees in the busing wars, one could cite Kevin White, Eddie McCormack, Bob Kiley, Peter Meade, Rick Kelleher, Bill Leary, Marion Fahey—Irish all.[12]

Indeed, the struggle in Arthur Garrity's courtroom often seemed to be an Irish morality play, fought out between various conceptions of what it means to be Irish in contemporary Boston. Representing the plaintiffs was Nick Flannery, whose far-flung service in Washington, New York, Detroit, Chicago and Mississippi qualified him as the cosmopolitan Irishman. Speaking for the State Board of Education was Sandra Lynch, the emancipated Irish woman. Faithfully representing Kevin White's ambivalence toward desegregation was Kevin Moloney, the political Irishman. And doing battle for the School Committee— after Hale and Dorr backed out in late 1974—was the indomitable J. J. Sullivan, playing the role of true Irishman.

James J. Sullivan began as if he were going to challenge John Kennedy for the title of super Irishman. A bricklayer's son, Sullivan grew up in the tough Mission Hill district of Roxbury, but went on to Harvard

College and Harvard Law School, worked for Henry Cabot Lodge, then
served as Assistant U.S. Attorney and City Corporation Counsel under
John Collins. But once Kevin White took office, Sullivan found himself
in political eclipse. Gradually, he resumed his earlier identity as a
Roxbury Irishman, a belligerent battler for traditional Celtic values
against the dreamy notions of social experimenters. A stocky, ruddy-
faced man with a sheaf of snow-white hair, Sullivan had warned when
he took over the School Committee case that he intended to try it as
an "adversary proceeding." And he kept his promise, but his adversary
was not so much the plaintiff as the judge himself, whom Sullivan
privately ridiculed. His taunts and gibes enraged Garrity, who seethed
in his chambers.

The Garrity–Sullivan skirmishes revealed the political nub of the case.
Sullivan was charging Garrity with being a traitor to his own kind, an
apostate who had forgotten that an Irishman's ultimate loyalty was to
his family, his clan, his turf, his blood. Garrity was accusing Sullivan's
clients of being false to a still higher value, to the requirement of their
faith that they love and respect all God's children. Arthur Garrity was
probably harder on his fellow Irish Catholics than a Yankee judge would
have been in such circumstances. To him, racial hatred and prejudice
were as much moral transgressions as drug peddling and pornography,
crimes for which he was a notoriously tough sentencer. From the bench
he lashed out at "the frenetic, hate-mongering fringe in South Boston."
He would not countenance that kind of conduct. If people thought he
was harsh, so be it. The dictates of their church required a certain
standard of conduct and he was going to hold them to it.

But even the bitterness at Arthur Garrity could not match the sense
of betrayal which many Boston Irish felt at Ted Kennedy's adamant
support of the Garrity order. For most of them, Jack Kennedy was still
a household deity, the young godling who by his sacrifice had released
them from much of the anxiety about being only half-American. Yet
that worship was always mixed with sour envy of the Kennedys. When
Ted, the questionable younger brother, seemed to turn on them, they
unloaded on him all the repressed resentment they could never admit
they had felt for Jack.

It all came to a head that day in September, 1974, when Ted suddenly
appeared on the platform of an anti-busing rally on City Hall Plaza.
That morning, a *Globe* columnist had urged Kennedy to speak at the
rally. "Senator," wrote Mike Barnicle, "you are the one man who can

heal the divisions that have arisen over the issue of busing. You have the one voice that can help keep this city calm, leaving the clear ring of justice and common sense in homes and streets where people sit uncertain ... you could tell them, Senator, that law knows no neighborhood, that justice is not confined to any one block, that fear must be put aside and the fact of law adhered to. And to you, Senator Kennedy, they would listen.''

But when the crowd on the Plaza recognized him on the platform— that distinctive mop of brown hair, his face tanned from a late summer weekend on the Cape—they began booing and jeering:

"Impeach him. Get rid of the bum!''

"You're a disgrace to the Irish!''

"Why don't you put your one-legged son on a bus for Roxbury!''

"Yeah, let your daughter get bused, so she can get raped!''

"Why don't you let them shoot you, like they shot your brothers!''

Ripe tomatoes and pungent eggs flew through the autumn air, splattering the pavement around him, flecking his blue pin-striped suit. Shouting with rage, one woman flailed at him with her fist, striking him on the shoulder. He stumbled, then righted himself and hurried on. An elbow caught him in the ribs. A man aimed a kick at his shins.

As Kennedy reached the Federal Building named for his brother and darted through the swinging door, his pursuers pounded on the tinted glass. All of a sudden, a large pane gave way, the jagged shards shattering on the marble floor as the demonstrators stepped back and cheered, shaking their fists over their heads.

In *All in the Family*, the narrator asks the Jack Kennedy figure, "I thought all that was supposed to have changed with you.''

And he replies, with that familiar irony, "Is that what you thought?''

Indeed, many Americans had allowed themselves to believe that John Kennedy's accession to the presidency completed once and for all the assimilation of the Irish into mainstream America. His style and grace, his dry wit and cool irony, his beautiful wife and handsome children all created the illusion that the rage and frustration of centuries of Irish life had been dissipated in "one brief shining moment" of Camelot. His assassination did not destroy this notion. For it was widely thought that Kennedy's breakthrough to the pinnacle of national power had created such a firm sense of acceptance, of *belonging*, among Irish-Americans that it would survive the loss of his physical presence. Nobody imagined that his example alone would make the once surly, choleric, quarrelsome Gaels cultivate the broad New England "A," put on tweed jackets and cordovans, read naval history and send their sons to Harvard. Yet political commentators and social historians believed that 1960 had marked a watershed in Irish-American history, a continental divide on whose broad, grassy forward slope the new breed of assimilated Irishman would gratefully accept the political standards and cultural mores of "the American consensus."[13]

For some—young veterans who had used their V.A. loans to purchase homes in the inner suburbs, prospered in business or the professions, and sent their children to B.C. or Holy Cross, if not to Harvard—it had done just that. But for many others, left behind in the shabby old neighborhoods, pitted against blacks and Puerto Ricans for scarce jobs and other opportunities which had once seemed their birthright, the fabled Kennedy magic had left only a legacy of soured dreams, blighted hopes.

From this perspective, Boston's busing struggle is more than a battle of black against white; it is a feud within the Irish political family.

Like Jimmy Kinsella, many Boston Irish these past few years have been lashing out at the Irish political traitors, "their own kind," distant cousins if you will, who have betrayed them. Like Jimmy Kinsella, they have asked in bewilderment, "What the hell has happened? What the hell has happened to my family?"

And with Phil, the others might have said, "I don't know. I guess we all grew up."

For against the old loyalties of his childhood, the new Irishman invokes a different allegiance, to political and social ideals which transcend ethnicity or neighborhood. There are many ways of describing this struggle, but in the space remaining I would like to advance one of them. One way of conceptualizing this fierce family feud is as a struggle between two competing ideals in American life.

This is a conflict as old as the nation itself—between the notion of community invoked by John Winthrop when he set out to found a "city upon a hill" in the Massachusetts Bay Colony, and the idea of equality enshrined in the Declaration of Independence.

In March, 1630, the ship Arbella set sail from Southhampton, England, with a company of Puritans bound for Massachusetts. During the voyage, the company's leader, John Winthrop, delivered a sermon expressing his bold vision of their community-to-be: "We must consider that we shall be like a city upon a hill. The eyes of all people are upon us." But what emerges most clearly from Winthrop's sermon is the extraordinary intensity of the community he foresaw: "We must be knit together in this work as one man," he wrote. "We must uphold a familiar commerce together in all meekness, gentleness, patience and liberality. We must delight in each other, make others' condition our own, rejoice together, always have before our eyes our commission and community in the work, our community as members of the same bond."[14]

On June 12, the Arbella landed at Salem, where an advance party of the Massachusetts Bay Company had established a commercial outpost in 1626. But Salem did not please them and, five days later, they set off to find a new site. After much dispute, they chose the narrow Charlestown peninsula between the mouths of the Charles and Mystic Rivers.

Thus, for a time, Charlestown became Winthrop's "city upon a hill." But the party remained only a few months. That fall, fleeing scurvy, the threat of French attack and a shortage of fresh water, they established settlements at Watertown, Roxbury, Medford, Saugus and, across the Charles River, on the Shawmut Peninsula, soon to be renamed Boston. Winthrop's dream of a single, consecrated city was dead.

But his notion of a Bible commonwealth lived on in the separate towns which now dotted the tidewater flats around Boston Bay. Fear of wild animals, Indians, wind, storm, fire and disease account in part for the intensity of their communal life, their almost desperate insistence on mutual obligations. But perhaps their greatest fear of all was of violating the "covenant," the sacred compact which the settlers made with God and each other. The covenant was the stone on which the community was built, the basis of its determination to become a "fellowship of visible saints." A townsperson who broke its stern commandments endangered not only himself, but all his colleagues, and risked bringing down God's wrath on the entire community.

Thus the intense pressure for conformity to a shared set of beliefs, customs and institutions. By the very act of joining the congregation the Puritan accepted not only one God and one religion, but one polity, one law, one allegiance. The town could not tolerate diversity; it could not live with aberration. So most towns took steps to guarantee homogeneity. Sudbury enacted resolutions to bar "such whose dispositions

do not suit us, whose society will be harmful to us." Dedham banned
"the contrarye minded."[15]

In 1634, a revived Charlestown voted at town meeting that "none
be permitted to sit down and dwell in the town without the consent of
the town first obtained." Even after a person was received into the
town, he could be expelled by a process known as "warning out."
Ironically, this fate befell Charlestown's very first inhabitant—Thomas
Walford, who had lived on the south slope of Breed's Hill even before
the original settlers arrived from Salem. Not surprisingly, Walford resented the intruders, particularly Winthrop's company. So in 1631 the
town ordered that Walford be fined ten pounds and expelled from the
town.

Clearly Boston during that period and well into the nineteenth century
was not the Athens of America which has lived so long in legend—the
open, generous, diverse, big-spirited seat of American democracy. If
anything it was the national Sparta—narrow, closed, intolerant, a community in quest not of democracy but of self-perfection. Even the abolitionists were modern Puritans, harsh purveyors of their own revealed
truth. Until 1850, it was the most homogeneous of American cities.
Boston had no room for strangers.

But as early as 1650, the germs of another Boston were already
breeding in its harbor waters. "Whoever would send anything to any
towne in New England," John Eliot wrote that year, should send it to
Charlestown or Boston, "for they are haven townes for all New England
and speedy meanes of conveyance to all places is there to be had."[16]

For Winthrop and his lieutenants, this growth of commerce presented
a dilemma. They knew that, if unchecked, individual entrepreneurship
would destroy the communal solidarity demanded by their covenant.
Yet, the Puritans had never regarded personal enrichment as sinful, for
material success was a sure sign of God's favor. Later, Winthrop would
write, "It was a sad thing to see how little of a public spirit appeared
in the country, but self-love too much." By the end of the century,
rampant individualism and the increasing specialization of a mercantile
economy had largely eroded Winthrop's dream. Trade, almost by definition, was a commerce with strangers. Homogeneity could not long
survive the demands of a colonial, ultimately a national, economy. The
tight little seventeenth- and eighteenth-century communities gradually
had to recognize the entitlements of American citizenship, among them
the equality of free men.

When Jefferson, in his draft of the Declaration of Independence, first proclaimed that "All men are created equal," his principal purpose was to assert the right of English Americans as Englishmen. As Richard Bland, a Virginia lawyer, put it, the colonists had "as natural a right to the privileges and liberties of Englishmen as if they were actually resident within the kingdom." For Jefferson—himself a slaveowner— and most of his contemporaries, that equality was not construed to include black Americans. But as the doctrine was invoked time and again to justify the colonists' liberation from British domination, it became increasingly difficult to ignore the analogous claim of blacks for their freedom. As a group of Massachusetts Negroes wrote in one petition, "Every principle which impelled America to break with England 'pleads stronger than a thousand arguments in favor of your humble petitioners'." In 1783, the Commonwealth's Chief Justice held that slavery was "incompatible and repugnant" to the natural rights of man. Massachusetts became the first state in the union to effectively abolish human bondage.[17]

But the recognition of such universal principles by courts and legislatures did not in itself destroy the counterclaims of what James Madison called "the spirit of locality." This older communalism survived side by side with the abstract ideals of American communalism. De Tocqueville recognized that Americans had not one but two political systems: "The one fulfilling the ordinary duties and responding to the daily and infinite calls of a community; the other circumscribed within certain limits and exercising an exceptional authority over the general interests of the country." For seventy years, this delicate balance prevailed, reassuring Americans that the demands of nationalism were compatible with the intimacies of community.

In the mid-nineteenth century, of course, the revolutionary settlement broke down, the centralizing impulse dashing on the hard rock of particularism. The battle was joined in the Lincoln-Douglas debates, in which Lincoln argued that the essence of democratic government was "the equality of all men" derived from natural law, while Douglas insisted it was the "principle of popular sovereignty," the right of American communities to decide fundamental issues, like slavery, for themselves. Ultimately, force of arms held the nation together and emancipated the slaves, but the tug of war between community and equality was by no means resolved. In one guise or another, it has persisted to this day.

In the flowering of 1960s idealism, Americans persuaded themselves that community and equality were not only compatible but mutually reinforcing principles. In the single year of 1964—as Diane Ravitch has pointed out—the Johnson administration secured passage of the Civil Rights Act and the Economic Opportunity Act. Among other things, the Civil Rights Act empowered the federal government to cut off federal funds to districts guilty of racial discrimination, an unprecedented role for the executive branch in the struggle for racial equality. The Economic Opportunity Act, with its guarantee of "maximum feasible participation" in community action programs, granted poor people an unprecedented opportunity to control their own communities. Impelled by the same benevolent impulses, passed by the same congressional coalition, they were twin expressions of the nation's conscience at mid-decade.

The nation's liberal mayors—among them, John Lindsay in New York, Carl Stokes in Cleveland, Joseph Alioto in San Francisco, and Kevin White in Boston—did their best to respond to both impulses.

Because his opponent in the 1967 run-off was Louise Day Hicks, Kevin White was immediately identified as a liberal on race. In fact, as he readily concedes, he had thought little about racial questions and the needs of the city's blacks before Martin Luther King's assassination in April 1968 compelled him to confront those needs on an emergency basis. In succeeding months, he responded with a blitzkrieg of attention: Lindsayesque walks up Blue Hill Avenue, with stops along the way to bounce a basketball with black kids; meetings with the militants of the Black United Front; an all-day conference on black employment; an economic development and housing program, supported by the city's business establishment, to provide $56 million for the city's poverty areas, principally in Roxbury and the South End; pressure on the city's banks to provide mortgages for blacks who wished to buy houses outside the inner-city ghetto; support for the Model Cities Program under its new black director, Paul Parks; efforts to refurbish Franklin Park; creation of the Mayor's Office of Human Rights, headed by a black director, to supervise the city's efforts in the Civil Rights field; and promotion of Herbert A. Craigwell, Jr., a black detective, over hundreds of white officers, to become a Deputy Superintendent of Police. The mayor's identification with the black community was so intense for a time that he became known in some white communities as "Mayor Black."

But well before King's assassination, White had been working hard to identify himself with the aspirations of the city's white neighborhoods. His predecessor, John Collins, had striven with skill and energy to redevelop Boston's aging and decrepit downtown, concentrating so much of his effort there that his slogan, "The New Boston," had come to mean for many, "The New Downtown." Sensing the depth of alienation this had produced, Kevin White dramatically shifted the emphasis, adopting "City of Neighborhoods" as his informal campaign slogan. His very first position paper that summer of 1967 called for a new neighborhood services department which, after his election in November, grew into the Little City Halls Program. Some Little City Hall managers—notably Fred Salvucci in East Boston and John Lynch in Jamaica Plain—proved such effective spokesmen for their communities that they persuaded the mayor to support those neighborhoods against powerful downtown interests. He joined the battle to insulate East Boston from a voracious airport. He enlisted in the struggle to halt the runaway state highway program before it drove its right-of-ways through any more working-class neighborhoods.[18] When tenants in Allston-Brighton began clamoring for rent control, the mayor introduced a bold ordinance in the city council. In the Fenway, the South End, Dorchester and Brighton, he helped neighborhood groups fend off the encroachments of non-profit, tax-exempt institutions to expand their plants at the expense of dwelling units or precious open space.

And so, for a brief time, it looked as if the mayor—like the nation—could have it both ways: marching arm-in-arm with community and equality into a new urban renaissance.

But soon the inherent tensions between community and equality reasserted themselves. Civil rights legislation sought to override local law or custom—often equated with bigotry—in the name of a national commitment to human rights. The poverty program, on the other hand, encouraged "community control" as an antidote to bureaucratic centralization. Or, as Diane Ravitch puts it, "those who pursue equality demand the right to be treated the same; those who pursue community demand the right to be different."[19]

It should be noted here that the national vogue for "ethnicity" is a by-product of this latest rage for community control. As with so many aspects of community, it was the blacks who first sought their ethnic "roots" as a means of developing self-respect. But "ethnicity" was quickly seized by Italians, Poles, Greeks and Irish as a potent weapon in their struggle to remain "different."

Boston, to be sure, has long had a high ethnic consciousness. Teddy White, in his autobiography, tells of the Irishmen who operated Boston's streetcars in his youth. "The motormen were all Irish," he writes. "Most were Galway men. They were proud of being men of Galway and they told me why men of Galway were different from men of Cork, or Tipperary, or Dublin. It sounded very much like Jewish talk—why Pinsk Jews were different from Warsaw Jews, or Odessa Jews, or Lvov Jews."[20]

But there is a tendency to romanticize Boston's rich ethnic mosaic. Only recently have we come to understand that the city's neighborhoods are somewhat less cohesive and homogeneous than they seem. Stephen Thernstrom, digging deep into census data, has made us aware of much hidden movement in and out of these supposedly impervious enclaves.[21]

But, though they are probably more fluid and diverse than we once thought, Boston's ethnic neighborhoods are real enough. And as the sixties became the seventies, they grew increasingly unwilling to accept bureaucratic dictates from outside—whether from urban renewal administrators, highway commissioners, port authority directors, university chancellors or bank presidents. Responsive to political pressure, such officials often accommodated themselves to the aroused neighborhoods during this period.[22]

But in 1974, the neighborhoods found themselves confronting an outsider—a federal judge—who was not directly responsive to political pressure. Kevin White likes to tell stories about the neighborhood people he met during his series of Kaffee Klatches that summer, people who told him he ought to get the judge to rescind his busing order. When the mayor said he couldn't do that, they simply didn't understand. After all, he'd helped stop the highways, slowed the airport's expansion, made urban renewal more responsive to community needs. Why couldn't he stop busing in the same way?

Well, of course, he couldn't. In 1974, Boston found itself locked into a fierce standoff between the demands of equality and community. The two ideals which had seemed to run parallel for much of the sixties had now turned at right angles and confronted each other head on. Eddie McCormack, encouraged by Kevin White and others, tried to accommodate the two in his Masters' plan, but the judge refused to buy critical elements of it. The city simply couldn't have it both ways any longer.

In these past few years, Boston has learned that it had to make some **hard** choices—between racial justice and self-determination, between equality of educational opportunity and neighborhood schools, between a black child's right to a desegregated education and a white mother's right to control her own child's destiny.

What makes Boston's experience during these past years rise to the level of genuine tragedy is precisely that these are not choices between right and wrong, or between judicial dictatorship and sound social policy, but between competing values, between right and right. No wonder that the two sides—so often two branches of the same Irish political family—have stared at each other in utter incomprehension, each accusing the other of madness and duplicity.

Notes

1. *The Last Hurrah* (Boston: Little Brown, 1954); *The Edge of Sadness* (Boston: Little Brown, 1961); *All in the Family* (Boston: Little, Brown, 1966). For critical analysis of O'Connor's work: Arthur Schlesinger, Jr., introduction to *The Best and the Last of Edwin O'Connor*, ed. Edmund Wilson and John V. Kelleher (Boston: Little, Brown, 1970), pp. 3-35; Hugh Rank, *Edwin O'Connor* (New York: Twayne Publishers, Inc., 1974).

2. O'Connor, *All in the Family*, pp. 408-16.

3. For background on the history and sociology of Boston's neighborhoods and ethnic groups: Michael P. Conzen and George K. Lewis, *Boston: A Geographical Portrait* (Cambridge, Mass.: Ballinger Publishing Company, 1976), pp. 23-27, 32-48; Oscar Handlin, *Boston's Immigrants: A Study in Acculturation* (New York: Atheneum, 1968; first ed., 1941); *City Wilderness*, ed. Robert Woods (New York: Arno Press, 1970; reprint of 1898 ed.); *Americans in Process*, ed. Woods (New York: Arno Press, 1970; reprint of 1902 ed.); Herbert Gans, *The Urban Villagers: Group and Class in the Life of Italian Americans* (New York: Free Press, 1962); Stephen Thernstrom, *The Other Bostonians: Poverty and Progress in an American Metropolis, 1880-1970* (Cambridge, Mass.: Harvard University Press, 1973); Yona Ginsberg, *Jews in a Changing Neighborhood: The Study of Mattapan* (New York: Free Press, 1978).

4. A significant number of Yankees remained in the city and continued to influence its public life. Some of them remained as residents in elite enclaves like Back Bay and Beacon Hill; others retained a financial or cultural role in the city even after moving away. Among the works dealing with Boston Yankees into the twentieth century: E. Digby Baltzell, *Puritan Boston and Quaker Philadelphia* (New York: Free Press, 1980); Geoffrey Blodgett, *The Gentle Reformers: Massachusetts Democrats in the Cleveland Era* (Cambridge, Mass.: Harvard University Press, 1966); Robert Cutler, *No Time for Rest* (Boston: Little, Brown, 1966); Frederick Cople Jaher, *The Urban Elite: Upper Strata*

in Boston, New York, Charleston, Chicago, and Los Angeles (Champaign, Ill.: University of Illinois Press, 1981); John P. Marquand, *The Late George Apley: A Novel in the Form of a Memoir* (Boston: Little, Brown, 1937).

5. Of related interest here: Richard Sennett and Jonathan Cobb, *The Hidden Injuries of Class* (New York: Vintage Books, 1972); and Daniel J. Friedman, *White Militancy in Boston: A Reconsideration of Marx and Weber* (Lexington, Mass.: Lexington Books, 1973).

6. Charles Wyzanski: longtime (1941-) justice of the Federal District Court, now senior justice. Eli Goldston: businessman and civic leader, President of Eastern Gas and Fuel Association.

7. Ruth Batson: black civil rights leader active in early voluntary busing programs including "Operation Exodus." Ellen Jack: black civil rights leader, Chairman of the Education Committee of the NAACP at the time of the desegregation case. James Breeden: Episcopal minister, civil rights leader, Assistant Superintendent, Boston Public Schools. Mel King: black civil rights leader, South End activist, Member Massachusetts House of Representatives (1973-1982), candidate for mayor, 1983. *Morgan* vs. *Kerrigan*: 379 Fed. Supp. 410, 1974; 401 Fed. Supp. 216, 1975.

8. Regarding Boston as an Irish city in the late 1950s: Murray Burton Levin, *The Alienated Voter: Politics in Boston* (New York: Holt, Rinehart and Winston, 1960); also, William V. Shannon, *The American Irish* (New York: The Macmillan Company, 1963).

9. W. Arthur Garrity: Justice of the Federal District Court in Boston (1966-), presiding justice in the school desegregation case. *The Boston School Decision: The Text of Judge W. Arthur Garrity's Decision of June 21, 1974* (Boston: The Community Action Committee of Paperback Booksmith, 1975).

10. Kenneth O'Donnell: assistant to President John F. Kennedy and Massachusetts political figure.

11. Frank Harris: member of Citywide Coordinating Council. John Driscoll: Boston lawyer, member of Coordinating Council, informal aide to Judge Garrity. William Looney: Boston lawyer, informal aide to Garrity.

12. William Leary and Marion Fahey served as Superintendents of Boston Public Schools, 1972-75 and 1976-79.

13. E. Digby Baltzell, *The Protestant Establishment: Aristocracy and Caste in America* (New York: Random House, 1966), esp. pp. xiv-xv.

14. Darret B. Rutman, *Winthrop's Boston: Portrait of a Puritan Town 1630-1649* (Chapel Hill: University of North Carolina Press, 1965), p. 48; also, Edmund Morgan, *The Puritan Dilemma: The Story of John Winthrop* (Boston: Little, Brown, 1958).

15. Richard Lingeman, *Small Town America: A Narrative History 1620–The Present* (New York: Putnam, 1980); Page Smith, *As a City Upon a Hill: The Town in American History* (New York: Alfred A. Knopf, 1966); Michael

Zuckerman, *Peaceable Kingdoms: New England Towns in the Eighteenth Century* (New York: Alfred A. Knopf, 1970); Kenneth R. Lockridge, *A New England Town: The First Hundred Years, Dedham, Mass. 1636-1736* (New York: Norton, 1970).

16. Perry Miller, *The New England Mind: From Colony to Province* (Cambridge, Mass.: Harvard University Press, 1953).

17. Arthur Zilversmit, *The First Emancipation: Abolition of Slavery in the North* (Chicago: University of Chicago Press, 1967), pp. 110-11, 114.

18. Frederick Salvucci: transportation planner and community activist, Assistant Director, Little City Hall Program 1971-74, Massachusetts Secretary of Transportation 1975-78. John Lynch: community planner and activist, Director Jamaica Plain Little City Hall 1969-75. See Alan Lupo, Frank Colcord, and Edmund P. Fowler, *Rites of Way: The Politics of Transportation in Boston and the U.S. City* (Boston: Little, Brown, 1971).

19. Diane Ravitch, unpublished paper given to School Desegregation Study Group, American Academy of Arts and Sciences, Boston, 1977.

20. Theodore White, *In Search of History* (New York: McGraw Hill, 1979), p. 38.

21. Thernstrom, *The Other Bostonians*; see also United Community Services and Action for Boston Community Development, *Five Ethnic Groups in Boston: Blacks, Irish, Italians, Greeks, and Puerto Ricans* (Boston, 1972).

22. Lupo, Colcord, and Fowler, *Rites of Way*; Peter Schrag, *Village School Downtown: Politics and Education: A Boston Report* (Boston: Beacon Press, 1967); Langley Carelton Keyes, Jr., *The Rehabilitation Planning Game: A Study in the Diversity of Neighborhood* (Cambridge, Mass.: MIT Press, 1969).

Conclusion

RONALD P. FORMISANO

> ... man is by nature a political animal; it is his nature to live in a state. He who by his nature and not simply ill-luck has no city, no state, is either too bad or too good, either sub-human or super-human—sub-human like the war-mad man condemned in Homer's words "having no family, no morals, no home...."
>
> Aristotle, *The Politics*

> It is not, perhaps, wholly accidental that the two political theorists who did the most to develop a descriptive political science were Aristotle and Machiavelli, who, though separated by eighteen centuries, both witnessed politics on the smaller, more human scale of the city state.
>
> Robert A. Dahl, *Who Governs?*

The Indians called the hilly peninsula Shamut. Englishmen, including the maverick Reverend William Blaxton who settled there in splendid isolation in 1625, knew it as Trimountain because of the ridge of three hills rising across its spine. In 1630 the Massachusetts Bay Company "planters," who had tried briefly to start a town nearby (at a place later known as Charlestown), barged in on Blaxton's solitude at Trimountain and renamed it Boston.

That was all the legal standing the town ever possessed or needed—its "christening" by the Court of Assistants on September 7, 1630. No act of incorporation came until the City of Boston came into existence in 1822, with the approval of its charter by the Great and General Court. In the next hundred years a town government evolved as the population grew to 15,000. By the middle of the next century Boston was the largest urban place in British North America. Though it soon lost that distinction to New York and Philadelphia, it remained the chief port, entrepôt, and virtual capital of New England.

It would not be expected that the colonial town would have much in common with the metropolis of 750,000 of the early twentieth century or the smaller city of a half million of the present. Indeed, a primary purpose of this collection of essays is to show the changing styles of urban politics over two centuries as they relate to changing social structure and political culture.

Yet G. B. Warden's iconoclastic and provocative essay seems to take as its text the well-known lines from Ecclesiastes 1:9,

> "What has been is what will be,
>   and what has been done is what will be done;
> and there is nothing new under the sun."

Warden's reminder that the seventeenth- and eighteenth-century town occupied itself with economic and social issues that are quite recognizable to Bostonians of today is refreshing. Yet his argument points to more than continuity and shows also the distinctive traits of the colonial town, thereby suggesting as well the changes Boston has experienced.

That insecurity and instability are prominent themes in Warden's account should not be surprising, given that the subject is a recently established frontier settlement poised on the edge of a wilderness and situated on a coastline a perilous ocean voyage away from the mother country. Yet in its own universe Boston was a place of importance, a provincial capital, whose Puritan founders had not suffered, even in the first years of precarious survival, from a lack of self-confidence and self-righteousness in their cause.

Though Puritan society was hierarchic and "lesser" members of the community were imbued with traditional English deference toward their "betters," Warden holds that seventeenth-century Boston operated essentially as a town meeting democracy. Those who wanted a voice, at least in the town meeting, probably could have it, even if they lacked the proper church or property qualifications.

Town politics possessed little autonomy, overlapping as it did, in a communitarian society, with social, economic, and religious elements. Most strikingly different from what was to come later was a government designed simply to reflect society. With annual elections, part-time officials having limited jurisdiction, and changing town by-laws, nothing like a specialized class of political leaders existed.

Politics was pragmatic and served the interests of individuals and groups, but nevertheless strong inhibitions still prevented politics from acquiring a markedly distinct and independent life of its own. This was a society, after all, in which religion was still more important than politics, a fact which is easy to forget regarding a place which has since acquired a reputation for making a religion of politics.

At the heart of colonial politics were "informal, person-to-person, face-to-face networks expectable in a small town of five to fifteen thousand people." Such networks would of course continue to exist and to be important into the 1980s. But in the seventeenth century they were primary and prevalent throughout the body politic, such as it was.

After 1700 confusion, uncertainty, and instability continued, but both the royal establishment (after 1692) and the Caucus (after 1720) brought order to politics as each vied for influence. These competing networks of influence were not at all the same things as later urban institutions such as machines or political parties, but they did contribute to making politics more organized and specialized. As Warden describes the process elsewhere, under the leadership of the Cookes, father and son, from 1710 to 1740, and then of the Adamses, father and son, the Caucus had an identity, persistence, and ability to marshall a significant number of votes in defense of its interests. These were clearly defined as representing the local, small-scale and traditional in the town (most notably in terms of such issues as no central markets, continued town meeting government, cheap money, and opposition to impressment). It is important to note that this politics had an upper-class, if not elite, leadership. It derived legitimacy from its representation of the traditional past, the "Old Cause," with its Congregational, frugal, independent characteristics, and on this basis of legitimacy, shrewd leadership and popular support was able to exist for decades despite the apparent weight of the cosmopolitan forces that were arrayed against it. The Caucus resembled later political instruments, in that as an extra-legal and improvised grouping it brought to bear an "outside influence" on town meeting politics and governance.

Similarly, during the Revolutionary era outside organizations such as the Loyal Nine, Sons of Liberty, the Merchants Club, and Committees of Correspondence were vital to the promotion of the patriot cause, and existed parallel to the Caucus and town meeting. After the Revolution special commissions and fixed administrative bodies imposed more stability than ever, and in the 1780s and 1790s Warden finds the town meeting declining in significance. Indeed, the first calls to abolish the town meeting and substitute a new city government were heard in 1784 and arose from the desire to make Boston's politics more "stable, consistent, organized, and elitist." The democracy of the town responded with riotous demonstrations against incorporation but, says Warden, "democratic irrationality and popular sentimentalism" would not be enough to sustain the town meeting and its days were numbered.

The opponents of city government may well have been hopelessly blocking the march of Progress, but it was not until 1822 that Bostonians were persuaded to accept a city charter, and, as Ronald P. Formisano shows, not without considerable turmoil and the eruption of anti-elite, populist social protest of far-reaching effect on politics.

Although Formisano focuses on an important period of transition (1790s-1830s) in which a Transportation and Communications Revolution arrived, and early industrialization began, he argues that changes in social and political structures were quite gradual.

Far more than the town meeting persisted into the nineteenth century. In the Federal era the ruling elite stubbornly clung to the modes and mores of a hierarchical society. Politics was still very much influenced by the fact that this was a culture in which a gentleman could be recognized by dress and manners. Town meeting politics was not what it had been before the Revolution, but vestiges of an older era, like the Faneuil Hall town meeting, lingered.

Politics combined both aristocratic and democratic elements, a culture which Formisano characterizes as "deferential-participant." More men participated in politics, by voting and serving in lower offices or in *ad hoc* election work, and more of them came from the middle or "middling" and lower-middle classes. The latter's voice was heard occasionally, too, especially at times of conflict among the elite or of popular excitement.

Although after 1800 the Federalist and Republican parties played a role in elections for state and, to a much lesser extent, federal offices, these first parties did not become deeply ingrained in the political culture, and did not influence local politics to any great extent. Town elections, meetings, and referenda operated almost in a sphere separate from Federal-Republican partisanship which originated in debates over national, foreign and domestic policy and which became merged with various religious, status, and geographic divisions among contending groups in Massachusetts.

In the early 1820s, after several unsuccessful attempts, Boston adopted a city charter. The decision coincided with, and partly stimulated, a good deal of popular unrest. Middle- and lower-class distrust of elite leadership erupted during the transition and anticipated more sustained, populist social movements that would become far more frequent and characteristic of nineteenth-century politics.

But the populace had not rejected the elite generally, nor had the elite withdrawn from politics. The most dominant force in the new city government of the 1820s were Patrician leaders of the old Federal elite, notably "The Great Mayor" Josiah Quincy who was a quintessential representative of New England Federalism. Yet Quincy's reign, like the decade itself, looked to the past and future, and pointed in often conflicting directions, both modern and traditional, rational-bureaucratic and highly personal. Deference persisted but now more often encountered challenges from movements and interest groups using explicitly egalitarian appeals.

In the 1830s the latter became the common rhetoric of mass political party organizations. Unlike the Federalists and Republicans earlier, the new Whig and Democratic parties soon made their presence felt in city politics, notably in the realm of nominations for city offices. By the late 1830s city elections, like state and federal contests, and like most elections of consequence throughout the country from this time on, were contested strictly along party lines. Party institutions would provide much of the structure of city politics for another century and more.

As important as these political changes were, they did not signify any significant changes in socio-economic power. If the essay by Formisano shows that forms and styles of politics changed, Frederic C. Jaher persuasively argues that the core social elite of Boston, its Brahmin upper class, maintained economic, social and cultural hegemony up to and beyond the Civil War. Further, unlike the upper crust of many other cities, it did not withdraw totally from the hurly-burly of party politics in what used to be called "The Age of the Common Man." If that term ever had any meaning, it applied far more to other cities than to Boston. By no means did the elite completely dominate political life, and their numbers in city politics, as Jaher shows, declined during the thirty years from 1830 to 1860. Indeed, elite representation became limited almost solely to the mayor's office, which Brahmins occupied from time to time, often as strong executives. But their influence remained particularly strong in party organizations, both as candidates and in the parties' inner circles, notably the Whig Party which dominated city and state politics into the 1850s.

Jaher points out that underpinning the upper class's political strength was the economic adaptation of a younger generation of Brahmins who were using their mercantile-commercial wealth to establish the new industry of manufacturing in the United States. They were, according to Jaher, "one of the rare mercantile upper classes that retained their standing by adapting to industrialism."

While diversifying economically, the Brahmins also adapted in politics. Their Federalist party had lost its dominance of Boston and the state in 1823-24, and by 1824 the election of John Quincy Adams to the Presidency, a former Federalist but now a Jeffersonian Republican, sealed its doom. Gradually, however, former Federalists and old Republicans became dominant in the coalition which supported Adams's re-election in 1828. Though the Adams men lost at the national level, they emerged as the dominant force in Massachusetts. Eventually they organized and identified themselves more and more in partisan terms, first as the National Republicans, then, in 1834-35, as the Whig Party. In these political movements and nascent institutions the Brahmin merchant-manufacturers, or often their lawyer-spokesmen, played an important role, both behind the scenes and publicly, particularly as candidates for Congressional seats.

In Boston itself, while the Brahmins' overt participation declined in city politics it rose in many other public areas of social and cultural endeavor, such as support for education, public health, or the arts. The sense of civic responsibility and community duty remained high among the elite, and in pursuing community welfare, Jaher points out, the Brahmins also frequently advanced their own interests. It was, however, an enlightened self-interest that has led historians to praise Brahmin Boston "as America's earliest and best provider of urban welfare."

Brahmin politicians of polish and culture continued to be elected to the mayoralty through the 1840s: Frederick O. Prince would be elected in the 1870s and a Josiah Quincy in the 1890s. But in the 1840s non-elite Bostonians such as small businessmen, grocers, and liquor dealers began to dominate the eight-member Board of Aldermen and the forty-eight-man Common Council. In the 1850s the mayoralty too shifted out of Brahmin hands and the men elected to the city's top office, while usually wealthy, tended to be self-made businessmen or entrepreneurs.

The decade before the Civil War also produced the first massive political reaction against the immigrant Irish Catholics. The latter had been noticeably present in Boston since the 1830s, and the antagonism of native Protestants was manifest as early as 1834 when an anti-Catholic mob burned the Ursuline Convent in Charlestown. In 1837 native fire companies had attacked Irish neighborhoods in the Broad Street riot and by 1844-45 a Native American party managed to break the Whig and elite hold on the mayoralty by appealing to fears and resentments against "foreigners" and "Papists." But it was in the 1850s that the Irish Catholics, whose increasingly numerous votes had been going to the Democrats, became an important reference group in the city's (and state's) politics. Ironically, the reaction against the growing Irish presence in the electorate resulted primarily from a temporary alliance of the Irish with the conservative wing of the Whig party, with whom they united to oppose and defeat a new constitution in 1853 proposed by a reform coalition of Democrats and Free Soilers.

A new native American political movement shortly appeared, electing Boston's mayor in December, 1853, and then in the 1854 fall elections winning a stunning triumph by carrying all state offices and almost the entire legislature. The Know-Nothing Movement was an amalgam of reaction and reform, nativism and egalitarianism, moralism and populism, mobilized principally by the native Protestant desire to hem in and roll back Irish Catholic influence. In the grass-roots upheaval of 1854-55 party politicians were swept aside, and amateurs and non-professional activists bearing a multitude of causes came forward. The Know-Nothings also gave sharp expression to anti-Southern and anti-slavery attitudes activated among many northerners by Congress's 1854 repeal of the Missouri Compromise (and passage of the Kansas-Nebraska Act). But the nativist, evangelical Protestant desire to control Irish Catholic influence constituted the central element in the first stage of the political realignment of the 1850s in which the old Whig party was swept away. In the next stage the Republican party would replace the Know-Nothings.

The politics of the city hardly became Republicanized overnight, however. In 1854 Boston elected a Know-Nothing as mayor, then a "Citizens'" candidate (1855, 1856), followed by a "Faneuil Hall" nominee (1857-1859), and in 1860 and 1861, as their Northern countrymen were electing the Republican Abraham Lincoln to the Presidency and then embarking on a Civil War to preserve the Union, Boston chose an outright Democrat to its chief executive office. Boston was never as Republican as the rest of the state and Boston Republicanism, moreover, was never as true-blue as "country" Republicanism.

In 1861 anti-slavery men and abolitionists in Boston, believing that neither Republicans nor Democrats of the city could be trusted to protect their rights of assembly and free speech, prompted their allies in the General Court to introduce a measure leading to appointment of Boston's police by state officials. Though the measure failed, and abolitionist meetings still were disrupted, the Civil War city administrations co-operated in providing money and services essential to mobilization for the federal war effort. And Mayor Frederick Lincoln (1863-66), earlier elected as a non-partisan "Faneuil Hall" candidate, but now identified as a Republican, acted forcefully to suppress the fierce anti-draft riot of the Irish Catholics in July, 1863.

The rioters in the North End were largely working-class artisans and poor laborers, but the Irish were developing increasingly a middle-class leadership. Their political assimilation was inevitable.

In 1859 they elected a common councillor in Boston, and several more in the 1860s before adding, in 1869, the first Irish Catholic alderman, from South Boston. Then in the 1870s Irish ward leaders became very important in the city's Democratic leadership and it was clear that it was only a matter of time before the Irish would have the votes to dominate the city's politics and claim its top offices.

The three essays by Geoffrey Blodgett, Paul Kleppner, and Constance Burns all deal with different aspects of the late nineteenth- and early twentieth-century transition from Yankee to Irish control of the mayoralty and most of the apparatus of city government. All three call attention to the complexity of the process and qualify what Blodgett calls the "folk memory" of a passionate and monolithic Yankee-Irish cleavage.

Blodgett focuses on the elements of the Yankee upper class who acted as mediators and cooperated with middle-class Irish leaders "to moderate the passion of power transfer." The Yankee population of Boston as a whole, of course, tended to vote Republican and for the most part to keep their distance, to put it mildly, from the Irish. But within the Democratic party's leadership, elite Yankees were still a significant group. The 1884 election of Hugh O'Brien as mayor brought about a reaction in the state and city that made the Irish ward leaders realize that the Yankee Democratic political leaders were still necessary and useful to them. Primarily out of pragmatism and partly from deference, then, Irish votes helped to elect Frederick O. Prince, Nathan Matthews, and another Josiah Quincy as mayor, and the Democrats captured the mayoralty during twenty of the last thirty years of the century.

The Yankee Democrats obviously benefited from the alliance, and since before the Civil War this group had turned to the Democratic party as a refuge and bulwark against the evangelicalism and moralism that frequently cascaded through New England politics. Yankee anti-evangelicals shared a common ground with Irish Catholic Democrats in "mutual aversion to the moral agenda of the new Republican party for purifying the social order, whether the object of purification was the Southern slave owner or the urban saloon." This was a cross-class and cross-cultural alliance, numerically unbalanced to be sure, against the moralist Protestant middle whose goals often found expression in the Republican party.

The Depression of the 1890s, Blodgett argues, created severe strains and ultimately broke down the working union of the Quincys and Maguires. There followed in the first decade of the next century intense Irish internal political war which "sometimes verged on ethnic fratricide." With the formation of the Good Government Association, however, Yankee-Irish polarization tended to develop and Irish factionalism did not prevent Irish leaders from aggressively pursuing the mayoralty, using Yankee reformism as a foil.

The new 1909 city charter was a typical reform of the Progressive era, taking power away from the wards and away from ethnic neighborhoods, while centralizing and rationalizing power in a stronger mayor's office, and creating non-partisan at-large elections for a smaller city council. In addition two state-appointed watchdog commissions, one for finance and one for appointments, institutionalized the legislature's distrust of the city and provided some insurance against the wrong kind of man—from the reformers' point of view—being elected mayor.

Even with these limitations, the mayor's office proved irresistibly attractive to ambitious Irish politicians. The irony of the 1910 election, as Blodgett sees it, was that the Yankee reformers, having just strength-

268 Ronald P. Formisano

ened the mayor's office and weakened the council, lost the executive post to Irish ward boss Fitzgerald while the GGA, at least for the time being, won a majority of the council.

Paul Kleppner also takes a skeptical view of the folk tradition of Irish-Yankee polarization and emphasizes, as few historians have done before, the differences *within* Irish Catholic ranks. Kleppner begins by pointing to strong Democratic party regularity in the period 1876-1905, but finds that Democratic consistency was greater when Yankees headed the city ticket rather than Irish candidates. In addition, Boston's Irish generally voted consistently more Democratic, and its native-stock voters less so, than the same groups in outstate Massachusetts. That the "Boston context" made a difference in these ways is not surprising. But Kleppner's other finding is particularly unsettling of folk memory and of conventional political wisdom.

When Irish candidates headed the Democratic city ticket both native-stock *and* Irish voters gave less support to the Irish Democratic candidate for mayor. Kleppner locates the causes of this arresting discovery in a deep-rooted factionalism among Irish sub-groups and rival ward chieftains, a factionalism which was shaped by the decentralized structure of city government and the working rules of the Democratic party. In the 1880s and 1890s, too, political clubs within the wards served as power bases for rival ward leaders and accentuated Irish and Democratic factionalism. So did the attempts of mayors Matthews and Quincy to strengthen the mayor's office.

Given the potential and reality of Irish factionalism, the GGA or "Goo Goo" counter-offensive against the rising Irish tide may have been a godsend that contributed mightily to Irish electoral unity. One might even suggest not too fancifully that if the Goo Goos had not existed, then John Fitzgerald, and if not him then surely James Curley, would have invented them. Curley certainly did his best to prolong their existence.

Indeed, according to Constance K. Burns's account of the critical 1910 mayoral election, the image of James J. Storrow which prevailed in that campaign was, for thousands of Bostonians, a compound of Storrow's own mistakes and Fitzgerald's ingenuity. But that is getting ahead of Burns's story.

Burns shifts the focus from Yankee and Irish Democrats to Yankee reformers or Progressives, and begins with an insight based on a comparative urban perspective. By the standards then prevailing in most

American cities, according to Burns, Boston's government was relatively honest and efficient, whether its mayor was Irish or Yankee. But
the impulse to reform was contagious, and if Boston did not experience
"urban problems" on the same scale as New York or Chicago, it did
have the classes and groups with a moralist outlook and reform ambitions.

The reformers, specifically the Public School Association, turned first
to Boston's schools. The potential for religious and ethnic conflict in
this sphere was great and had been fierce in times past. Protestant–
Catholic antagonism drifted in and out of school politics in the period
1900-1910, too, but under the creative leadership of the elite Yankee
businessman, J.J. Storrow, the PSA controlled this potentially explosive
division. "Reform" in the schools tended to be pluralist, pragmatic,
and accommodationist.

But "reform" in city politics, led by the GGA and the Finance
Commission, tended to be adversarial. Its first objective was to change
the rules of city politics by getting a new charter and a strong mayor,
and its second was to elect Storrow to an office tailor-made for the
"right kind" of mayor. Storrow, unfortunately, according to Burns,
put aside the conciliatory and pragmatic policies that had served well
in schools' politics (and in the charter campaign) and adopted the Goo
Goo style of attacking Irish politicians as a threat to Boston's well-
being. Burns regards this as playing into the hands of Fitzgerald, who
had already outmaneuvered the reformers by endorsing the new charter
as the first step in his campaign to regain the mayor's office, now even
more attractive to him than in 1905. Burns reinforces the views of
several historians regarding the pivotal nature of the 1910 election as
consummating the political shift underway throughout this period. She
also adds to our understanding of how folk legends, of that election
and earlier events, have blurred the various ways that political leaders
of that generation, from both sides of the cultural divide, tried to transcend an ethnic politics based on group antagonism.

For the next fifty years after 1910, as William Shannon points out,
the Irish clearly controlled the politics of the city. Shannon's essay
introduces this period, and explores the historic cultural and emotional
underpinnings of Irish group politics. He comments perceptively on the
different values of native Protestants and Irish Catholic immigrants, and
appreciates how the latter's experience as an oppressed people had
necessarily developed in them "formidable talents for political conspiracy and political agitation." While violence and rebellion had been

an inevitable part of political culture in Ireland, in the United States the politics of organization, compromise, and accommodation proved most valuable. Nevertheless, elements of the rebel style also had their political uses and were exploited by Fitzgerald and especially by Curley.

In the 1870s and 1880s the Irish had produced a generation of leaders who were bridge-builders and brokers and who were also polished enough to be acceptable to the Yankees. Hugh O'Brien, the first Irish mayor (1885-1888), was a successful businessman, the last of his kind to become chief executive, while Patrick Collins (1901-1905) was the last college-educated mayor for over half a century. There was a blending of local and cosmopolitan interests in political organization as a vigorous ward organization tapped the politically concerned at the local level and the leadership represented them to the cosmopolitan city.

The O'Briens and Collins were somewhat in awe of Brahmin culture and achievements, but Fitzgerald and Curley employed very different strategies, rhetoric, and style. Fitzgerald was something of a transitional figure, half-way between an O'Brien or Collins and a Curley. He presented himself as a feisty Irishman and exploited cultural politics, but was restrained in comparison to Curley.

The latter, a major, often dominant force in Boston from 1913 to 1949, Shannon depicts as essentially responding to the popular needs, both psychic and practical, of an Irish subculture which, despite its numbers and political majority, largely remained a "minority" in status and self-perception. Curley, as everyone knows, criticized and derided Yankee culture, thereby, venting frustration and resentment that had seethed for generations, and providing the Irish first of all with a "politics of catharsis." In addition, however, Shannon's functional analysis also reveals that Curley provided a politics of social service, implementing where he could the "elements of a rudimentary welfare state," and also played the showman in a politics of entertainment.

Durable and flamboyant as Curley was, other men also won election as mayor during the decades when he was in and out of city hall. Maurice Tobin and John Hynes, for example, represented an alternative in the businesslike and administrative style of O'Brien or Collins. Their election, and the voters' frequent rejection of Curley, did not signal any loss of what the Irish had attained as the dominant (though divided) political majority. They consolidated, rather, the politics of social service, as well as a politics of patronage and personal loyalty.

Though the Irish constituted the single most important group in Boston's politics, somewhat as the Yankees had earlier, it was also apparent early in this period that other groups were playing a role in the city's politics. In 1937, for example, Tobin defeated Curley by putting together support from middle-class Irish, Yankees, and most of the Jewish voters, anticipating the kind of coalitional politics that would become characteristic of a more pluralistic Boston of the 1960s and 1970s.

In Shannon's view the basic styles of Irish leadership were set as early as the late nineteenth century. However much individuals might differ, the strategies remained the same. Yet to a degree Shannon, and other contributors to this volume, see Curley's style as regressive, almost atavistic.

Charles Trout, on the other hand, offers a much more positive interpretation of Curley, but like Shannon draws important distinctions among leadership styles. Curley's authority as a leader, according to Trout, derived from his "charismatic" representation of the Irish underdog rising and overcoming in Yankee Boston. Curley built his career initially on the assertion of the worth and normality of Irish political values, but as he aspired to enlarge his public stature he found a wider "legitimacy" denied him. Trout's analysis of Curley's lifelong quest for legitimacy makes Curley understandable as less of a maverick, less idiosyncratic, and as more of a representative figure.

Similarly, Trout maintains that Curley deserves credit, despite the aura of petty graft and seedy corruption which clung to him, as a genuine Progressive reformer who anticipated the New Deal, and who, during the Roosevelt years, did not get the recognition he deserved for supporting socially progressive legislation. Trout portrays Curley's concern for the neglected and damaged members of industrial society as genuine, and his criticism of business abuses and his concern for the general public would now be called consumer advocacy.

Martha Wagner Weinberg's essay brings the reader full tilt into contemporary political culture. Although the most recent in a long line of Irish mayors, Kevin White, elected four times from 1967 to 1979, has survived by assembling core electoral support from "liberals, blacks, and Italians," and, after 1975, "the elderly." Even by 1967 the city's population had shifted so significantly that White was elected by a coalition that was not based on an Irish majority. It is clear that Boston's *electoral* politics, at least, have changed.

White himself is not easy to categorize, employing as he does a variety of styles with which to govern and to campaign. The politics of catharsis as practiced by a Curley have obviously receded, yet White was not simply an accommodator or administrator. As Weinberg points out he used both traditional and cosmopolitan methods of building coalitions and implementing policies. He flaunted his "machine" but also was a innovator interested enough in policy to attract to his administrations a long line of liberals and academics.

At the same time there is much that is familiar in the three major reasons Weinberg offers to explain White's durability. First, his diverse experience and personality and his flexible style were important. White was in some ways a bundle of contradictions, but all the elements of his personality and style derived from his political-social environment and he used them to good advantage.

Second, says Weinberg, White was lucky. Although Weinberg may have underestimated White's political deftness in side-stepping the bullet of desegregation-busing, as well as other issues that might have brought him down, one can well imagine that White might not have survived them. Any durable politician has to have luck. Finally, White assembled power in a system in which power is increasingly dispersed. In 1979 White virtually advertised the fact that his campaign apparatus and the city administration were "folded into one large organization." This was White's response to an ambivalent electorate which was "increasingly skeptical of those who seek power" but also which was "anxious for strong political leadership." White chose to come on strong. It might be argued, though, that even this ambivalence was not new, and that both tendencies—skepticism, even rejection of power seekers, and desire for strong leaders—co-existed many times in the past, and that earlier mayors similarly took a direct approach.

It is appropriate that J. Anthony Lukas's final chapter focuses not on a particular mayor but on what surely is the city's major social problem in the last quarter of the twentieth century—race relations. It is fitting, too, given the emphasis on internal conflict among the Irish which has been prominent in several essays, that Lukas should interpret the conflict over busing as a "family" conflict within the Irish subculture. Boston's blacks took the initiative in raising the question of segregated schools in the early 1960s, and race, and racial attitudes are of fundamental importance in understanding the controversy that simmered through the 1960s and then erupted in the 1970s. But Lukas emphasizes the crucial role of class within the Irish group, with the Garritys and Kennedys at the upper end of the class-status scale promoting integration, and the supporters of Hicks, Kerrigan, and Bulger at the other end opposing it.

Lukas sees the desegregation controversy as a fierce family feud and a class struggle, and also as a contest between "two competing ideals in American life," between, in brief, community and equality. In a few paragraphs Lukas succinctly reviews the historic tension between these two ideals from the first settlements of the Puritans in the 1620s down through the nineteenth and twentieth centuries.

Kevin White, as a conciliator, compromiser, and consensus-builder, tried to balance both, and succeeded to a degree in attracting votes from Boston's blacks as well as from voters of Irish and other ethnic backgrounds. But Lukas concludes that community and equality inevitably come into conflict, and Boston "has learned that it [has] to make some hard choices—between racial justice and self-determination, between equality of educational opportunity and neighborhood schools, between a black child's right to a desegregated education and a white mother's right to control her own child's destiny."

The politics of the town and city were affected always by the "rules of the game," though during the seventeenth and eighteenth centuries society and politics were so closely intertwined that the rules were not particularly important. Politics did not have much of an autonomous existence until the mid-eighteenth century or so, though that process advanced considerably with the American Revolution.

From the 1780s to 1822 the form of government itself constituted a political controversy, with cosmopolitan elites tending to favor incorporation as a city and a scrapping of the old-fashioned town government. They wanted greater centralization of power within Boston, especially a stronger executive which would direct and shape the city's physical and economic development. As the city grew, and as "growth" and "improvements" became shibboleths of the nineteenth century, it was only a matter of time before the pro-city forces had their way.

Still the 1822 city charter was not won without considerable controversy, and the new rules were somewhat ambiguous about how strong the new mayor should be. Josiah Quincy (1823-28) began to move the town truly into the more rationalized apparatus of a city and brought great energy and personal presence to the executive, often in the service of traditional goals. Quincy tried to hold on to the organic wholeness that had suffused the town earlier, even as he patched and innovated to repair and replace what was lost as the sense of community and personal responsibility disappeared.

Quincy promoted economic development, erected buildings, and reorganized government branches, and most of all he taxed and spent. Though the voters quickly turned to less energetic men (though mostly of the same social background) who retrenched and consolidated, "The Great Mayor" had set a pattern.

In 1854 a populist reaction against the centralist tendencies Quincy had set in motion took effect in a charter revision which took power away from the mayor and gave it to an expanded board of aldermen. The wards emerged with greater representation on the board, council, and School Committee, and by the late nineteenth century mayors increasingly strained to expand the scope of their office. As several of the essays here make clear, the decentralized city government, and the similarly structured party organizations, had a profound effect on the expression of social divisions and interest-group goals in the city's politics.

Political parties had played an important part in nominating and electing officers since the 1830s. Yet many mayors, even during the heyday of partisan politics in Boston (1835-1909) won office after being nominated not by Whigs, Democrats, or Republicans, but by "Citizens" groups, on coalition tickets and non-partisan platforms. At the aldermanic level partisan identity still meant a great deal during the second half of the nineteenth century, based as it often was on powerful ethnic, religious and class divisions. The mayor's office, however, more often went to men whose supporters downplayed their candidate's partisan identity.

In 1909 a new charter removed political party from the formal operation of the city's politics, and at the same time swung the city back to a stronger mayor and a more centralized government. In requiring non-partisan elections and in weakening ward representation, Boston followed a national trend of the "Progressive Era" by trying to take "politics" out of government and make it rational and efficient. Reform elements wanted also to minimize Irish influence, a strategy which backfired as Irish ward bosses quickly moved to capture the newly strengthened mayor's office.

The 1909 charter change increased the mayor's power at the expense of the council, while abolishing the two legislative branches and replacing them with a single, nine-member council elected at large. In 1923-24 the pendulum swung back to decentralization when voters approved a council of twenty-two elected from each of the city's wards. This neighborhood-based council lasted until 1949 when by referendum the voters again installed a nine-member, at-large council. Subsequently Keven White tried, unsuccessfully, to change the charter to increase the power of the mayor (at the expense of the school committee), while recent changes in the 1980s have restructured representation so that the council and school committee are elected partly by district and partly at large, restoring influence to local neighborhoods.

Rule changes had been pursued earlier to try to counter the consequences of Irish-Democratic political majorities, notably after the 1884 election of Hugh O'Brien when the state legislature decided to take away from the city the power of appointing its own police chief and placed it instead in the hands of a state commission. Yet reformers and partisans had proposed this shift more than twenty years earlier, when mayors were still safely Yankees but nevertheless distrusted by legislators representing rural and small town constituents, or perhaps Worcester or Springfield, who thought big city politicians corrupt no matter what their cultural background. In addition, the intense social conflicts of the Civil War era inspired the early proposals to give control of Boston's police to the state, but when partisanship became reinforced by clear-cut ethnic and religious distrusts, then the measure passed quickly.

It is useful to recall that the Irish–Yankee conflict is often given too much causative primacy in the city's history. Though the withdrawal of the Yankee elite from politics roughly coincided with the arrival and political assimilation of the Irish, the Brahmin retreat sprang from a great many other causes. It also came later and more gradually than in other cities, as Brahmins hung on in the mayor's office, and were prominent in endowing and staffing various private–public institutions.

Yet before the Civil War the process known as the "suburbanization of the elite" was already underway in Boston and its surrounding countryside. Many middle- and upper-middle-class families of property frequently transferred their domiciles to Brookline and other towns to avoid paying high city property taxes. Continuing into the twentieth century, the consequences of suburbanization became of vast import for all of

American politics after World War II. In Boston, however, the relative absence of the status elite from the city became a disadvantage especially during the desegregation conflicts of the 1960s and 1970s.

Other Northern cities, and some border cities such as St. Louis and Baltimore, desegregated their public schools with far less social turmoil, and no violence, in sharp contrast to events in Boston in 1974-75. The reasons for this are many and complex, though foremost among them would be the intransigence of the Boston School Committee in the decade before Garrity's decision. Aside from the personal attitudes of committee members on racial issues, the committee, chosen in at-large elections, functioned as an elevator for ambitious politicians and also provided the last significant patronage influence independent of the mayor. In other cities where desegregation went smoothly, school committees tended to be appointive, or also felt the restraining influence of high-status elites. In St. Louis, for example, prestigious leaders took a leading role in public advocacy of moderation, pragmatism, and accommodation. In Boston, these "blue-ribbon types" were generally not to be seen. Though they might work or do business in it, the city's problems were not theirs. Of course in Boston few of the society's top leaders from any realm, official or unofficial—with the exception of a federal judge and the Boston *Globe*—risked getting "out front" on desegregation.

Expressions of shock over the incongruity of racial violence in "The Cradle of Liberty," the "Athens of America," hotbed of abolition, and in a place with a reputation for culture and learning, betray vast ignorance of Boston's past and present, as well as lack of any comprehension of the long-standing intractability of the problem of racism in American society. Yet having said that, and having reminded ourselves for the umpteenth time of the deep-rooted tribal identities of Boston's subcultures, of the scars left by the Yankees' assumption of caste (i.e., genetic) superiority over everyone and especially over the Irish, and the seeming inability of the Boston Irish to lose (as William Shannon put it) their minority mentality, the contradiction between the school wars of the 1970s and Boston's communal-civic-traditions is still difficult to ignore.

Lost in the focus on the great transition from Yankee to Irish is the recognition that Boston's tradition of an activist city government, one which taxes and spends rather heavily and which aims to promote community prosperity, has spanned the entire history of the city. The most famous Brahmin mayors were taxers, spenders, and doers. One need only mention the name Josiah Quincy, and such a mayor can be found in the 1820s, and 1840s, and 1890s. Although in some very different ways and for quite different purposes, James Curley and Kevin White were also taxers, spenders, and doers. It may be objected that Curley was far too ethno-centric, too particularist, and hopelessly corrupt, and does not deserve to be mentioned with the others, particularly the third Quincy, whose progressive vision transcended ethnic and religious antagonisms. Yet Curley too used the power of government to aid not only particular groups and clients but also to strengthen the community as a whole. Even his severest critics would not deny that he was, when he could be, a taxer, spender, and doer.

Thus the rules of the game of Boston politics have been written and re-written as various religious, status, economic, ethnic and racial groups have dominated or simply grown strong enough as political entities which could not be ignored. But the rules have not simply expressed the majority will or the unsuppressible demands of particular minorities. They have functioned also independently of competition for power, status, and tangible resources; they have acted as shapers of that very competition because they have been part of a political culture—or political cultures—developing over many generations.

Boston's politics, as our title says, has evolved and changed through the centuries. It has contained too patterns or cycles of continuity within that evolution.

Bibliographical Essay

At first glance it seems surprising that so politically conscious a city as Boston, with so long and prominent a political history, possesses so sparse a literature on its politics. It is a condition that Boston shares with most other large American cities. The reasons for such oversight reflect the canons of historical study in the United States, as well as the fact that the study of American politics has been nationally oriented, and its building blocks have been the states, either individually or in their informal groupings as regions.

The works included here are those important secondary sources that deal with the politics of the city either as their principal focus or, more commonly, as part of a larger focus. Primary sources may best be approached through the bibliographies of these secondary works.

There is no comprehensive account of the city's political history, but good, general introductions are: Michael P. Conzen and George K. Lewis, *Boston: A Geographical Portrait* (Cambridge, Mass.: Ballinger Publishing Company, 1976), and Walter Muir Whitehill, *Boston: A Topographical History*, 2nd ed. (Cambridge, Mass.: Harvard University Press, 1968); and still valuable is Henry Cabot Lodge, *Boston* (New York: Longmans, Green and Co., 1892). More cumbersome but packed with details are: Justin Winsor, ed., *The Memorial History of Boston, Including Suffolk County, Massachusetts, 1630-1880*, 4 vols. (Boston: James B. Osgood and Company, 1880-81), and Albert P. Langtry, ed., *Metropolitan Boston: A Modern History*, 4 vols. (New York: Lewis Historical Publishing Company, Inc., 1929).

The period from the founding of Boston in 1630 through the end of the seventeenth century may be considered a prepolitical era that had important implications for later political development. The best introduction to it is Darrett B. Rutman's *Winthrop's Boston: Portrait of a Puritan Town, 1630-1649* (Chapel Hill: University of North Carolina Press, 1965). A fine comparative view of Boston contrasting it to the closed corporations characterizing other town governments is Jon C. Teaford, *The Municipal Revolution in America: Origins of*

Modern Urban Government, 1650-1825 (Chicago: University of Chicago Press, 1975).

Rutman saw the covenanted community passing by the end of the first generation, but for Bernard Bailyn it began to dissolve a generation later when wealth and diversity worked to diminish the sense of commonweal present earlier. For Bailyn's view, *The New England Merchants in the Seventeenth Century* (Cambridge, Mass.: Harvard University Press, 1970). In *The Character of the Good Ruler: Puritan Political Ideals in New England, 1630-1720* (New Haven, Ct.: Yale University Press, 1970), T. H. Breen argues that an enduring division of "two New Englands" was produced by the intrusion of "alien" institutions and people with the arrival of the British establishment after 1700.

The first political period began in 1700 when the British crown belatedly extended its mandate over the Bay Colony and lasted until the expulsion of the imperial forces in 1776, surely a dramatic way to conclude any period. A splendid history of the entire era is G. B. Warden's *Boston 1689-1776* (Boston: Little Brown, 1970). Another work viewing this entire period and also providing histories of New York and Philadelphia is Gary B. Nash, *The Urban Crucible: Social Change, Political Concerns and the Origins of the American Revolution* (Cambridge, Mass.: Harvard University Press, 1979). Other works providing insight into Boston politics during the Revolution include: Robert E. Brown, *Middle Class Democracy in Massachusetts, 1691-1789* (Ithaca, N.Y.: Cornell University Press, 1955); Hiller B. Zobel, *The Boston Massacre* (New York: W. W. Norton, 1978); Benjamin W. Labaree, *The Boston Tea Party* (New York: Oxford University Press, 1964); John C. Miller, *Sam Adams: Pioneer in Propaganda* (Stanford, Calif.: Stanford University Press, 1960; originally pub., 1936); Bernard Bailyn, *The Ordeal of Thomas Hutchinson* (Cambridge, Mass.: Harvard University Press, 1975); Stephen E. Patterson, *Political Parties in Revolutionary Massachusetts* (Madison: University of Wisconsin Press, 1973); and Richard D. Brown, *Revolutionary Politics in Massachusetts: The Boston Committee of Correspondence and the Towns, 1772-1774* (Cambridge, Mass.: Harvard University Press, 1979).

The politics of Boston during the early national period must be approached mostly through works dealing with Massachusetts, but which have some references to Boston: James Banner, *To the Hartford Convention: The Federalists and the Origins of Party Politics in Massachusetts, 1789-1815* (New York: Alfred A. Knopf, 1970); Paul Goodman, *The Democratic-Republicans of Massachusetts* (Cambridge, Mass.: Harvard University Press, 1964); and Ronald P. Formisano, *The Transformation of Political Culture: Massachusetts Parties, 1790s-1840s* (New York: Oxford University Press, 1983).

Boston politics in the 1820s are covered rather directly in Robert A. McCaughey's fine biography of "The Great Mayor," *Josiah Quincy 1772-1864: The Last Federalist* (Cambridge, Mass.: Harvard University Press); of some use too is Quincy's own account of Boston's history, *A Municipal History of the Town and City of Boston, 1630-1830* (Boston: C. C. Little and J. Brown, 1852). Among the many biographies shedding light on the entire early national period are: Samuel Eliot Morison, *Harrison Gray Otis, 1765-1848: Urbane Federalist* (Boston: Houghton Mifflin Company, 1969); and Carl Seaburg and Stanley Patterson, *Merchant Prince of Boston: Colonel T. H. Perkins, 1767-1854* (Cambridge, Mass.: Harvard University Press, 1971). For this era, too, Harold and James Kirker's delightful *Bulfinch's Boston, 1787-1817* (New York: Oxford University Press, 1965), should not be ignored.

The antislavery agitation, the social upheaval of the 1850s, and the era of the Civil War and Reconstruction are not at all adequately represented in the historial literature from a Boston viewpoint. But Oscar Handlin's classic study of the beginnings of massive Irish immigration does contain important chapters dealing with its political consequences: *Boston's Immigrants: A Study in Acculturation* (New York: Atheneum, 1968; originally pub. 1941); similarly helpful, Ronald Story, *The Forging of an Aristocracy: Harvard and the Boston Upper Class, 1800-1870* (Middletown, Ct.: Wesleyan University Press, 1980).

Specialized histories also can take the reader through the middle decades of the nineteenth century and reveal a great deal about Boston's politics, including: Roger Lane, *Policing the City: Boston, 1822-1885* (Cambridge, Mass.: Harvard University Press, 1967); Robert H. Lord, et. al., *History of the Archdiocese of Boston in the Various Stages of its Development, 1604 to 1943* (Boston: Boston Pilot Publishing Co., 1944); and Charles Phillips Huse, *The Financial History of Boston: From May 1, 1822 to January 31, 1909* (Cambridge, Mass.: Harvard University Press, 1916). A parallel administrative history is John Koren, *Boston, 1822 to 1922: The Story of Its Government and Principal Activities During One Hundred Years* (Boston: City of Boston Printing Department, 1922).

For the late nineteenth century Geoffrey Blodgett's *The Gentle Reformers: Massachusetts Democrats in the Cleveland Era* (Cambridge, Mass.: Harvard University Press, 1966), is an essential starting point, while important dimensions of the era's social history may be gleaned from Sam Bass Warner, *Streetcar Suburbs: The Process of Growth in Boston 1870-1920* (Cambridge, Mass.: Harvard University Press, 1962); and in the well-known novel by John P. Marquand, *The Late George Apley* (Boston: Little Brown, 1937).

The Progressive period lacks its own history, so again state studies and other works are useful, for example, Richard M. Abrams, *Conservatism in a Progressive Era: Massachusetts Politics, 1900-1912* (Cambridge, Mass.: Harvard University Press, 1980). For the 1920s, similarly, see J. Joseph Huthmacher, *Massachusetts People and Politics, 1919-1933* (Cambridge, Mass.: Harvard University Press, 1959). Highly readable and containing insights into Boston's politics is Francis Russell, *A City in Terror—1919—: The Boston Police Strike* (New York: Viking, 1975).

If Boston lacked a strong Progressive movement during the first decades of the twentieth century, it also did not benefit as much as it might have from the New Deal, as Charles Trout shows in *Boston, The Great Depression and the New Deal* (New York: Oxford University Press, 1977). For ethnic group reactions to World War II, see John F. Stack, Jr., *International Conflict in an American City: Boston's Irish, Italians, and Jews, 1935-1944* (Westport, Ct.: Greenwood Press, 1979).

For the colorful and controversial James Michael Curley, the literature is disappointing. His autobiography, *I'd Do It Again* (Englewood Cliffs, N.J.: Prentice Hall, 1957), is superficial; Reinhard Luthin's chapter in *American Demagogues* (Boston: Beacon Press, 1954), is very critical, while William V. Shannon's references to Curley in *The American Irish* (New York: Macmillan, 1966), are moderately so. For the classic work of fiction based loosely on Curley's career, see Edwin O'Connor, *The Last Hurrah* (Boston: Little Brown, 1955).

For the post-1945 era, Murray B. Levin, *The Alienated Voter: Politics in Boston* (New York: Holt, Rinehart and Winston, 1962) emphasizes corruption and declining participation; Edward Banfield and Martha Derthick, eds., *A Report on the Politics of Boston* (Cambridge, Mass.: Joint Center for Urban Studies, 1960) also stress issueless politics and the lack of leadership. Derthick extends her analysis to Mayor John Collins' administration (1959-67), noting signs of change, in a chapter in *Big City Politics: A Comparative Guide to Political Systems*, eds. Banfield and Derthick (New York: Random House, 1968).

The good feelings resulting from increased government intervention and economic revival are captured in Walter Muir Whitehill, *Boston in the Age of John Fitzgerald Kennedy* (Norman: University of Oklahoma Press, 1966), while negative reactions to urban renewal and to highway building as displacement of the working class and the poor are depicted and explained in Langley Carelton Keyes, Jr., *The Rehabilitation Planning Game: A Study in the Diversity of Neighborhood* (Cambridge, Mass.: MIT Press, 1969), and Alan Lupo, Frank Colcord, and Edmund P. Fowler, *Rites of Way: The Politics of Transportation in Boston and the U.S. City* (Boston: Little, Brown, 1971).

Under Collins's successor, Kevin White (1967-83) the demographic changes in the city became pronounced and the shift to a new political era unmistakable. A new population mix evolved with a suburban exodus and a professional and minority influx, the implications of which are described in Edgar Litt, *The Political Cultures of Massachusetts* (Cambridge, Mass.: MIT Press, 1965). White's politics are described by Philip Heymann and Martha Wagner Weinberg in "Paradox of Power: Mayoral Leadership and Charter Reform in Boston," in Walter Dean Burnham and Weinberg, eds., *American Politics and Public Policy* (Cambridge: MIT Press, 1978). White's early ventures in developing neighborhood support are described by Eric A. Nordlinger in *Decentralizing the City: A Study of Boston's Little City Halls* (Cambridge: MIT Press, 1972).

The implications of the black population growing from 5 percent in 1950 to 30 percent in 1980 have been considerable. The court-ordered desegregation (busing) that began in 1974 produced considerable upheaval. Alan Lupo describes the conflict's early years, with considerable historical background, in *Liberty's Chosen Home: The Politics of Violence in Boston* (Boston: Little Brown, 1977); for a sociologist's approach, with emphasis on South Boston, see Emmett H. Buell, Jr., *School Desegregation and Defended Neighborhoods: The Boston Controversy* (Lexington, Mass.: D. C. Heath and Company, 1982). In 1983 there was a major black contender for mayor in the person of Melvin H. King, and new charter arrangements which created district elections promising to elect significant numbers of blacks and Hispanics to the City Council and School Committee. King tells of the changing role of blacks in his recent book, *The Chain of Change: Struggles for Black Community Development* (Boston: South End Press, 1981).

Index

About the Contributors

RONALD P. FORMISANO is Professor of History at Clark University and the author of *The Birth of Mass Political Parties: Michigan, 1827–1861*, and *The Transformation of Political Culture: Massachusetts Parties 1790s-1840s*.

CONSTANCE K. BURNS was the Director of Forum 350, The Boston Political History Project. She is currently doing research on the age of Progressive Reform in Boston.

GEOFFREY BLODGETT is Professor of History at Oberlin College and the author of *The Gentle Reformers: Massachusetts Democrats in the Cleveland Era*. He is working on a study of the two administrations of Grover Cleveland.

FREDERIC COPLE JAHER is Professor of History at the University of Illinois, Champaign-Urbana. His works include *The Urban Establishment: Upper Strata in Boston, New York, Charleston, Chicago, and Los Angeles, Doubters and Dissenters* and (editor) *The Age of Industrialism in America: Essays in Social Structure and Cultural Values*.

PAUL KLEPPNER is Presidential Research Professor of History and Political Science and Director of the Social Science Research Institute at Northern Illinois University. He is the author of *The Cross of Culture: A Social Analysis of Midwestern Politics, 1850-1900*; *The Third Electoral System, 1853-1892: Parties, Voters and Political Cultures*, and *Who Voted? The Dynamics of Electoral Turnout, 1870-1980*.

J. ANTHONY LUKAS is a Pulitzer prize-winning author and journalist. His chapter in this book grew out of work he has done for a forthcoming book on three Boston families in the decade after Martin Luther King's death.

WILLIAM V. SHANNON is University Professor and Professor of History and Journalism at Boston University. He is former United States Ambassador to Ireland and is the author of *The American Irish: A Political and Social Portrait*.

CHARLES H. TROUT is Dean of Faculty and Provost at Colgate University. He is the author of *Boston, The Great Depression, and The New Deal*, and is currently engaged in writing a biography of James Michael Curley.

G. B. WARDEN is former Director of the Cambridge Historical Society and author of *Boston, 1689-1776*.

MARTHA WAGNER WEINBERG is Associate Professor of Political Science at the Massachusetts Institute of Technology. She is author of *Managing the State* and co-editor (with Walter Dean Burnham) of *American Politics and Public Policy*.